Media Ethics
Beyond Borders

A Global Perspective

"The complexity and contentiousness of developing university ethical standards is at the core of this collection, which makes the point that the discussion must, however, begin somewhere in attempting to overcome these barriers.... This collection ... [takes] the first steps toward the goal of a global media ethics." – *Journalism and Mass Communication Quarterly*

Media Ethics Beyond Borders explores the construction of an ethics for news media with global reach and impact. Addressing the current media revolution that blurs geographical, cultural, and temporal boundaries, this work considers how urgent global issues and the power of global communications prompt the need for a media ethics without borders - a media ethics that is global in its principles and in its understanding.

But difficult questions arise: Do universal values exist in journalism? How would a global media ethics accommodate the cultural, political, and economic differences around the world? Can a global ethic based on universal principles allow for diversity of media systems and cultural values? What should be the principles and norms of practice of global media ethics?

This collection of essays by international media ethicists provides leading theoretical perspectives on such questions, considering the major issues and applies the ideas to specific countries, contexts and problems. The result is a rich source of ethical thought and analysis on questions raised by contemporary global media. The book is required reading for anyone who takes seriously the responsibility of global media for a troubled planet.

Stephen J.A. Ward is the James E. Burgess Chair in Journalism Ethics and director of the Center for Journalism Ethics at the School of Journalism and Mass Communication, University of Wisconsin in Madison. He was previously director of the Graduate School of Journalism, University of British Columbia in Vancouver, Canada. His research interests include global journalism ethics, the philosphical foundations of media ethics, and theories of objectivity.

Herman Wasserman teaches media and cultural studies at Newcastle University, UK, and is associate professor extraordinary of journalism at Stellenbosch University, South Africa. He is a former Fulbright Scholar at Indiana University, and a former fellow of the Ethics Colloquium at the University of Missouri School of Journalism. He is the editor of *Ecquid Novi: African Journalism Studies* and on the editorial boards of several journals, including the *Journal of Mass Media Ethics* and the *Journal of African Media Studies*.

Media Ethics Beyond Borders

A Global Perspective

Edited by
Stephen J.A. Ward and
Herman Wasserman

Routledge
Taylor & Francis Group

NEW YORK AND LONDON

Published 2010
by Routledge
270 Madison Ave, New York, NY 10016

Simultaneously published in the UK
by Routledge
2 Park Square, Milton Park, Abingdon, Oxon OX14 4RN

Routledge is an imprint of the Taylor & Francis Group, an informa business

First published by Heinemann Publishers (Pty) Ltd, 2008

Printed and bound in the UK on acid-free paper by
TJ International Ltd, Padstow, Cornwall

Library of Congress Cataloging-in-Publication Data
Media ethics beyond borders : a global perspective / edited by Stephen
J.A. Ward and Herman Wasserman.
p. cm.
Includes bibiliographical references index.
Journalistic ethics. 2. Mass media—Moral and ethical aspects. I. Ward,
Stephen J. A. (Stephen John Anthony), 1951- II. Wasserman, Herman, 1969-
PN4756.M36 2010
174.907—dc22
2010003038

ISBN10: 0-415-87887-X (hbk)
ISBN10: 0-415-87888-8 (pbk)
ISBN10: 0-203-85307-5 (ebk)

ISBN13: 978-0-415-87887-6 (hbk)
ISBN13: 978-0-415-87888-3 (pbk)
ISBN13: 978-0-203-85307-8 (ebk)

Contents

Preface

Media Ethics Beyond Borders is the result of a roundtable on global media ethics held at the Stellenbosch Institute for Advanced Study (STIAS) at the University of Stellenbosch, South Africa, in March 2007. Over three days, an international group of 13 leading media ethicists and scholars presented papers that became the chapters of this volume. The ethicists came from the United States, Canada, Finland, Taiwan, Egypt, Ethiopia, Zambia, and South Africa. The papers sparked such stimulating discussion that it led to the idea of publishing the contributions.

The idea for a roundtable was developed during a conversation between Stephen Ward and Herman Wasserman at a conference of the International Communication Association in Dresden, Germany, in the summer of 2006. The motivating idea was to provide a forum that advanced the emerging field of global media ethics. It was decided that the session should be held in a developing country such as South Africa, because of the under-representation of the Global South in the field of media ethics.

Ward and Wasserman became the co-organisers of the project and approached Prof Bernard Lategan, director of STIAS, to host the roundtable. Valuable financial support was also received from the University of Stellenbosch's then Deputy Vice-Chancellor for Research, Prof Walter Claassen; the Dean of Arts and Social Sciences, Prof Hennie Kotzé; and the University's International Office. Colleagues at the University of Stellenbosch's Department of Journalism, especially Lizette Rabe and Arnold de Beer, gave of their time and expert advice, and Wiana de Beer was in charge of logistics. We thank STIAS and the University for their generous and far-sighted support for the roundtable, and for their continuing support.

We thank the participants especially for giving generously of their time and resources to attend the roundtable, and for enduring an accelerated editing and publishing schedule. Unfortunately, Prof Kaarle Nordenstreng could not participate in the book project due to other commitments and Profs Ying-Chun Hsieh and Ching-Chen Hsieh of Taiwan had to withdraw their paper from the book due to illness. We are grateful to Prof Nick Couldry who joined the project after the roundtable and contributed a chapter. We would also like to thank Heinemann Publishers and Claudia Bickford-Smith for her enthusiasm and interest in our project, and Silvia Raninger for her expert copy editing under time pressure.

Biographies of Authors

Fackson Banda is associate professor to the SAB LTD-UNESCO Chair of Media and Democracy at Rhodes University, South Africa. He has taught at the University of Zambia, apart from practising broadcast journalism at the Zambia National Broadcasting Corporation (ZNBC). He introduced the widely read "Media Discourse" column into Zambia's *Post* newspaper. His research interests include political economy of communication, civic education and journalism, media policy and institutions, African political thought and African media, and postcolonial theory.

Clifford G. Christians is the Charles H. Sandage Distinguished Professor, Research Professor of Communications, and Director of the Institute of Communications Research at the University of Illinois-Urbana. He is the author or co-author of *Media Ethics: Cases and Moral Reasoning* (8th edition); *Good News: Social Ethics and the Press*; *Communication Ethics and Universal Values*; *Moral Engagement in Public Life: Theorists for Contemporary Ethics*; *Responsibility in Mass Communication* (3rd ed.); *Jacques Ellul: Interpretive Essays*; and the *Handbook for Mass Communication*.

Nick Couldry is Professor of Media and Communications at Goldsmiths College, University of London. He is the author or editor of seven books, including most recently *Listening Beyond the Echoes: Media, Ethics and Agency in an Uncertain World* (Paradigm Books, USA, 2006) and (with Sonia Livingstone and Tim Markham) *Media Consumption and Public Engagement: Beyond the Presumption of Attention* (Palgrave Macmillan, 2007).

Pieter J. Fourie has a doctoral degree in communication science from the University of South Africa and is senior professor in communication science at the same university, where he was also head of the Department for 17 years. He is the author and editor of a number of key works in the field of South African media studies, including the first publication in South Africa in the field of visual communication and semiotics, *Beeldkommunikasie: Kultuurkritiek, ideologiese kritiek, en 'n inleiding tot die beeldsemiologie* (McGraw-Hill, 1983) and *Aspects of film and television communication* (Juta, 1988). He is editor of the research journal

Communicatio: South African Journal for Communication Theory and Research and sits on the editorial boards of a number of other research journals. He was the president of the South African Communication Association for a number of years. In 2003, he was awarded the South African Academy of Science and Arts' Stals Prize for his contribution to the development of communication science in South Africa. In 2007 he was elected Fellow of the International Communicology Institute.

Ali Mohamed is a PhD candidate in Communication Studies at McGill University (Montreal). His current research focuses on digital media and the public sphere. In particular, he is exploring the potential of new communication technologies to enable new configurations of news production and emerging forms of political communication with respect to the public sphere in non-democratic contexts. His research interests also include the impact of the new media news environment, the major changes in the professional roles, and the credibility of news in relation to the impact of new communication technologies on an audience. He holds a Bachelor in Communication and Journalism from Cairo University, Egypt and a Master of Arts in Communication Studies from Assiut University, Egypt.

Shakuntala Rao is Professor of Communication at State University of New York, Plattsburgh, USA. She received her PhD from University of Massachusetts-Amherst, USA. Her articles and review essays have appeared in *Journal of Mass Media Ethics, Journal of Communication, Visual Communication Quarterly, Howard Journal of Communication, Journal of Broadcast and Electronic Media, Journal of Communication Inquiry, Global Media and Communication* and *Journal for the Society of Social Research*. She is currently associate editor of *Journal of Global Mass Communication*. Her primary areas of research are global media ethics, popular culture and postcolonial theory. She has been involved in training and in conducting workshops on ethics for print and television journalists in India, Pakistan, Kazakhstan and the US. She is also a regular columnist for one of the largest newspapers in India, *The Tribune*, where her columns on media appear every month.

Gebremedhin Simon is Dean of the Faculty of Journalism & Communication at Addis Ababa University, Ethiopia. He recently contributed the country report on Ethiopia for the BBC World Service Trust's African Media Development Initiative (AMDI).

Stephen J. A. Ward is the James E. Burgess Chair in Journalism Ethics and director of the Center for Journalism Ethics at the School of Journalism and Mass Communication, University of Wisconsin in Madison. He previously was director of the Graduate School of Journalism, University of British Columbia in Vancouver, Canada. He has a PhD in Philosophy from the University of Waterloo, Ontario. His research interests include global journalism ethics, the philosophical foundations of media ethics, and theories of objectivity. He is the author of *The Invention of Journalism Ethics: The Path to Objectivity and Beyond*, which won the 2005–2006 Harold Adams Innis Prize from the Canadian Federation for the Humanities and Social Sciences for the best English-language scholarly book in the social sciences. He is associate editor of the *Journal of Mass Media Ethics* and principal investigator of a study into the public communication of controversial science. His articles and reviews have been published in periodicals such as the *Journal of Mass Media Ethics*, the *Harvard International Journal of Press and Politics*, and *Journalism Studies*. He serves on seven editorial boards for media ethics and science journals, is a media ethics columnist and is the founding chair of the Ethics Advisory Committee of the Canadian Association of Journalists. He has 15 years of experience as a foreign reporter, war correspondent, and newsroom manager.

Herman Wasserman teaches media and cultural studies at Newcastle University, UK and is associate professor extraordinary of journalism at Stellenbosch University, South Africa. He is a former Fulbright Scholar at Indiana University, USA, and a former fellow of the Ethics Colloquium at the University of Missouri School of Journalism. He is editor of *Ecquid Novi: African Journalism Studies* and on the editorial board of several journals, including the *Journal of Mass Media Ethics* and the *Journal of African Media Studies*.

Lee Wilkins teaches media ethics at the University of Missouri School of Journalism. Her research focuses on the moral development of journalists and ethical decision making. She is co-author, with Renita Coleman, of *The Moral Media: How Journalists Reason about Ethics* and numerous articles and book chapters focusing broadly on ethics, particularly the relationship of journalism to democratic government. She is a member of the founding editorial board of the *Journal of Mass Media Ethics* and currently serves as editor of that publication. Wilkins earned her doctorate in political science at the University of Oregon and has worked as a reporter and editor on newspapers in several states in the US. She has won three teaching awards at the University of Missouri, and before moving to Missouri, she taught at the University of Colorado-Boulder for 11 years.

Introduction:
Why a Global Media Ethics?

Stephen J. A. Ward and Herman Wasserman

Is it possible for media ethics to extend beyond borders? These ten essays discuss, debate, and critique the very idea of a global media ethics that crosses physical and cultural boundaries. It is the idea of a new ethics for a journalism that is global in reach and impact. A media ethics without borders does not yet exist. It is an idea, a movement, an urgent possibility, and a controversial and ambitious proposal.

But while a global media ethics does not yet exist, it is vital that we try to imagine ways in which it might be brought into being, and what it would look like. We need to consider the construction of a global media ethics because of rapid and disorientating change. We live amid a media revolution that blurs geographical, cultural, and temporal boundaries. Urgent global issues and the power of global communications point to the need for a media ethics that is global in its principles and in its understanding of media. This media-connected world brings together a plurality of different religions, traditions, ethnic groups and values. Tensions propagate. Global problems deepen.

A global-minded media is of value because biased and parochial media can wreak havoc in a tightly linked global world. By the same token, media that claim to be 'global' yet fail to acknowledge the ways in which their ethical perspectives are influenced by their own cultural, historical or political positioning, will be unable to help us make sense of the world in which we live. Unless reported within its proper context, North American readers may fail to understand the causes of violence in the Middle East, or ethnic conflict in Africa. Jingoistic reports can portray the inhabitants of other regions of the world as a threat. Biased reports may incite ethnic groups in a region to attack one another. In times of insecurity, a narrow-minded, patriotic news media can amplify the views of leaders who stampede populations into war or the removal of civil rights for minorities.

With global reach comes global responsibilities. We need a cosmopolitan journalism that reports issues and events in a way that reflects this global plurality of views and the power relations between them; to practise a journalism that helps different groups understand one another better. Journalism with a global perspective is needed to help citizens understand the daunting global problems of poverty, environmental degradation, technological inequalities, and political instability. These problems require concerted global action. A successful appreciation of the problems that face the world, and what actions are necessary, requires reporting from an informed and nuanced transnational perspective.

However, to recognise the urgency of global media ethics is only the start. To agree that news media have global responsibilities does not mean that we have a clear and defensible list of global duties for journalists around the world. To speak of a global media ethics is not to provide a systematic framework of principles, standards, and best practices. Moreover, the idea of global media ethics raises tough theoretical and practical questions. Are there universal values in journalism or in news media? How would a global media ethics do justice to the cultural, political, and economic differences around the world?

The authors in this book address these difficult questions. They provide theoretical perspectives on major issues, and apply their ideas to specific countries, contexts and problems. Their reflections, analyses, and arguments are divided into three sections.

In Section One, the authors address the most theoretical and philosophical questions. Clifford G. Christians opens the book by arguing that a global media ethics should be based on an 'ethics of universal being'. The overarching framework for a media ethics without borders should be a universal ethics of human dignity, truth, and non-violence. These principles themselves are grounded in the sacredness of human life. Without these ethical foundations, relativism undermines our conception of the good, and makes our practices arbitrary. How can we condemn evil communities or irresponsible media practices except through widely accepted principles?

Lee Wilkins seeks to answer the question: How is work, particularly journalism, influenced by the moral growth of individuals? Wilkins looks at what neuroscientists understand about how the human brain thinks about morality. On this foundation, she places a feminist theory of care infused with an authentic sense of duty. She reviews the findings of moral development research applied to journalists. Her argument is that the organic human brain includes a hard-wired capacity for moral action influenced by an environment that shapes professional ethical response, particularly at the intersection of care and duty. This is one fruitful path by which a universal (or at least international) understanding of media ethics could be articulated and investigated.

Stephen J. A. Ward asks whether ethical journalists violate their principles of objectivity and independence when they report as patriots, especially in times of conflict. In a global world, how much ethical weight should we accord claims that journalists must be patriots to their country? Ward argues that patriotism challenges the notion that journalists can act as global citizens for a media ethics beyond borders. He develops a theory of moderate, democratic patriotism that is compatible with ethical journalism within a nation. Ward then develops a theory of 'global patriotism' for global journalists, where the first duty is to serve humanity at large.

Nick Couldry develops a framework for a media ethics from the point of view of *all* citizens. Using neo-Aristotelian virtue ethics, Couldry argues that we need a global media ethics that no longer separates media producers from media consumers. In an era where developments in media technologies have blurred the distinction between media production and consumption, media ethics can no longer be seen as a debate that only concerns 'insiders' in the media industry. Media ethics, Couldry emphasises, needs to be recast for an era when all of us have a stake in responsible media.

In Section Two, a group of authors consider how theories that advance universal values and principles for journalism relate to critical and postcolonial perspectives. How can global principles be 'local' or 'glocal'? How can a global ethics deal with issues of power, colonialism, and the diversity of media cultures? Herman Wasserman argues that supposedly universal values for media such as the concept of 'human dignity' have to be interpreted and applied not only within local contexts but also applied in relation to a global set of power relations within which media producers, audiences, and participants are mutually interdependent. Such a global picture would have to be enriched with a complex understanding of cultural, economic, and social factors that have impacted on how human dignity is understood in various contexts.

Like Wasserman, Shakuntala Rao approaches the question of global media ethics from the perspective of postcolonial theory. She argues for an 'epistemic syncretism' where media practitioners can combine Western theories of media ethics with theories derived from local traditions and religious life. For Rao, the point is not to pitch the global versus the local, or Western versus indigenous. Rather, she argues that the local should bear upon the universal in a non-coercive way. We should not reject the non-Western and the indigenous as non-theoretical. Instead, we should accept them as theory and as equally capable of analysing the media's ethical practices.

In his chapter, Pieter Fourie sounds a cautionary note against the postcolonial approaches to media ethics followed by Wasserman and Rao. Although Fourie acknowledges that the idea of postcolonial studies to decolonise Western epistemology may accentuate the need for an African perspective, he emphasises that such an appeal to indigenous knowledge should take account of the realities of cultural assimilation and globalisation. Having pointed out dangers associated with indigenous approaches to media ethics, Fourie argues for a normative ethics that is based on difference and diversity.

In Section Three, two authors ask about how media ethics operates in Zambia and Ethiopia, while a third author explains how the principles of Islam support the basic ideas of global ethics. Fackson Banda discusses the concept of 'glocalisation' and applies this theoretical construct to media ethics. In his discussion of how the 'globalisation' of media ethics becomes enmeshed with the specific context in which journalism is practised, Banda draws on the different historical trajectories that have altered the texture of media ethics in Zambia – from colonialism, to postcolonialism to globalisation. Banda illustrates the tensions that exist between global, often Euro-American, libertarian ethical values of journalism and the context-based peculiarities of process, ideology, and concept. He concludes that the question is no longer whether or not globalisation has any impact on the local practices of journalism ethics, but rather about the degree of glocalisation or hybridisation of the criss-crossing experience.

Ali Mohamed examines how the newspaper publication of the Danish cartoons of the Prophet Mohammed raises the issue of freedom of expression in the context of globalisation, cultural pluralism, and a new media that enables the rapid circulation of controversial images across borders. His essay explains how a reading of the primary Islamic scriptural sources reflects Islam's support for the common ethical value of freedom of expression but also the responsibility it entails. Mohamed uses Islamic principles to evaluate the Danish cartoon case, and he describes how the application of these principles may differ from other ethical approaches.

Gebremedhin Simon discusses media ethics in Ethiopia and draws links between that country's media ecology and codes of media ethics. By referring to examples from the Ethiopian media, Simon argues that media ethics are culturally sensitive and that local realities and circumstances have a significant, if not deciding, impact on how media ethics will be manifested in a local context.

This book is based on the belief that ethicists, media scholars, journalists, and members of the public in different countries need a sustained and critical dialogue on how media ethics can be reformed and re-invented to address the new conditions of journalism and public communication. This radical rethinking of the principles and standards of media ethics will not be accomplished today or even tomorrow. Many conceptual and practical obstacles must be overcome. However, the hope is that, in time, this search for a global media ethics will lead to fundamental change in how we think about media ethics, and how we act as global communicators.

This book does not claim to be comprehensive. It could not possibly include all of the perspectives on global media ethics from every part of the world. Yet, this book does claim to be an exploration into the barely chartered terrain of the ethics of the future. It is an invitation to readers to join the robust and growing debate on the prospects of a media ethics beyond borders.

SECTION I

Universals, Theory, and Global Ethics

The Ethics of Universal Being[1]

Clifford G. Christians

We live in a world of unrelenting conflict and face a monumental challenge in producing a legitimate ethics. On the theoretical side of this difficult task, we need to be certain about our moral foundations. Without a defensible conception of the good, our practices are arbitrary. How can we condemn violent practices such as suicide bombings in the name of jihad except through widely accepted principles? We are stunned at the blatant greed and plundering of the earth, but without norms we are only elitists and hot-tempered moralists. Conflicts among people, communities, and nations need principles other than their own for their resolution. A credible ethics, as a minimum, must be fundamentally transnational in character.

Within communications, revolutionary changes are underway in media technologies. Digital information systems now dominate industrial societies worldwide. An ethics of integrity for media professionals must be developed in an era of overwhelming electronic instruments. The origins of media ethics are rooted in print technology. Journalism ethics in its contemporary form has included broadcast media and made some advances in understanding visual literacy. The dominant ethical issues in news, persuasion, and entertainment have been articulated in a pre-digital context. Now the media ethics agenda must be developed for the cyber world of search engines, online networking, and computer data bases. Some issues are new, some amplify or transform moral principles of the past, and others create new levels of complexity. And with a philosophical foundation in place, the difficult choices can be made more responsibly. A thin parochial ethics is obviously inadequate for coming to grips with today's global technologies. As a *Media Ethics Beyond Borders* takes shape in this volume, the overarching framework is a universal ethics of human dignity, truth, and non-violence, these principles themselves grounded in the sacredness of human life.

Within the turbulence at present – political, economical, and cultural – this paper argues for universalism in ethics. It demonstrates that the modernist construction is no longer credible. Enlightenment rationalism contending for absolutes across time and space has been exposed as imperialistic, oppressive of non-Western perspectives, and exclusively male. The subjective-objective dichotomy on which it is based is no longer epistemologically viable. While media ethics has generally depended on the ethics of rationalism, in the search of a universal foundation in a global world, reviving the modernist version is not viable.

However, an ethics of universal being is an alternative. It enables us to start over intellectually with the holistic notion of humans as humans-in-relation, rather than with a truncated notion of humans as rational individuals. It speaks against the claims of both philosophical and cultural relativism. It is held together by a pretheoretical commitment to the purposiveness of life in nature, defined in human terms as the sacredness of life. In our systematic reflection on this underlying perspective, three ethical principles emerge as entailed by it – human dignity, truth-telling, and non-violence. Instead of the individual autonomy of ethical rationalism, ethics begins with its opposite – universal human solidarity. And from that starting point, we enter our own communities and work professions with standards to guide our decisions and behaviour.

I. Relativism

Ethical rationalism has been the dominant paradigm in ethics. Through reason the human species is distinctive and through rationality moral canons are legitimate. In this view, timeless moral truths are rooted in human nature and independent of the conventions of particular societies. In this form, the Enlightenment mind established absolutist ethical systems that made relativism inconceivable, Immanuel Kant's categorical imperatives being the pre-eminent example.

The idea of a common morality known to all rational beings has had its detractors, of course. David Hume (1739, 1963), for example, took seriously the multiplying discoveries of other cultures in the 18th century. He recognised within the framework of empirical philosophy that these diverse conceptions of the good life might turn out to have nothing in common.

But it was Friedrich Nietzsche (1944–1900) who developed a totalising assault on moral values in the 19th century. In his first book *The Birth of Tragedy* (1872), Nietzsche insisted that "only as aesthetic phenomena are life and the world justified" (1967a, pp. 5, 24). He announced a philosophy beyond good and evil that "places morality itself not only in the world of appearances but even among deceptions, as semblance, delusion, error, and interpretation" (1976a, Preface, cf. Nietzsche, 1976b).

Over against the traditional belief that ethics was essential for social order, Nietzsche argued that moral values had become worthless. In his *Will to Power* (1967c) there is no longer an answer to the human "why" and this nihilism means the "end of the moral interpretation of the world" (pp. 1–2). Because he was questioning God's existence, and with it the viability of moral commands,

Nietzsche turned to aesthetic values that need no supernatural sanction. "One can speak of beauty without implying that anything ought to be beautiful or that anybody ought to create the beautiful" (Kaufmann, 1968, p. 130).

These oppositional voices in the 18th and 19th centuries, rooted in Hume and Nietzsche, have burgeoned into a wholesale attack, so that in our own time, immutable and universal imperatives have been generally discredited. Ethical rationalism has been exposed as the "morality of a dominant gender and class" (Outka and Reed, 1993, p. 4). Defending an abstract good is no longer seen as beneficent, but rather as imperialism over the moral judgments of diverse communities.

The modernist project to establish reason and truth as everywhere and always the same has failed. The concept of norms themselves has eroded. Metaphysical certitude has been replaced by philosophical relativism. Moral principles are presumed to have no objective application independent of the societies within which they are constituted.

1.1. Language

Communications is one crucial laboratory for addressing this predicament. Communications is not a discipline *per se* with a discrete subject matter; it is a pervasive scholarly orientation that is integrative rather than specialised. Communications makes possible all cultural forms, all community life and socio-political institutions without being absorbed into any of them. Therefore, in today's wide-ranging assault on the foundations of knowledge, the communication infrastructure has no place to hide. Nietzsche was a philologist and today's conundrums typically come to a head at the nexus of language theory and theories of culture.

In Wittgenstein's (1953, 1956) linguistic naturalism, for example, the search for an abstract essence entangles us in a maze of propositions that lead finally to the point where the essentialist turn was taken in the first place. Instead of essentialism, we can only claim in mathematical proofs, "this is what we do. This is use and custom among us, a product of our natural history" (Wittgenstein, 1956, sec. 63, p. 20; cf. 1953, pp. 116–123). The same appeal to custom is alleged to hold when it comes to moral language and communication. Objects and events situated in time and space contain all the facts there are. Moral standards, therefore, are only intelligible within their own lingual context.

Jean Baudrillard is a contemporary example. Baudrillard is centrally concerned about the consequences of saturating ourselves with signs and images. In Baudrillard's *Simulations* (1983), the massive development of media technologies has shifted modern civilisation from production to reproduction, from economic and political institutions to hyperreality. We create cybernetic models to organise our experience, but a reversal occurs and reality arises from them instead. Rather than producing a meaningful view of the world, electronic culture creates a black hole into which all objective meaning disappears. Images are refined and manipulated technologically until they have no referent in reality outside them.

Differences between the real and the copy become obscure, and, in fact, implosion has occurred. The simulacra have been inverted. The world of codes and networks – the hyperreal – becomes the real instead. Time-honoured distinctions disappear – between the real and the unreal, reality and image, centre and periphery, fact and fiction, news and drama, information and propaganda, and between signifier and signified. Implosion makes such concepts meaningless. Whatever can be digitalised and codified becomes the frame of reference for technological societies. Our understanding of the human is reduced to codes, signals, DNA models, and the Human Genome Project.

In our day, morality has appeared to reach the end of the line. The social fashion is to be emancipated from moral standards and to disavow moral responsibility. We are witnessing the demise of the ethical, living in what Nietzsche (1996) calls the era beyond good and evil. In summarising the postmodern argument against ethics, Zygmunt Bauman uses Nietzsche's perspective: ethics in postmodern times has been replaced by aesthetics (Bauman, 1993, pp. 178–179). Popular culture gets caught up in the technological imperative, producing the visually interesting, creating programmes at times of artistic wholeness, but driven by the conditions of aesthetic space rather than ethics.

There are major paradoxes in these analyses of language and communications. But underneath the overwrought claims, they speak in concert against the totalising conditions of knowledge that the 18th century fostered – against metaphysics, universal reason, ethical systems, correspondence views of truth, and essentialist theories of human nature. And cultures feeding from the Enlightenment worldview now face a crisis of validation. What still counts as legitimate knowledge? There are no widely accepted rational means for people committed to different beliefs to debate them constructively. Transhistorical certitude has been replaced by philosophical relativism, that is, by the presumption that moral principles have no objective application independent of the societies within which they are constituted.

Nihilism (no moral truths exist) and scepticism (moral propositions cannot be justified) are prevalent responses as well.

1.2 Philosophical Anthropology

At this critical juncture in its history, the Enlightenment's progeny needs to examine once again whether a universal moral order is conceivable and intellectually defensible. In fact, it has to recover the very idea of moral universals itself. And this must be done without presuming first foundations, without the luxury of an objective metaphysical reality from which to begin. The only legitimate option is an ethics that is culturally inclusive rather than biased toward Western hegemony. The future of communication ethics, in Seyla Benhabib's terms, depends on whether a "post Enlightenment defense of universalism, without metaphysical and historical props, is still viable" (1992, p. 3; cf. 2002).

Rather than move uncritically from objectivity to subjectivity or from correspondence to coherence views of truth, I believe resolution emerges from philosophical anthropology.[2] The modernist period coopted moral issues into epistemology, and when modernity's cognitive system went bankrupt, moral imperatives were destroyed also. But if normativity is adequately understood in terms of our human wholeness, an ontological ground for ethics is once again viable in the contemporary context. Therefore, the question for metaethics: Are there global principles or a moral order or master norms that belong to our humanness? The philosophy of communication itself offers the possibility of discovering something ontologically – rather than epistemologically – universal. For communication to occur beyond mere transmission, the human being must be able to recognise in the "otherness" of its representations that which is

> universal in them….A communicative subject must actually know universals, not in the sense of…abstract generalizations, but with the capacity to grasp precisely the universality imminent in the particular….The communicative mind must be able to assimilate that universality of something 'other', without thereby losing self-identity, that is to say, without itself becoming something universal (Henrici, 1983, p. 3).

Beyond epistemological relativism in the Nietzschean tradition, cultural relativity is unquestioned and celebrated across a wide range of the social spectrum – that is, the right and valid are known only in local space and native languages. A context that is intelligible, a proposition that is true, an argument that is valid, and judgments of right and wrong are accepted as such by a culture's internal criteria. And therefore such concepts, propositions, arguments, and judgments have no validity elsewhere. Moral realists of various kinds still exist, of course, but they no longer define the public agenda. Our crusades for individual rights, national interest, and for ethnic identity, in their latent effect, nourish the relativistic mind and help establish its givenness (cf. Masolo, 2004, p. 496). For most philosophers, there is no other avenue to self-respect. On the concrete level, relativism carries the day, and any work on universals faces a crisis of validation. The most compelling pathway is ontology, an ethics of being.

2. Sacredness of Life as Protonorm

The German philosopher Hans Jonas illustrates one strategy for establishing the idea of universal norms in ontological terms. He turns to nature rather than to modernist foundationalism rooted in a static, Newtonian cosmology. Natural reality has a moral claim on us for its own sake and in its own right. The philosophical rationale for human action is reverence for life on earth, for the organic whole, for the physical realm in which human civilisation is situated.

The Enlightenment worldview assumed that humans alone are conscious and purposeful and that nature is spiritless. Jonas contradicts this dichotomy. In his perspective, purpose is embedded in the animate world and its purposiveness is evident "in bringing forth life. Nature evinces at least one determinate goal – life itself" (Jonas, 1984, p. 74). Thus, Jonas concludes, "showing the immanence of purpose in nature . . . with the gaining of this premise, the decisive battle for ethical theory has already been won" (p. 78).[3]

Our duty to preserve life is to be understood as similar in kind to parents' responsibility for their children. It is an obligation "independent of prior assent or choice, irrevocable, and not given to alteration of its terms by the participants" (Jonas, 1984, p. 95). When new life appears, the forbears do not debate their relationship to it as though the offspring is neutral protoplasm and their responsibility a matter of calculating the options. Parental duty to children is an archetype of the natural accountability Jonas thus establishes – an *a priori* ought, grounded ontologically, an obligation that is timeless and non-negotiable.

Human responsibility regarding natural existence contributes the possibility of intrinsic imperatives to moral philosophy. It demonstrates the legitimacy of concluding that collective duty can be cosmic, primordial, and irrespective of our roles or contracts. Through the preservation of life as the ground for human responsibility, Jonas has established normative discourse to help contradict the postmodern assumptions that metaphysical truths do not exist and that no 'ought' can be derived from being.[4]

Jonas gives the preservation of life a taken-for-granted character. Our human identity is rooted in the principle that "human beings have certain inescapable claims on one another which we cannot renounce except at the cost of our humanity" (Peukert, 1981, p. 11). Rather than generating an abstract conception of the good, the primal sacredness of life is a catalyst for binding humans universally into an organic whole. In Peukert's terms, given the oneness of the human species, our minimum goal must be

> a world in which human beings find ways of living together which enable every individual to work out a lifestyle based on recognition and respect of others, and to do so ultimately in a universal perspective not confined to small groups or nations…. Universal solidarity is thus the basic principle of ethics and the normative core of all human communication (p. 10).

In other words, there are protonorms that precede their reification into ethical principles. There is at least one primordial generality underlying the logos of systematic thought. And its universal scope enables us to avoid the divisiveness of appeals to individual interests, cultural practices, and national prerogatives. The sacredness of life, evident in natural being, grounds a responsibility that is global in scope and self-evident regardless of cultures and competing ideologies.[5]

In a study of ethical principles in 13 countries on four continents, the sacredness of human life was consistently affirmed as a universal value (Christians and Traber, 1997). Our duty to preserve life is taken for granted, outside subjective experience. The scientific view of the natural world cannot account for the purposiveness of life itself. Reverence for life on earth is a pretheoretical given that makes the moral order possible.

The veneration of human life is a protonorm similar in kind to the proto Germanic language – *proto* meaning beneath – a lingual predecessor underlying the Germanic languages as we know them in history. Reverence for life on earth establishes a level playing ground for cross-cultural collaboration on the ethical foundations of responsible communication. Various societies articulate this protonorm in different terms and illustrate it locally, but every culture can bring to the table this fundamental norm for ordering political relationships, and such social institutions as the media. Its dynamic and primordial character contradicts essentialist and static views of human nature. It represents a universalism from the ground up.

3. Application to Communications

The communications context is especially appropriate for understanding the scope and character of reverence for life. Within a symbolic cultural theory of communication, the complex relationships become clear among human interaction, our global oneness, and the web of life as a whole.[6]

Martin Buber (1970) makes the dialogic primal in his famous lines, "In the beginning is the relation" (p. 69) and the relation is "the cradle of actual life" (p. 60). He intends the relation ontologically as a category of being. Human relationships, not individuals per se, have primacy. "Persons appear by entering into relation to other persons" (p. 112). "The one basic word is the word-pair I-Thou" (p. 3). Rather than arguments and concepts, this embodied connection gives moral anchorage. For Emmanuel Levinas, as described by Olthuis,

> the face of the Other commands me not to kill….The face is the epiphany of the nakedness of the Other, a visitation, a coming, a saying which comes in the passivity of the face, not threatening, but obligating. My world is ruptured, my contentment interrupted. Here is an appeal from which there is no escape, a responsibility, a state of being hostage. It is looking into the face of the Other that reveals a call to a responsibility that is before any beginning, decision or initiative on my part (1997, p. 139; cf. Levinas, 1979, 1981).

Moreover, in Levinasian terms, when I turn to the face of the Other, I see not only flesh and blood but the whole of humanity – dialogic communication understood as intersubjective universalism.

Paolo Freire (1969/1973) insists on the same integrated unity: "I cannot exist without a not-I; in turn the not-I depends on that existence." "There is no longer 'I think' but 'we think'," he writes. It is the "we think" that establishes the "I think" and not the contrary. "This co-participation of Subjects in the act of thinking is communication….Communication implies a reciprocity which cannot be broken" – giving and receiving, comprehending and creating, teaching and learning (pp. 137–139). Communication is a process with a double function – I-Thou or I-It – but never one element in isolation. Communication is not the transference of knowledge but a dialogic encounter of subjects creating it together. Freire's approach to communication presumes and articulates an explicit ontology of radical humanness.

Buber, Freire, and Levinas categorically reject the Enlightenment's dichotomies, its dualisms between self and language, the isolation of the individual from society, and its rupture of subjective and objective. Concrete human existence is embedded in the vitalistic order as a whole; we nurture I-Thou relationships with the natural world as a dimension of our corporeality in general and through our sense perception in particular. Although he does not attribute consciousness to trees, for example, Buber speaks of a mutuality that occurs in the ongoing oscillations of I-Thou and I-It relations: "It can happen, if will and grace are joined, that as I contemplate a tree I am drawn into a relation, and the tree ceases to be an It" (p. 58). "Relation is reciprocity...and there are three spheres in which the world of relation arises: life with nature...life with men... life with spiritual beings" (pp. 56–58). This is an incarnational worldview – one explicitly social, which extends the personal to the supreme reaches of the universe and shapes an environmental ethics as well. It is the only counter-Enlightenment philosophy of communication that explicitly meets the challenge of J. B. Lotz (1963):

> The ontology of Being dominated by the person differs greatly from an ontology of Being dominated by the thing....Ontology must be rescued from submersion in things by being thought out entirely from the viewpoint of person and thus of Being (pp. 280, 294).

The dialogic tradition sweeps epistemology into anthropology. We understand reality when we get inside the self that is bonded-in-relation and embedded in purposive nature.[7]

This is a philosophy of communication not limited to hermeneutics and semantics but one that is decidedly

> anthropological or more exactly anthro-ontological. For one thing, language presupposes corporeality for vocal utterances to be articulated and pronounced. For another, language necessarily refers to a world perceptible to the senses and common to the speaker; it implies their common being-in-the-world (Henrici, 1983, p. 2).

Mediated systems, from this perspective, are inescapably human creations as well. In literary works or cinema, the indispensable features of their inner dialectics – the point of departure, plot, setting, overall tone, and resolution of conflicts – are all value driven and either engage a culture's value system or they cannot be understood.

Contrary to another Western dualism – humans as body and mind – the dialogic worldview is trinitarian, including the spirit. Or, instead of spirit, this third dimension is called *psuchee* or the moral imagination. Each of the three is a *conditio sine qua non* in a dialogic understanding of the human. To the rational and biological aspects, dialogic theory adds the symbolic, the interpretive domain, centered in the *psuchee*. This is a holistic human being where the various dimensions of our humanness come to expression in and through one another. One humanly integrated whole of three distinct dimensions is harmonised into a unique species without exception. We are unitary beings with our various human capacities depending on and interacting with one another.

This third feature – the interpretive – was recognised by the classical Greeks as the primordial home of language. From the mythological Hermes, inventor of language, they coined the term *hermeneia* (hermeneutics, interpretation). Aristotle's genius brought hermeneutical consciousness into focus as a constituent feature of the human species, and in the *Nicomachean Ethics* he gave the interpretative art its richest meaning.[8] *Hermeneia* is not theoretical knowledge *(episteme)* nor is it practical skill *(techne)* because it concerns more than habit and utility (cf. Gadamer, 1965/1975, pp. 274–289). In making a moral decision, Aristotle argues, *hermeneia* discerns the appropriate action, in the right amount, and with proper timing. This is Aristotelian language confirming that we are moral beings with an orienting system beyond the senses, yet one differing from formal logic.

Certainly, moral insight *(phronesis)* in Aristotle's ethics has a rational, cognitive element. Moral insight arises from "the ability to deliberate and consequently to believe through deliberation that something is or is not to be done" (Engberg-Pederson, 1984, p. 152). However, *phronesis* is not merely a static grasp of "true universal propositions," but is necessarily practical "in the sense of actually leading to action" (pp. 168–169). It presumes desire and will. "Reasoned argument is not sufficient" to make us act nobly; it only makes us see in particular situations what acts "we already want to do" (p. 135). Rather than automatically applying a universal good lodged in the intellect, through moral insight humans discover "what should be done in situations in which this is not yet clear" (p. 238). The point of ethical theory is "action as opposed to mere knowledge", and therefore, *phronesis* presupposes a "desiderative state; it is necessarily motivational" (pp. 238–239; cf. Farrell, 1993, ch. 2).

Aristotle's tripartite human, and the wholistic being presupposed by the universal sacredness of life, enter theorising from different perspectives but overlap around the interpretive modality. While Aristotle's human being was understood in essentialist terms and the sacredness of life is non-essentialist, they agree on the level of communication theory that moral rules exist independently of human judgment and action.

Language has the same human home as morality in the centre of our being. Neither can be isolated in the *cogito*. In dialogic theory, communication rests not in *episteme* or the monads but in the interpretive capacity, the spirit. Discourse is born of conscience. A fulsome anthropology of organic wholeness moves language from its Enlightenment site in cognition to an interpretive axis in values and worldviews – or, as the centre of our being is sometimes called – to the human spirit.

If the interpretive domain is lingual, and if language is the matrix of community, then human bonds are not constituted by reason or action but through finding common meaning in *hermeneia*. The commonplace, "we're with you in spirit", reflects the powerful truth that our species' oneness is born along the stream of consciousness. We resonate through our spirit cross-culturally to the moral imagination of others everywhere.

The sinews that hold the world together are moral – we are connected as a human whole, spirit-to-spirit. Contrary to what functionalism contends, our international web is not primarily political power or economic interdependence or information technology but a commitment of conscience that preconditions the ethos of these external apparatuses. Our mutual humanity is energised by moral obligations that activate our conscience toward the bondedness we share inescapably with others.

Such protonorms as reverence for life can only be recovered locally and inscribed culturally. Language situates them in history. Master norms are of a universal order conceptually speaking; they reflect our common condition as a species. Yet human beings enter them through the immediate reality of geography, ethnicity, and ideology. We distinguish between the universal and particular as we do with a windowpane, knowing there is a decisive break yet recognising that the universal realm is only transparent in the local. Through protonorms we have an answer to relativism, while allowing for multiple realisations in different cultures. Buber's (1965) earthiness protects us from a naïve and sterile universalism: "A legitimate philosophical anthropology must know that there is not merely a human species but also peoples, not only a human soul but also types and characters, not merely a human life but also stages in life" (p. 123).

An ethics of universalism situated in creatureliness entails a thicker view of moral judgments. Rather than privileging an individualistic, transcendental rationalism, moral commitments are inscribed in our worldviews through which we share a view of reality and establish human community. This ontological model is actually close to the way the moral imagination operates in everyday life and refuses to separate moral agents from all that makes them unique. Instead of constructing a purely rational foundation for morality, our mutual human existence across cultural, racial, and historical boundaries is the touchstone of ethics. The moral order is positioned fundamentally in the creaturely and corporeal rather than the conceptual. "In this way, ethics…is as old as creation. Being ethical is a primordial movement in the beckoning force of life itself" (Olthuis, 1997, p. 141).

To postmodernists and other detractors, universalist positions have discredited themselves because they have seemed to breed totalitarianism. Those who claim inside knowledge of universal, transcendental truth, typically seek to convert or control dissenters. Universalism is said to threaten diversity, whereas relativism liberates us to reject all oppressive claims to truth. In light of this objection, it must be reiterated that the protonorm of the sacredness of human life is not a foundational *a priori*. This universal, in fact, belongs to a different category, philosophically speaking, than that of objectivist absolutes. Adherence to presuppositions is

> a matter of commitment, not epistemic certainty. We initiate any inquiry or action with…presuppositions because we must do so, not because they have been demonstrated. One's commitments are always open to question, and thus are liable to be modified or replaced. But one cannot proceed in any enterprise with taking something as given (Johnstone, 1993, p. 7).

Cartesian rationalism and Kant's formalism presumed noncontingent starting points. Universal human solidarity does not. Nor does it flow from Platonism, that is, the finite participating in the infinite and receiving its essence from it. Without a protonorm of universal scope, ethical theory and practice are trapped in the distributive fallacy – one ideological bloc presuming to speak for the whole.

A commitment to universals does not eliminate all differences in what we think and believe. Normative ethics grounded ontologically is pluralistic. The only question is whether our values affirm the human good or not. With universal theory, there is a frame of reference for interpreting and measuring communities. Standards are essential for forming the common good. Communities turn in on themselves; they are not all legitimate. Matthew Hale's white supremacist World Church of the Creator and the Michigan militia are communities for condemnation. The question is whether our communities affirm the sacredness of life.

This is worldview pluralism, which allows us to hold our beliefs in good faith and debate them openly rather than be constrained by a superficial consensus. The standard of judgment is not economic or political success but whether our worldviews and community formations contribute in the long run to truth-telling, human dignity, and nonmaleficence. Ethical principles grounded in being do not obstruct cultures and inhibit their development. On the contrary, they liberate us for strategic action and provide a direction for social change.

4. Basic Principles

The primal sacredness of life is a protonorm that binds humans into a common oneness. And in our systematic reflection on this primordial generality, we recognise that it entails such basic ethical principles as human dignity, truth, and nonviolence.

4.1 Human Dignity

The universal reverence of life, in fact, presupposes the strongest possible definition of human dignity as

> the respect-worthiness imputed to humankind by reason of its privileged ontological status as creator, maintainer and destroyer of worlds. Each self shares in this essential dignity insofar as it partakes in world-building or world-destroying actions. Thus human dignity does not rest on intention, moral merit, or subjective definitions of self-interest. It rests on the fact that we are, in this fundamental way that is beyond our intention, human....To assert dignity is to both acknowledge the factuality of human creative agency and to accept responsibility for its use (Stanley, 1978, pp. 69–70).

Different cultural traditions affirm human dignity in a variety of ways, but together they insist that all human beings have sacred status without exception. Native American discourse is steeped in reverence for life, an interconnectedness among all living forms so that we live in solidarity with others as equal constituents in the web of life. In communalistic African societies, *likute* is loyalty to the community's reputation, to tribal honour. In Latin-American societies, insistence on cultural identity is an affirmation of the unique worth of human beings. In Islam, every person has the right to honour and a good reputation. In Confucius, veneration of authority is necessary because our authorities are human beings of dignity. Humans are a unique species, requiring within itself regard for its members as a whole. Respect for another person's dignity is one ethical principle on which various cultures rest.[9]

From this perspective, one understands the ongoing vitality of the Universal Declaration of Human Rights issued by the United Nations General Assembly in 1948. As the Preamble states, "Recognition of the inherent dignity and of the equal and inalienable rights of all members of the human family is the foundation of freedom, justice and peace in the world" (Universal Declaration, 1988, p. 1). Every child, woman, and man has sacred status, with no exceptions for religion, class, gender, age, or ethnicity. This common sacredness of all human beings regardless of merit or achievement is the shared commitment out of which we begin to generate notions of a just society.

4.2 Truth

Truth-telling is another basic ethical principle that follows from the ontological grounding of ethics in the sacredness of life. Language is the primary means of social formation and, therefore, human existence is impossible without an overriding commitment to truth. The most fundamental norm of Arab Islamic communication is truthfulness. Truth is one of the three highest values in the context of the Latin-American experience of communication. In Hinduism, truth is the highest *dharma* and the source of all other virtues. Among the Sushwap of Canada, truth as genuineness and authenticity is central to its indigenous culture (Cooper, 1996). Living with others is inconceivable if we cannot tacitly assume that people are speaking truthfully. Lying, in fact, is so unnatural that machines can measure bodily reactions to it. When we deceive, Dietmar Meith argues, the truth imperative is recognised in advance: "Otherwise there would be no need to justify the exceptions as special cases....Those who relativise truthfulness, who refuse to accept it as an ethical principle, indirectly recognise it as generally valid" (Meith, 1997).

In Sissela Bok's (1979, cf. p. 19) terms, deception is as blatant, destructive, and morally outrageous as physical assault. In an intellectual trajectory connecting to Aristotle, the positive worth of truth-telling has been generally accepted at face value, with deception an enemy of the human order: "Falsehood is in itself mean and culpable, and truth noble and full of praise" (Aristotle, bk. 4, ch. 7). Though often only a rhetorical flourish and reduced in meaning, media codes of ethics typically appeal to truth as the cornerstone of social communication; they reflect in their own way its intrinsic value. As a primary agent of the symbolic theatre in which we live, the public media have no choice but to honor this norm as obligatory to their mission and rationale. The result is a richer epistemology than minimalist notions of accurate representation and objectivist ways of knowing. Truth-telling is axiological rather than a problem of cognition *per se* and integrated into human consciousness and social formation.[10]

4.3 Nonviolence

Nonviolence – a commitment to living together peacefully – is likewise a non-negotiable imperative rooted in the sacredness of life. In fact, Mahatma Gandhi and Martin Luther King, Jr., developed this principle beyond a political strategy into a public philosophy. According to Philippe Nemo, in Emmanuel Levinas, interaction between the self and the Other makes peace normative. "The first word of the Other's face is 'Thou shalt not kill.' It is an order. There is a commandment in the appearance of the face, as if a master spoke to me" (Levinas, 1985, p. 89). In the face-to-face encounter, the infinite is revealed. The Other's presence involves an obligation to which I owe my immediate attention. In communalistic and indigenous cultures, care for the weak and vulnerable (children, sick, and elderly), and sharing material resources, are a matter of course. Along with *dharma, ahimsa* (nonviolence) forms the basis of the Hindu worldview.

Darrell Fasching's comparative study of religions identifies hospitality to strangers as a common commitment, "giving birth to a cross-cultural ethic of non-violent civil disobedience…through movements of liberation which seek to protect the dignity of those who were treated as strangers" (Fasching, 1995, p. 15; cf. 1993). The public's general revulsion against physical abuse in intimate settings, and our consternation over brutal crimes and savage wars, are glimmers of hope reflecting this principle's validity. Out of nonviolence, we articulate ethical theories about not harming the innocent as an obligation that is cosmic and irrespective of our roles or contracts.[11]

5. The Challenge

If we could establish master norms, such as justice, truth, and nonmaleficence, we would have a frame of reference for critiquing media conventions and codes of ethics. It would ensure that the issues addressed in our pedagogy and theorising would be stitched into the common morality. Instead of seeking consensus about prescriptive maxims, master norms of this sort would favour intersubjectivity models and theoretical paradigms that are gender inclusive and culturally diverse. Rather than debilitating relativism, we would have a more vigorous response to the classic paradox – that is, one cannot insist on philosophical relativism without rising above it, and once outside it you have given it up.

Normative ethics grounded in a universal protonorm is a complex architecture. And to shape our communication theory and media practice more effectively by basic principles – themselves universal by virtue of their inscription in an underlying protonorm – more experiments are needed that come to grips with our moral obligation in global terms. Some glimmers of that consciousness are emerging over the environment; abusing one's share of the world's resources has now taken on moral resonance; global warming is no longer a political football but a public responsibility. But statecraft, demands for health care, educational strategies, military weapons, modes of transportation – all should be brought to judgment before the ultimate test. Do they sustain life, enhance it long term, contribute to human well-being as a whole? The challenge for the mass media is not just political insight in news and aesthetic power in entertainment but moral discernment.

In other words, does news discourse designed to irrigate public debate also connect the issue to universal norms, speaking not only to our minds but revivifying the spirit? Does the press graft the deeper questions underneath the story onto our human oneness? In the process of invigorating our moral imagination, the ethical media worldwide enable readers and viewers to resonate with other human beings who also struggle in their consciences with human values of a similar sort. Media professionals have enormous opportunities for putting this universal protonorm to work, through the sacredness of life enlarging our understanding of what it means to be human. This is discourse that irrigates public debate, refusing simply to focus on politics or entertainment *per se* but connecting the issues to universal norms, speaking not only to our minds but vivifying the spirit, grafting the deeper questions underneath the story onto our human oneness.

Conclusion

In asking whether universal truths are possible, I have centered on the irrevocable status of human life. If one understands the nature of history, language, and our dialogical personhood as cultural beings, human sacredness is inescapable. And as we come to live inside universal human solidarity, we recognise that a basic list of ethical principles is entailed by it – social justice, truth-telling, nonmaleficence, and possibly others.

Ethical theory is concerned not only with defining the central issues but also with determining the authentic grounds of moral standards. If no such grounds exist, what can be done? Therefore, rather than introduce a set of moral maxims but leaving their anchorage unattended, I have focused on a protonorm inscribed in being. Without such a primordial norm and the ethical principles derived from it, how can we argue that bombing a federal building in Oklahoma City is wrong, that the wanton slaughter of Rwandese in a refugee camp is morally outrageous, that killing journalists in El Salvador is despicable, that ransacking the earth's ecosystem is evil? On what grounds are terrorists condemned for trying to achieve political ends by assassinations? How can we despise Hitler or praise the protectors of Anne Frank? Without a commitment to norms that are beyond one's own self-interest, moral claims are merely emotional preferences. Without a protonorm on behalf of human solidarity, history is but a contest of arbitrary power.[12]

Communication ethics at this juncture has to respond to both the rapid globalisation of communications and the reassertion of local identities. It is caught in the apparently contradictory trends of cultural homogenisation and cultural resistance. Transnationalism has tribalism's fury. As we theorise universal models of communication ethics, it is the integration of globalisation and ethnicity that is today's extraordinary challenge. Through the sacredness of life we can make our way constructively at the intersection of the global and multicultural.

Czech president Vaclav Havel has understood more clearly than most of us that this present historic juncture requires a new vision cosmic in scope. "We are rightly preoccupied" he says, "with finding the key to ensure the survival of a civilisation that is global and at the same time clearly multicultural" (Havel, 1994, p. 614; cf. 1989). We fret over the possibility of "generally respected mechanisms of peaceful coexistence" and wonder "on what set of principles they are to be established." Many believe that this central political task at the end of the century "can be accomplished through technical means....But such efforts are doomed to fail if they do not grow out of something deeper, out of generally held values" (Havel, 1994, p. 614; cf. 1997). In Havel's terms, appeals at international forums for human rights and freedom are meaningless if they do not derive from respect for "the miracle of Being, the miracle of the universe, the miracle of nature, the miracle of our own existence" (p. 615). The ethics of being contributes to Havel's project. Through human solidarity rooted in a universal reverence for life, we respect ourselves and genuinely value the participation of others in a volatile age where "everything is possible and almost nothing is certain" (p. 614).

Notes

1 An early version of this paper was presented as a plenary address at the convention of the International Association of Mass Communication Research in Potoroz, Slovenia, on 29 June 1995 (cf. Christians, 1995). Another early version introduced a book of essays on universal values and was situated within the Enlightenment-modernity context rather than vis-à-vis relativism (Christians and Traber, 1997).

2 For a review of the important literature since Max Scheler's *Man's Place in Nature* in 1928, see Schacht (1990). A classic essay is Ricoeur (1960). Michel Foucault (1973) indirectly recognises the implications of focusing the issues in human terms by considering the contemporary era "the end of man" (p. 385, cf. ch. 10). For Foucault, "the idea of 'man' as an interpretive conceptual invention" is no longer viable (Schacht, 1990, p. 158).

3 Jonas' purposive life is fundamentally different from the teleological view of nature that was the basis of Aristotelianism for centuries. It does not entail essentialist natural phenomena ordered by intrinsic design. It does not presume that natural objects are substances consisting of form and matter.

4 In rejecting postmodernist claims that metaphysical truths do not exist, Jonas is not repeating traditional views of ethics grounded in the nature of the human and a static universe: an Aristotelean grounding of ethics in the nature of the human psyche, a Platonic anchor in the tripartite nature of the soul, or a theistic view of the world as a moral order under God. Instead of assuming a fixed and unchanging universe, Jonas speaks of purposive life on this side of Einstein, Freud, and Darwin.

5 The term 'sacredness' is standard in religious vocabulary, referring to deity. But it is also an anthropological term with its etymology from the Latin sanctum, meaning 'set apart'. The protonorm is presuppositional, pretheoretical, deep, primordial. On that level, sacredness as a term grants extraordinariness to human life, but is not invoking the higher level of organised religion, its doctrines, and institutions.

6   The dialogic philosophy of communication described in this section illustrates this revolution in the philosophy of language. Dialogic theory is interpretive, symbolic, contextual, and interactionist, in contrast to the traditional paradigm, which is verificationist, sentential, and formal. This section contributes to the basic thesis that the most difficult questions of metaethics require a struggle over the philosophy of language. It demonstrates that a radically human philosophy of communication (rather than a theory modeled on machine systems or mathematical formulae), one that is radically opposed to monologic and transmission theories, can enable us to take Hans Jonas' first-level approximation about responsibility for life and develop it into a complex protonorm. For an introduction to the theoretical issues regarding a dialogic approach to language and mind, Gadamer's (1965/1975) work is particularly helpful. As Richard Bernstein summarises it, "Gadamer's entire project of philosophical hermeneutics can be read as an attempt to recover . . . the quintessence of our being [as] dialogical" (Bernstein, 1986, p. 65; cf. Shin, 1994).

7   Even though our affirmation of life is embedded in our being, there will be those who refuse to acknowledge it. It fulfils our humanness to affirm it, but could be rejected as alien to my freedom or preferences. Some may claim a higher or deeper reason to kill rather than affirm or reflect the protonorm. All moral systems must account for human evil, and appealing to universals does not deny its existence. Whenever rejection occurs, because one believes in the protonorm's ubiquity, the response can still be in life-affirming terms on the grounds that evil has crusted over it rather than eliminated it.

8   Aristotle found *hermeneia* worthy of a major treatise by that title, *On Interpretation*, and he outlined a formal theory in his *Rhetoric.*

9   This understanding of human dignity rivals that of Kant in complexity, but without claiming an essentialist human nature. In the Kantian formula, one acts so that one treats humanity as an end and never as a means only. In Kant's *Groundwork*, rational nature exists as an end in itself and therefore every rational creature is to be respected as such. Humans are not victims of their inclinations nor determined by the forces of nature. Humans are a distinct species who choose rational ends by rational means, with rational choice therefore the ground of morality. Thomas Hill summarises Kant this way: "Moral conduct [in Kant's view] is the practical exercise of the noble capacity to be rational and self-governing, a capacity which sets us apart from the lower animals and gives us dignity" (1973, p. 449). While acknowledging Kant's influential work on human dignity, the argument here is that its formalism and essentialism are dependent on a Newtonian cosmology and are not sustainable on this side of Darwin, Freud, and Einstein.

10 For elaborations on this nonobjectivist definition of truth as authentic disclosure and interpretive sufficiency, see Christians (2003) and Christians (2004).

11 For detail theoretically on nonviolence and the application of this principle to media practice, see Christians (2007).

12 Over the last decade, the social ethics of Agnes Heller, Charles Taylor, and Edith Wyschogrod, and the feminist ethics of Nel Noddings, Carol Gilligan, Seyla Benhabib, and Martha Nussbaum have made a major impact on ethical theory. Their achievements are of crucial importance for defining the issues in communication ethics as well. Social and feminist ethics make a radical break with the mainstream morality of individual rights. Their communitarian commitment fits hand in glove with an interactive philosophy of communication, whereas atomistic ethics is at odds with it (Koehn, 1998,

ch. 4). Truth is understood as authenticity in a social context, and its validity is freed from the correspondence tradition. Confidentiality and promise keeping are no longer encumbered with Enlightenment privatism. Noddings' *Caring* (1984) makes the I-Thou encounter normative. Edith Wyschogrod's (1990) *Saints and Postmodernism* serves as a counterpoint to benign politics, working as she does on human struggles under conditions of oppression. However, for all their apparent achievements in the particular, on what grounds do we endorse contemporary work in social and feminist ethics except as they presuppose and apply universal solidarity? Without their contributions to human dignity, truth-telling, or nonviolence, why should we not insist on maintaining the rationalist canon instead? Why should any post-Enlightenment turn be considered an intellectual advance, rather than endorsing a cynical will of the stronger or a nihilism in which no right or wrong is conceivable?

References

Baudrillard, J. (1983). *Simulations.* (P. Foss, P. Patton, & P. Beitchman, Trans.). New York: Semiotext(e).

Bauman, Z. (1993). *Postmodern ethics,* Oxford, UK: Blackwell.

Benhabib, S. (1992). *Situating the self: Gender, community and postmodernism in contemporary ethics,* Cambridge, UK: Polity Press.

Benhabib, S. (2002). *The claims of culture: Equality and diversity in the global era.* Princeton, N.J.: Princeton University Press.

Bernstein, R. (1986). *Philosophical profiles: Essays in a pragmatic mode.* Philadelphia, Pa: University of Pennsylvania Press.

Bok, S. (1979). *Lying: Moral choice in public and private life.* New York: Vintage Random House.

Bok, S. (1995). *Common values.* Columbia, Miss.: University of Missouri Press.

Buber, M. (1965). *Between man and man.* (Ronald G. Smith, Trans.). New York: Macmillan.

Buber, M. (1970). *I and thou [Ich und Du].* (Walter Kaufmann, Trans.). New York: Scribner.

Christians, C. (1995). The problem of universals in communication ethics, *Javnost [The Public],* 2(2), 59–69.

Christians, C. & Traber, M. (eds.). (1997). *Communication ethics and universal values,* Thousand Oaks, Calif.: Sage Publications.

Christians, C. (2003). Cross-cultural ethics and truth. In J. Mitchell, (ed.), *Mediating meaning: Studies in media, religion and culture* (pp. 293–313). Edinburgh: T. and T. Clark.

Christians, C. (2004). The changing news paradigm: From objectivity to interpretive sufficiency. In S. Iorio, (ed.), *Qualitative research in journalism: Taking it to the streets* (pp. 41–56). Mahwah, NJ: Lawrence Erlbaum.

Christians, C. (2007). "Non-violence in philosophical and religious ethics", *Javnost-The Public,* 14(4), 5–18.

Cooper, T. (1996). *A time before deception: Truth in communication, culture, and ethics.* Santa Fe, N. Mex.: Clear Light Publishers.

Dower, N. (1998). *World ethics: The new agenda.* Edinburgh, UK: Edinburgh University Press.

Engberg-Pederson, T. (1983). *Aristotle's theory of moral insight.* Oxford, UK: Clarendon.

Farrell, T.B. (1993). *Norms of rhetorical culture.* New Haven, Conn.: Yale University Press.

Fasching, D. (1993). *The ethical challenge of Auschwitz and Hiroshima.* Albany, N.Y.: State University of New York Press.

Fasching, D. (1995). "Response to Peter Haas," *The Ellul Forum,* 14 (January).

Freire, P. (1970). *Pedagogy of the oppressed.* (Myra B. Ramos, Trans.). New York: Continuum. Original work published 1968.

Freire, P. (1973). *Education for critical consciousness.* New York: Continuum. Original work published 1969.

Gadamer, H. (1975). *Truth and method [Wahrheit und Methode].* (G. Barden & J. Cumming, Trans.). New York: Seabury. Original work published 1965.

Havel, V. (1989). *Living in truth.* Ed. J. Vladislav. London: Faber & Faber.

Havel, V. (1994). Post-modernism: The search for universal laws. *Vital speeches of the day,* 60(20) (August 1), 613–615.

Havel, V. (1997). *The art of the impossible: Politics as morality in practice.* New York: Knopf.

Hill, T. E., Jr. (1973). "The hypothetical imperative," *Philosophical Review*, 82, 429–450.

Hume, D. (1739). *Treatise of human nature*, London: J. Noon.

Hume, D. (1963). *Enquiries concerning the human understanding and concerning the principles of morals.* Oxford, UK: Clarendon Press. Original work published 1748, 1751.

Johnstone, C. L. (1993). Ontological vision as ground for communication ethics: A response to the challenge of postmodernism. Paper presented at a convention of the Speech Communication Association, Miami, Florida, November.

Jonas, H. (1984). *The imperative of responsibility.* Chicago, Ill.: University of Chicago Press.

Kaufmann, W. (1968). *Nietzsche: Philosopher, psychologist, anti-Christ,* Princeton, N.J.: Princeton University Press.

Koehn, D. (1998). *Rethinking feminist ethics: Care, trust and empathy.* New York: Routledge.

Levinas, E. (1985). *Ethics and infinity: Conversations with Philippe Nemo.* (R. A. Cohen, Trans.). Pittsburgh, PA: Duquesne University Press.

Lotz, J. B. (1963). Person and ontology, *Philosophy Today*, 7 (Winter), 279–297. Reprinted from *Scholastik*, 38(3), 335–360.

Masolo, D.A. (2004). Western and African communitarianism: A comparison. In K. Wiredu, (ed.)., *A companion to African philosophy* (pp. 483–498). Oxford: Blackwell.

Mieth, D. (1997). The basic norm of truthfulness: Its ethical justification and universality. In C. Christians & M. Traber, (eds.), *Communication ethics and universal values.* (pp. 87–104). Thousand Oaks, Calif.: Sage.

Miner, R. (2004). *Truth in the making: Creative knowledge in theology and philosophy.* London: Routledge.

Nietzsche, F. (1966). *Beyond good and evil.* (W. Kaufmann, Trans.). New York: Random House. Original work published 1886.

Nietzsche, F. (1967a). *The birth of tragedy.* (W. Kaufmann, Trans.). New York: Random House. Original work published 1872.

Nietzsche, F. (1967b). *On the genealogy of morals.* (W. Kaufmann & R. J. Hollingdale, Trans.). New York: Random House. Original work published 1887.

Nietzsche, F. (1967c). *Will to power: Attempt at a revaluation of all values.* (W. Kaufmann, Trans.). New York: Random House. Original work published 1880.

Nussbaum, M. (2000). *Women and human development: The capabilities approach.* Cambridge UK: Cambridge University Press.

Nussbaum, M. (2001). *Upheavals of thought: The intelligence of emotions.* Cambridge UK: Cambridge University Press.

Olthuis, J. H. (ed.). (1997). *Knowing other-wise: Philosophy at the threshold of spirituality.* New York: Fordham University Press.

Outka, G. & Reeder, J.P. Jr. (1993). *Prospects for a common morality.* Princeton, N.J.: Princeton University Press.

Peukert, H. (1981). Universal solidarity as the goal of communication, *Media Development*, 28(4), 10–12.

Polanyi, M. (1968). *The tacit dimension.* Garden City, N.Y.: Doubleday.

Ricoeur, P. (1967). The antinomy of human reality and the problem of philosophical anthropology. In N. Lawrence and D. O'Connor, (eds.), *Readings in existential phenomenology* (pp. 390–402). Englewood Cliffs, N.J.: Prentice-Hall.

Ricoeur, P. (1973). Ethics and Culture: Habermas and Gadamer in Dialogue, *Philosophy Today*, 17, 153–165.

Schacht, R. (1975). *Existentialism, existenz-philosophy, and philosophical anthropology.* Pittsburg, Pa.: University of Pittsburg Press.

Schacht, R. (1990). Philosophical anthropology: What, why and how, *Philosophy and Phenomenological Research*, 50, 155–176.

Shin, K. (1994). *A hermeneutic utopia: H.-G. Gadamer's philosophy of culture.* Toronto, Ont.: Tea for Two Press.

Stanley, M. (1973). *The technological conscience: Survival and dignity in an age of expertise.* Chicago, Ill.: University of Chicago Press.

Universal Declaration of Human Rights. (1988). In *Human rights: A compilation of international instruments.* Geneva: Centre for Human Rights.

Wiredu, K. (1996). *Cultural universals and particulars: An African perspective.* Bloomington, Ind.: Indiana University Press.

Wittgenstein, L. (1953). *Philosophical investigations.* Oxford, UK: Basil Blackwell.

Wittgenstein, L. (1956). *Remarks on the foundation of mathematics.* Oxford UK: Basil Blackwell.

Wyschogrod, E. (1990). *Saints and postmodernism.* Chicago, Ill.: University of Chicago Press.

2 Connecting Care and Duty: How Neuroscience and Feminist Ethics can Contribute to Understanding Professional Moral Development

Lee Wilkins

1. Introduction

This chapter is an attempt to provide a theoretically based answer, with some empirical support, to this question: How is work, particularly journalism, influenced by the moral growth of individuals?

Potential answers link two literature subsets: the literature of moral development as it applies to journalism and public relations, and feminist ethical theory. However, because the goal of this chapter is a universal approach, the route taken to link these two separable parts of the literature begins with a single constant: the human brain and what neuroscientists understand about how humanity thinks about morality. On to this foundation is placed a feminist theory of care infused with an authentic sense of duty. Finally, the chapter reviews the findings of moral development research applied to journalists and suggests some additional questions. The broad argument is that the organic human brain includes a hard-wired capacity for moral action influenced by an environment that shapes professional ethical response particularly at the intersection of care and duty. The goal of this theoretical work is to delineate one fruitful path by which a universal (or at least international) understanding of media ethics could be first articulated and then investigated both philosophically and empirically. Readers should be aware that, while there is significant empirical support for some of the work reviewed here, other posits have yet to be tested. This interdisciplinary conversation between philosophy and psychology includes false starts and fragmentary understandings. The chapter attempts to connect some fragments, but it is work that will continue for many decades.

2. The Untested Assumptions of Moral Development

Moral development research makes some important assumptions that are seldom addressed in the literature but which are nonetheless central.

- All human beings have the capacity for moral thinking. This capacity for moral thinking is similar to the human biological capacity for language.
- Moral thinking is linked to experience. This link has both internal and external implications. Internally for the autonomous adult, experiences inform individual decision-making, creating habits of mind and action. Experience is also part of culture and the creation of cultural meaning – the external component.
- Moral thinking can be both general and particular. There are general moral questions – Is it right to lie or to kill? – to which all human beings have a response. But, there are particular elaborations of moral questions – Is it ever appropriate for a journalist to deceive a source who is attempting to deceive the journalist? – to which professionals must respond.

Keeping these assumptions in mind, a lens through which research on moral development can be unpacked is as follows:

MA=f(o)e.[1]

MA stands for **moral action** which includes both reasoning and response; **F** stands for function – the next two elements interact synergistically rather than summatively;

O stands for the human **organism**, the biological entity with the capacity for moral thought influenced by individual experience and life within a particular culture and political system;

E stands for the external **environment**. "The new biology recognises the importance of environment in influencing even basic biological structures in the brain," (Tancredi, 2005, p. 24). This chapter suggests that the world of work, specifically journalism, constitutes an important part of any professional's environment, one that over the years could be expected to have an impact on thinking, particularly in the professional domain.

The organism and the environment are dynamic.[2] They function in a synergistic way; they are mutually interactive on multiple levels. Moral growth and moral thinking, as reflected in various behaviours, can and should change over time. Different environments may support or retard different qualities and rates of moral growth.

The goal of moral development research is to clearly articulate influences on the human organism which is itself responding to the environment. Next, the chapter will briefly review some research on the organism, place that research within a philosophical context, and then, returning through the theoretical lens of **MA=f(o)e**, suggest potential paths for additional empirical and theoretical work.

3. The Moral Organism: Hard-Wired for Fair

Aristotle wrote elegantly about mature character, but was relatively silent on how that character emerged – before habituation. Darwin believed that one of the significant differences between human beings and other animals was what he called "the moral sense", a rudimentary awareness of right and wrong. Late in the last century, Wilson referred to this pre-cognitive inclination as "the moral spark" (Wilson, 1993). Moral development theorists Piaget (1965) and Kohlberg (1981, 1984) documented that people grew as moral beings along relatively predictable paths but were silent about whether those paths were founded on an internal bedrock of moral grammar. If these collective insights are taken seriously, then a crucial question for 21st century philosophy must become: Does the human being, through evolution and genetics, have a species specific and hence universal, hard-wired capacity to consider right and wrong in a way different from animals, including the higher apes and intelligent species such as dolphins?

Harvard neuropsychologist Marc D. Hauser answers that question in the affirmative. In his book, *Moral Minds: How nature designed our universal sense of right and wrong* (2006), Hauser contends that, "we evolved a moral instinct, a capacity that naturally grows within each child, designed to generate rapid judgment about what is morally right or wrong based on an unconscious grammar of action....These ideas draw on insights from another instinct: language," (p. xvii). Phrased another way, what neuroscientists attempt to understand is what the organic brain brings to the moral mind (Gazzaniga, 2005). Based on a variety of experiments and observations of both children and adults in multiple contemporary cultures, Hauser asserts that all human beings are endowed with a "moral faculty – a capacity that enables each individual to unconsciously and automatically evaluate a limitless variety of actions in terms of principles that dictate what is permissible, obligatory or forbidden," (p. 16). This does not mean that human beings don't make ethical mistakes, just as human beings make grammatical or word usage errors or misunderstand some statements entirely; nor does Hauser's concept of a 'moral faculty' mean that there is one right answer.

Hauser concludes that human beings are hard-wired for 'fair' in much the way that John Rawls described justice as fairness (1971). To illustrate the various experimental findings, Hauser develops three avatars – a Kantian creature, that functions through logic and the application of principle, a Humeian creature, that functions through emotion, and a Rawlsian creature, which blends the two. Each of the creatures has been put to experimental test in the past decade by various neuroscientists.

Responses to word problems provide evidence that human moral thinking includes significant elements of the Kantian creature – the rational, principled approach to moral decision-making. "What emerges from these cases is a key insight: It is impermissible to cause an intended harm if that harm is used as a means to a greater good. In contrast, it is permissible to cause harm if that harm is only a foreseen consequence of intending to cause a greater good" (p. 120). This is the Kantian creature at work: regard people as an end in themselves rather than as a means to an end. Other experiments suggest that human hard-wiring contains a significant element of emotion: "...as David Hume intuited, and as the neuroscientist Antonio Damasio has emphasised more recently, rational thought often relies on an intimate handshake with the emotions," (p. 189). "When someone is willing to act on a moral belief, it is because the emotional part of his or her brain has become active when considering the moral question at hand," (Gazzaniga, 2005, p. 167). Emotional conflict provides a telltale signature of an ethical dilemma and is essential to its resolution (Hauser, p. 223). A Humeian creature who can feel emotions such as disgust, can attach those emotions to morally repugnant actions. These emotional responses (such as disgust) are common in all cultures, further indication that the Humeian creature is both species specific and universal.

Another element of justice as fairness is the ability to see things from another's point of view. "Studies of empathy unambiguously show that our capacity to take another's perspective influences our behavior," (Hauser, p. 195). Axlerod's (1984) work on the evolution of cooperation provides another sort of empirical support for the role of empathy: knowing how someone else will respond can promote cooperative as opposed to competitive behaviours and those cooperative responses are quite robust, even under environmental pressure. Fairness is connected to cooperation and thus is essentially tied to human society. "Whereas we inherited a largely selfish nature from our ancestors, we also evolved a uniquely human psychology that predisposes us toward a different form of altruistic behaviour: strong reciprocity....As defined by the leading proponents of this position, strong reciprocity is a 'predisposition to cooperate with others and to punish those who violate the norms of cooperation, at personal cost, even when it is implausible to expect that these costs will be repaid either by others or at a later date,'." (p. 82).[3]

Neuropsychology has been unable to locate a singular, physiological moral organ in the brain. Studies using MRI technology suggest, "Unambiguously, when people confront certain kinds of moral dilemmas, they activate a vast network of brain regions, including areas involved in emotion, decision-making, conflict, social relations, and memory ....What these brain-imaging studies do show is that when we experience conflict from competing duties or obligations, one course of conflict comes from the dueling voices of the Kantian and Humean creatures," (p. 222). Hauser concludes that the way humanity has evolved to deal with this conflict is to develop a temperate (in the Greek sense) Rawlsian creature who enters the moral conversation not just to mediate between reason and emotion but to guide resolution down a line of actions that promote fairness and strong reciprocity. Animals have pieces of this biological grid (De Waal, 1996); only human beings appear to have developed the complete grammar and to pass it on in the form of biological inheritance.

The theory that humankind's ability to enact justice as fairness based on hard-wiring suggests that such behavior should emerge early in childhood, that it involves the ability to consciously delay gratification, and that responses to issues such as permissible harm would vary across cultures but that the core question – when is harm permitted – would remain. There is substantial experimental and anthropological work to support each contention. The moral faculty is also permeable to education and experience. "The main point is that the moral faculty may guard its principles but once its guard has been penetrated, we may use these principals to guide how we consciously reason about morally permissible actions. If this captures the link between operative moral principles and our moral actions, then we will have identified an important difference between the moral and linguistic domains of knowledge," (p. 159). This body of work responds to significant lacuna in moral development analysis: why authority matters in the first place, how children learn to attach the words 'good' and 'bad' to specific actions, how stages of moral development might be better defined and what promotes movement from stage to stage (Hauser, 2006).

Of course, there is much more to be done – in the lab and outside it. Hauser's effort, as broad ranging as it is, fails to consider the impact of hormones on human response – particularly violence – a crucial issue in any discussion of instinctual moral response. Hauser also spends so much time building the case of a human-centred moral faculty that he spends almost no time discussing how that faculty can be thwarted. There is much evidence, from Milgrim's experiments (which Hauser discusses) to Lifton's (1986) work on Nazi physicians (which Hauser does not mention), to indicate that a human moral instinct can be undermined and overwhelmed in many ways. And, because his work, by ethical constraint, must use non-invasive techniques, the role of neural transmitters and other cell-level, bio-chemical reactions, are absent in the volume.

Nonetheless, his interpretation of the evidence about the human mind is provocative and evocative. If human beings are indeed hard-wired for 'fair', then some understandings of ethics can be universalised through the species. If the human species is uniquely cooperative and reciprocal in a moral sense, then community is more than just implicated: it is essential. "We should look not for a universal ethics comprising hard-and-fast truths, but for the universal ethics that arises from being human, which is clearly contextual, emotion-influenced, and designed to increase our survival," (Gazzaniga, 2005, p. 177). If there is a bedrock of instinctive moral understanding, a link between rationality and emotion that is characteristic of the empathetic Rawlsian creature, then studying moral development and the influences on it can help articulate the complexity of moral thinking and growth throughout the human lifetime. Hard-wired for 'fair' means moral development has a solid foundation on which to build.

However, hard-wired for 'fair' is only a framework. But it is a framework with a central assumption: fairness is relational. It involves others. Professionals still need to decide what constitutes fairness and what to be fair about. They must be clear about their connections and their relationships, just as the theory **MA=f(o)e** implies. Answers to these questions are neither hard-wired nor instinctual. They demand philosophical theory, an approach centred in relationships and the mutual web of dynamic obligation such theory implies.

4. Feminist Theory: Strong Care Informed by Duty

Reducing moral thinking and decision-making exclusively to instinct is silly. Yet, much of the philosophical work on the ethics of care is based on a metaphor that is – or at least appears to be – instinctual. Specifically, Noddings (1984/2003) and Tronto (1995) lodge care in the mother/child relationship, particularly the relationship of the mother to the infant and the young child. Noddings (1984/2003) describes the concept of "one caring" as based on empathy, which she refers to as "engrossment" or filling oneself with the emotions of the other (p. 10). Both scholars lodge care in the concrete circumstances of the moral actor, and each agrees that care has an emotional quality. All owe a great deal of their insight to the work of psychologist Carol Gilligan in her study of women deciding whether to abort.

In in-depth interviews, Gilligan found that the women making this crucial moral choice spoke *In a different voice* (1982). That voice viewed ethical reasoning through the lens of care – first for self, then for others, and finally for universal principals (a movement from concerns with goodness to questions of truth and authenticity) for both self and others to which all could agree. These ways of caring did not emerge as part of the hierarchical stages that both Piaget and Kohlberg had documented. Instead, these ways of considering care emerged from the questions women asked themselves as they tried to make this particular decision. All were rooted in relationships – the relationship of the woman to the fetus, the relationship of the woman to the father (if known), and the relationship of the woman to herself. Gilligan's moral theory of care argued for "knowledge seeking grounded in and inspired by a concrete, caring relationship" (Steiner & Okrusch, 2006, p. 114). Care is not gendered. Gilligan (1977; 1982) specifically noted that moral adulthood requires the ability to use "two different moral languages, the language of rights that protects separations and the language of responsibilities that sustains connection," (Gilligan, 1982, p. 210).

Other scholars have expanded on these concepts. Tronto (1995) distinguished "four phases of care, each of which has a concomitant 'value': caring about, attentiveness; taking care of, responsibility, caregiving, competence; and carereceiving, responsiveness." Some, but not all feminist scholars, argue that care is not an exclusively private or interpersonal concern. Tronto, Koehn (1998) and others suggest that care can involve culture, including its institutions and its politics, on multiple levels. "Tronto insisted that integrating care and compassion with justice brings highly political questions to the fore," (Steiner & Okrusch, 2006). Indeed, some feminist scholars have insisted that larger political structures, for example historic power relationships, influence the most intimate of caring relationships, for example marriage (DesAutels & Waugh, 2001).

Still, the mother/young child metaphor haunts the theory thereby creating some confusion and making something less than the best case for it. Particularly as applied to questions outside intimate relationships, such as the role of care in professional ethics, feminist ethics needs something more than the foundational dualistic mother/child bond to sustain it.

Drawing again from concrete experience, journalists employing a feminist ethic may find a more informative parallel in a different sort of caring relationship: parenting a teenager.

First, unlike breastfeeding, dads parent teens, too. This lodges feminist professional ethics firmly in the camp of care rather than in a setting of gendered care. Second, the work of parenting a teenager centers around helping to develop an autonomous adult while continuing to provide nurture and supporting essential, if complicated, physical needs. Third, teenage psychological development hinges on peer relationships, which means community expectations and norms become an element of parenting. A communitarian insight here is essential: teens come to discover and test who they are in relation to a community of others of which parents are an important but not singularly important part. For teens, community does precede self.

Parenting a teenager is a negotiation between empathic care and the promotion of autonomy in community. A crying baby calls forth what psychologists have termed empathetic distress from the adults who hear it. The cry of an angry, rebellious, self-willed and overconfident teenager (a description of teens that appears to be universal regardless of culture) produces distress. What parents call on to respond in such situations is empathic care informed by and implemented with duty. Furthermore, parents cannot do this without some community support.

Gilligan's formulation of feminist ethics relies on actions that must be taken – either abort or carry the fetus. These actions are linked to obligations to self and others, what philosophers call duty. Because parenting teenagers is truly a process of caring duty, W. D. Ross' (1930) explication of duty as multiple duties, some of which are affirmative, seems a particularly appropriate philosophical approach to buttress professional care (Patterson & Wilkins, 1991; Meyers, 2003). Ross, like feminist scholars, asserted duty was grounded in relationships. Second, Ross is what philosophers refer to as an intuitionist, in other words he believed that some duties – what he labeled the *prima facie* duties – are intuitively grasped. Robert Audi (2004) explains intuitionism this way:

> Consider intuitionism in the weak (and rough) sense of the view that an irreducible plurality of basic moral judgments can be intuitively and non-inferentially justified. Such a view can be non-rationalist, taking intuitions to be non-inferential responses to perceptual experience and thereby resting on empirical grounds for moral judgments or principles….
>
> Can an empiricist intuitionism account for the strength that intuitive moral justification may have? Recall two points: First it is only general principles that even rationalist intuitionists take to be self evident….Second, and more important, since…the major intuitionists are not committed to denying, and tend to grant, that justification for believing moral propositions is defensible, a further obstacle to their being empirical is eliminated" (Audi, 2004, p. 55).

Ross's *prima facie* duties are: nonmaleficence and keeping promises. These *prima facie* duties have more moral weight then the affirmative duties: fidelity, reparation, gratitude, justice, beneficence, and self-improvement. Ross (unlike some of his critics) did not worry much about the origin of intuition. Today, neuroscience may be uncovering the origin of intuition in a profound way. Ross, instead, explored how multiple duties could be employed in real life, noting that duties do compete and that, depending on the morally relevant facts, some would be more applicable than others. In application to professional ethics, affirmative duties strongly suggest that certain actions be taken, an approach that parallels the ethics of care. The appeal of Ross is that "he provides a universalist contextualism: universal in abstract *prima facie* duty, contextual in actual duty. And, this position, it seems to me, is a far more accurate reflection of humans' moral reasoning, both in fact and in capability. Persons can, I think, grasp universal moral truth at the abstract level, but our moral decision making in actual cases is fraught with uncertainty and ambiguity. Ross, better than any other theorist, captured this tension," (Meyers, 2003, p. 93).

Being a caring journalist means providing the sort of information that allows citizens to create community – even if there are elements of that community with which the individual journalist would disagree. While much of the literature on professional journalistic ethics emphasises the decisions one ought not to take (e.g. Patterson & Wilkins, 2005; Christians et al., 2006; Bivins, 2004), a 'care informed by duty approach' would also emphasise potential choices, the affirmative link between journalism and democracy, and the need for journalism that nurtures a more just community (Christians, Fackler, Ferre, 1993). Even professional ideals such as objectivity, either in its traditional formulation or in more recent, critical work (Ward 2005), could find a philosophical basis in caring: care enough to nurture social and political discovery and development, one reading of the affirmative duties of gratitude and beneficence.

One additional insight from the work on cognitive development helps provide a bridge from this person-centred approach to the larger professional world. One of the most startling findings in *Women's Ways of Knowing* (Belenky et al., 1986), was that women who had been subject to violence (specifically physical abuse and/or rape) and poverty appeared permanently stalled in their intellectual and moral development. This human response was not universal, but it was common, evidence that the environment in general, poverty, or specific trauma, rape, can profoundly influence future individual development. These insights apply to individuals and communities equally. In other words, there are some environments – think gulag or concentration camp – which make caring and development far more difficult than others – think a peaceful democracy or a functioning city government. The environment here has an impact on the organism, which is reciprocal, symbiotic, and far from neutral, particularly when evaluated from a duty-based perspective.

The theoretical lens of feminist ethics, understood through the metaphor of parenting a teen rather than an infant, is particularly relevant to the institutional relationship between journalism and democratic functioning. Further, feminist ethics as informed by multiple duties provides a strong handshake between the profession's goals, institutional demands, and the individual circumstance that characterises ethical choice for journalists and their news organisations.

Feminist ethics and duty-based thinking provide the internal basis for moral action within the individual organism. If the organism itself is hard-wired for 'fair' as neuroscience suggests, then the theoretical building blocks to discover and investigate the impact of other elements of the external environment are now in order. The goal is to discover whether the dynamic external environment, specifically membership in a profession and professional expertise, can permeate the organism's ethical predispositions (hard-wiring) and learning to result in moral action.

5. Moral Development: A Review of Current Findings

The founding question of moral development theory centres on how human beings respond to real ethical choices. The field has progressed through qualitative methods using small research cohorts and in-depth interviews. However, in the 1970s, James Rest, employing Kohlberg's theory, developed a paper-and-pencil test to measure moral development. This test, called the Defining Issues Test, has been subsequently been administered in more than 1 000 studies in multiple cultures, although most of the work has been done in the US.[4] The original DIT scholars focused their research on professions with a large moral component including health professionals. They suggest the DIT is especially good at measuring decision-making in uncertain situations but did not focus on either duty or care. From its inception, the DIT included a 'journalism based' scenario.

The DIT creators labeled journalism an 'emerging profession', even though US journalists are not subject to licensure or review boards like two of the ancient professions, medicine and law (Rest & Narvaez, 1994, p. xi). Published work began with a pilot study of 72 journalists (Coleman & Wilkins, 2002); other studies followed. Since the results of this work are reported in depth in other places, the following review focuses on the highlights of the studies in total (Coleman & Wilkins, 2002, 2004; Wilkins & Coleman, 2005, 2006), with an emphasis on the questions the studies raise.

- Journalists scored fourth highest among all professionals tested (Coleman & Wilkins, 2002; Wilkins & Coleman, 2005); public relations professionals scored sixth highest (Wilkins & Coleman, 2006). Both groups scored higher than professions with more required formal education.

Table 1: Mean P Scores of Various Professions

Seminarians/philosophers	65.1
Medical students	50.2
Practicing physicians	49.2
Journalists	48.1 to 48.68
Dental students	47.6
Public relations professionals	46.2
Nurses	46.3
Lawyers	46
Graduate students	44.9
Undergraduate students	43.2

Pharmacy students	42.8
Veterinary students	42.2
Navy enlisted men	41.6
Orthopaedic surgeons	41
Adults in general	40
Business professionals	38.13
Accounting undergraduates	34.8
Accounting auditors	32.5
Business students	31.35 to 37.4
Advertising professionals	31.64
Public relations students	31.18
High school students	31
Prison inmates	23.7
Junior high students	20

(Compiled by the authors from individual published studies and
data supplied by the Center for the Study of Ethical Development)

- Findings focusing on journalists and public relations professionals are generally consistent with the larger literature. Among them: Religiosity was consistently and negatively correlated with high quality moral reasoning among journalists. Religious fundamentalism had the same negative effect on the public relations professionals. It is fundamentalist views – rather than religion itself – that appear to be the issue. While those who said they held fundamentalist views showed significantly lower levels of ethical reasoning, those who said they were deeply religious did not show any differences from those who said they were less religious.
- The larger literature of the field suggests that liberal political ideology correlates with higher level moral thinking. This was true for public relations professionals, but not for journalists.
- Gender, age and education were not predictors of higher-level moral thinking, consistent with research in the field and with Gilligan's framing of the ethics of care. Education approached statistical significance. This finding may be a statistical artifact, as the samples of journalists and public relations practitioners were very homogenous in terms of educational attainment. There is no ready explanation for the lack of an effect of age considering the research cohorts ranged from 18 to 75.

One common feature of the studies cited above is the use of domain-specific dilemmas, a research approach that was initially discouraged until DIT results became consistent across multiple professions, scholars and decades (Rest, Narvaez, Thoma, & Bebeau, 1999). However, domain-specific stories can be more predictive of behaviour (Rest & Narvaez, 1984; Rest, Narvaex, Bebeau, & Thoma, 1999), an important finding since much anecdotal study of professional ethics exposes the fissures between 'knowing what to do' and 'doing it'. The studies of journalists and public relations professionals reviewed here used domain-specific dilemmas and found that expertise in an area leads to high quality ethical reasoning about those topics. A study of advertising practitioners, however, showed exactly the *opposite* results (Cunningham, 2005).

Thus, professional expertise appears to support higher-level moral thinking, a specific environmental impact on moral action. Other environmental influences appear to include education. Age and gender do not appear to influence professional moral development.

Even though the DIT is framed as a largely rights and responsibilities exploration, open-ended responses in the studies described above make an important place for care. "Second, the responses that centred on stakeholders also revealed the sense of connection that the participants felt toward both the subjects of the story – primarily the children – and their readers. Kohlberg's description of moral development does not neatly account for the ethical import of connectedness. However, this notion can be explained by the insights of Gilligan and others …. Connection provided the participants with a reason to run the photo (the dominant decision) and to withhold it (due primarily to privacy and considerations of long-term harm). Both 'final' decisions were based in ethical theory, yet called on connection as an additional element with moral weight. For these participants, that moral weight also spoke to the potential impact of the photo, and hence to journalistic role and the impact of publicity, " (Wilkins & Coleman, 2005, 62).

At the most elementary analytic level, the **MA=f(O)e** formulation helps to explain the foregoing descriptive results. These studies suggest respondents combine care and duty in a professional setting – one informs the other and reasoning is incomplete without both. The responses also implicate fairness and strong reciprocity within roles and individual choices. The journalists/public relations practitioners involved mentioned institutional relationships – between the individual and the workplace and between journalists and democratic society. Reasoning that invoked both care and duty extends theory and could also be tested empirically. Robust findings – ones that shared some commonalities across cultures – could begin to explicate how journalists working in different environments, for example a parliamentary as opposed to a constitutional democracy, could employ such reasoning and help more clearly delineate the impact of what is specifically cultural compared with more fundamental understandings (Rao & Lee, 2003). If the findings of neuroscience are correct, this sort of dynamism is to be expected. Additional research could explore how different elements of the dynamic dominate moral actions at specific times of life or within specific roles. Just as important, although more troubling from a philosophical perspective, would be empirical findings that are entirely culturally relative in content.

These findings from studies of professionals also suggest that the ability to reason at a high level ethically reflects the sort of domain-specific knowledge that characterises a profession in the philosophical sense. If studies of other journalists, particularly journalists with a different 'home' culture, produce similar results, then the case for professional status is enriched. Thinking well ethically could be considered an element of profession-specific knowledge, one that foregrounds relationships between people in various roles and among democratic institutions.

Journalism and public relations may be professions that have emerged, in the same way that engineering and others emerged at the beginning of the previous century.

Thinking through the lens of **MA=f(o)e**, another approach to the study of moral development has been to devise controlled experiments to see what sorts of interventions or manipulations can help improve people's ethical reasoning. This sort of theorising moves moral development from the descriptive to the predictive. Most typically, researchers look to educational interventions such as ethics courses (Cabot, 2005). However, scholars also have examined two influences in the professional environment: race and the presence of photographs.

- White journalism majors were significantly more likely to use lower quality ethical reasoning when the story subjects were black than when they were white (Coleman, 2003). Black journalism majors were not (Coleman, 2005). The black future journalists showed the same level of reasoning regardless of the race of the story subjects. Minimally, these results focus attention on the impact of domestic culture on ethical thinking, a question that must be investigated internationally as well.
- Visual information significantly improved participants' ethical reasoning. Two experiments, which included photographs of story subjects, identified thinking about the people affected by an ethical situation as important (Coleman, in press). This finding, which may be linked to an ability to literally envision specific stakeholders, is intellectually and emotionally connected to care. How such understandings are 'resolved' similarly can call upon duty. This work could be extended to examine whether moving images, which have a different impact on memory and retention than do still photographs (Lang, 2000), similarly influence ethical thinking. Since decades of work in neuroscience has found that the presence or absence of visual information alters reasoning, part of the organic functioning of the human brain, investigation of the dynamic interaction between visual information and moral action seems essential.

In sum, the journalists and public relations practitioners who participated in these studies found dynamic ways to blend caring about story subjects, clients, their organisations, and society at large with the various professional duties, central among them truth-telling, avoiding harm and furthering democratic functioning. Theoretically their responses point to the outcome of an ethic of strong care informed by duty. Care emerges from the daily experiences of professional work; connecting that work to larger duties became a central element in the application of universal principles, something these professionals demonstrated considerable expertise in. Thus, while care informed by duty may not be the dominant understanding of feminist ethics in philosophy, professional journalists and public relations practitioners appear to have adopted the approach and in many cases become expert in its application. As one public relations firm owner noted, "We have fired clients, but we have never fired a journalist". In this one short statement, care – for the firm, for the future – is informed by the duty to tell the truth in a way that leads to action that is philosophically and professionally defensible. This professional stance appears to be defined by a willingness to adopt a caring posture to others and to professional institutions. These findings also suggest descriptive and predictive extensions of the research based on the **MA=f(o)e** formulation.

6. Professional Moral Development: Where Do We Go?

Relatively few studies have examined development throughout the first four decades of human life (Levinson, 1986) or moral development in people past the age of 35 to 40 (Belenky, 1986; Gilligan, 1982). Levinson's work devotes some attention to the impact of work on development, and in that study, work was emphasised as marking some sorts of moral growth rather than as an influence on that growth. The same is true of *Women's Ways of Knowing* (Belenky, 1986).

Only Erikson (1963) has provided any sort of life-long theoretical map. That theory is linked with life experience in general, and only at certain times focuses on specific actions, for example the ability to establish and maintain adult, intimate relationships. However, Erikson's theory also establishes a profoundly influential place for the environment, in his words the society into which human beings are born and function. Erikson provides some tantalising suggestions about what sort of external influences may spur moral adult development and growth. He notes, "…We must expand our scope to include the study of the way in which societies lighten the inescapable conflicts of childhood with a promise of some security, identity, and integrity. In thus reinforcing the values by which the ego exists … societies create the only condition under which human growth is possible….Yet, political, economic and technical elites, wherever they have accepted the obligation to perfect a new style of living at a logical point in history, have provided men with a high sense of identity and have inspired them to reach new levels of civilisation" (Erikson, 1950/1963, pp. 277–278). While the use of the word 'elite' here would make some journalists wince, this chapter suggests that, by virtue of their centrality to self-governance and culture, the work of journalism provides individual members of the profession with the sense of identity and inspiration of which Erikson speaks.

Another group of psychologists – without the lens of Freudian psychoanalysis – have come to remarkably similar conclusions. When Gardner, Csikszentmihalyi and Damon (2001) note that journalism is a profession profoundly out of joint with itself, they also summon notions of identity, roles, and professionals' goals as they are influenced by the world of work in which contemporary people spend so much of their adult lives. By interviewing professionals 'at the top of their game', Gardner and colleagues assured themselves of a 'sample' that included individuals with both professional vision and a professional career informed by life experience. These journalists worked and yearned for a profession that was reconnected to its goal of providing sustenance to political society. They cared deeply that democracy succeed and believed their profession was essential to that success. They saw themselves reflecting that connection but stymied by the powerful economic factors currently influencing media organisations – a professional crisis that parallels the individual, internal crises that Erikson suggests must be reconciled to promote growth. Authentic alignment meant creating new institutions, expanding the functions of existing institutions, reconfiguring membership in existing institutions, reaffirming the values of existing institutions, and taking personal stands (pp. 212–218). In his subsequent book, *Five Minds for the Future*, Gardner (2007) connects the ethical mind to work, suggesting that the ethical mind in the workplace must discover a sense of mission, find appropriate models, evaluate internally whether current choices reflect these models, and evaluate externally whether the profession as an institution is furthering the mission. These suggestions are not so far removed from the final four stages of Erikson's adult moral development. Future research should investigate the impact of work on moral growth. One element of such an investigation could be a further analysis of how professionals are balancing care and duty in their daily work lives as well as in their aspirations for their work. A possible approach is as follows:

Table 2: Stages of Adult Moral Growth Linked to Professional Moral Development:

Erikson	Gardner et al.
Identity vs role confusion	Reaffirming the values of institutions;
	Discovering a professional mission;
Intimacy vs isolation	Expanding institutional roles; finding and
	being a role model;
Ego integrity vs despair	Creating new institutions; testing moral
	action for internal consistency and against
	external professional norms.

Investigating these parallels leads to the following suggestions for non-hierarchical stages of work-related moral growth:

Entry into the profession: Learning professional norms, following the professional rules

During this phase of professional development, the first few years of professional work, the 'new' journalist learns the norms of the particular workplace and the profession at large. This would reflect the 'conventional schema' outlined by Thoma, et al., and moral development would be characterised by progressively more sophisticated thinking about issues confronting the individual journalist as opposed to the news organisation. In this stage, a relatively static understanding of duty – with emphasis on negative duties – would dominate issues of care, with perhaps the exception of self care.

Ethical reflection also would be characterised by individual identification with and commitment to a professional mission (Perry, 1970). Learning to think like an ethical professional (or to fail to think like one) dominates here.

The novice: Conflict and compromise between institutional norms and professional understandings

The beginner becomes more expert. More complex assignments will raise more complex moral questions. Role models, or lack thereof, are acknowledged. Organisational norms may chafe; this level of discomfort may spur additional and distinct ethical reflection. Promotion into some sort of management position, or other forms of becoming influential within news organisations, will raise questions of identity and power. Identity expands to include the larger profession in addition to the individual and the individual news organisation. Intellectually, the individual must balance competing demands that will stress individual notions of identity and care with organisational membership. The struggle here is to not let duty overwhelm care in the sense that Weber describes when discussing bureaucratic functioning.

The seasoned professional: The development of and connection to a professional vision

During this phase, the expert journalist will be much more autonomous in terms of daily and long-term assignments. Further, the choices such autonomy presents will reflect a long-term vision for the professional's contribution to the news organisation and the larger culture. Ethical thinking will consider an expanded range of stakeholders as well as both long-term and short-term impacts. Care and duty come into deeper balance. Conversely, it is in this stage where, if the journalist is in a management role, external demands may overwhelm the ethical inner vision. Universal principles (or an abandonment of them) will be at the forefront of ethical choice.

The mentor and steward: 'In it' for oneself or 'in it' for others

This phase of professional development will be characterised through the integration of personal ideals with professional ones. Professionals at this stage of their careers will 'self actualise' (Maslow, 1950) through their work but that self-actualisation will include a significant focus on others, either through organisational duties and responsibilities or through informal mentoring of junior and/or senior colleagues. Care is at the forefront here. Conversely, the lure of unenlightened self-interest may begin to dominate. Care for 'other than self' would be absent. Ethical considerations will focus on justice at the individual, organisational or social level. Courage and innovative thinking that includes a moral vision will be evident for some professionals at this stage of their careers. Morally-informed leadership can emerge from this level of professional development. Changing organisations, for a variety of ethically-informed reasons, may become a major part of professional efforts at this stage.

Conclusion

The expert journalist, at the height (or depth) of accomplishment, seems to be a long way from neuroscience. Yet, without the inborn capacity for moral action, moral development and its offshoot, professional moral development, make little sense. Philosophers from many ages have provided insights into the general morality, but for professions with acknowledged social missions and obligations, the balancing of duty and care can be both a guide and a goad to moral growth. A dynamic work environment, which surely characterises any journalistic organisation or system in this century, adds both stumbling blocks and opportunities. In a world-wide web of communication, only universal understandings of the ethical impetus and execution of specific roles make sense, however they are articulated within a specific organisation or culture. By looking systematically at the human organism as it finds itself with a professional mission in a dynamic environment, it will become more possible to understand how the elements of **MA=f(o)e** inform each other. It is the connection among them, as opposed to the dominance of any single element, that is crucial for analysis and theorising. The ethical lessons of work – just like the ethical lessons of home and hearth – are unlikely to remain compartmentalised for many professionals, journalists among them. Understanding this complex interaction, particularly when it is informed by the moral imagination, remains an important goal for scholars interested in professional, ethical growth.

For journalists, whose work is now slingshotted around the world by satellite and the internet, attention to universal foundational professional principles is required. But that demand arises from two distinct sources; audience members embedded within a particular political system and culture – who need to know what to expect and why – and journalists themselves, who through technological and economic convergence are being asked to reinvent their profession. Global communications technology and the economics of multi-national corporations do not immediately bring to mind morality and ethics. But, for journalists to reinvent themselves in a way that places public service at the core of professional autonomy within community, ethics must serve as a base as well as a marker of professional growth. Ethics allows tools and economics structures to be informed by purpose. Purpose, in turn, invokes duty; public service invokes care. Inventing a global journalism is not the work of a single act, but of a lifetime of many professionals. How the human organism accepts these challenges, places them within a culture and a profession, and then decides is likewise a shared project for professionals and scholars.

Notes

1 This framing of moral action is adapted from one developed by Davies in 1964 to explain political behaviour.
2 Dynamism should be understood as the ability of an organism (or a culture) to resolve problems effectively, in multiple ways that are not readily predictable. The following examples illustrate dynamism: human beings with brain injury caused by stroke often gradually regain much or all brain function. Even though certain areas of the brain have 'died', the adult brain is capable of rewiring itself to reclaim speech or movement. This 'rewiring' does not occur along only one predictable, well understood or even 'mappable' path. Human neurological function is dynamic. Similarly, acupuncture works through use of pressure points. The routes between these pressure points is not predictable; there are multiple 'ways' to get between points and the effectiveness of the treatment is not conditioned on certain routes or any specific number of routes. Acupuncture illustrates the dynamism of the human nervous system. Ecological systems are similarly dynamic.
3 Hauser sources this quotation as follows: "Strong reciprocity is pure altruism and uniquely human" (Fehr & Fischbacher, 2003; Fehr & Henrich, 2003; Gintis, 2000; Gintins, Bowles, Boyd, & Fehr, 2003).
4 For a detailed review of the DIT, its development, scoring, general findings, etc., consult Coleman & Wilkins, in press, *Handbook of Mass Media Ethics*, New York: Taylor & Francis.

References

Aristotle. *Nicomachean Ethics.* Translated by J.E.C. Welldon, Buffalo, N.Y.: Prometheus Books, 1987.
Audi, R. (2005). *The good in the right: A theory of intuition and intrinsic value.* Princeton, N.J.: Princeton University Press.
Belenky, M., Clinchy, B., Goldberger, N., Tarvle, J. (1997). *Women's way of knowing: The development of self, voice.* New York: Basic Books.
Christians, C., G., Ferre, J. P., & Fackler, M. (1993). *Good news: Social ethics and the press.* New York: Oxford University Press.
Coleman, R. (2003). Race and ethical reasoning: The importance of race to journalistic decision making', *Journalism & Mass Communication Quarterly*, 80(2), 295–310.
Coleman, R. (2005). *Color blind: Race and the ethical reasoning of African Americans on journalism dilemmas.* Paper presented at the AEJMC Conference, San Antonio, Tex., Aug. 10–13, 2005.
Coleman, R. (in press). The effect of visuals on ethical reasoning: What's a photograph worth to journalists making moral decisions? *Journalism & Mass Communication Quarterly.*
Coleman, R., & Wilkins, L. (2002). Searching for the ethical journalist: An exploratory study of the ethical development of news workers, *Journal of Mass Media Ethics* 17(3), 209–255.
Coleman, R., & Wilkins, L. (2004). The moral development of journalists: A comparison with other professions and a model for predicting high quality ethical reasoning, *Journalism & Mass Communication Quarterly*, 81(3), 511–527.
Davies, James C. (1964). *Human nature in politics.* New York: John Wiley & Sons.
De Waal, F. (1996). *Good natured: The origins of right and wrong in humans and other animals.* Cambridge, Mass.: Harvard University Press.
Erikson, E. (1963). *Childhood and society.* New York: W. W. Norton & Sons. Original work published 1950.
Gardner, H. (2007). *Five minds for the future.* Cambridge, Mass.: Harvard Business School Press.
Gardner, H., Csikszentmihalyi, M., & Damon, W. (2001). *Good work: When excellence and ethics meet.* New York: Basic Books.
Gazzaniga, Michael S. (2005). *The ethical brain: The science of our moral dilemmas.* New York: HarperCollins.
Gilligan, Carol. (1982). *In a different voice: Psychological theory and women's development.* Cambridge, Mass.: Harvard University Press.

Hauser, Marc D. (2006). *Moral minds: How nature designed our universal sense of right and wrong.* New York: HarperCollins.

Hume, D. (1978). *A treatise of human nature.* Oxford: Oxford University Press. Original work published 1739.

Koehn, D. (1998). *Rethinking feminist ethics: Care, trust and empathy.* New York: Routledge.

Kohlberg, L. (1981). *Essays on moral development, Vol. 1: The philosophy of moral development.* New York: Harper & Row.

Kohlberg, L. (1984). *The psychology of moral development: The nature and validity of moral stages.* San Francisco, Calif.: Harper & Row.

Lang, A. (2000). The limited capacity model of mediated message processing. *Journal of Communication* 60(1), 46–70.

Levinson, D. J. (1986). *The seasons of a man's life.* New York: Ballantine.

Lifton, R. J. (1986). *The Nazi doctors: Medical killing and the psychology of genocide.* New York: Basic Books, Inc.

Meyers, C. (2003). Appreciating W. D. Ross: On duties and consequences, *Journal of Mass Media Ethics,* 18(2), 81–97.

Milgrim, S. (1974). *Obedience to authority: An experimental view.* New York: Harper & Row, Publishers.

Noddings, N. (1984). *Caring: A feminine approach to ethics and moral education.* Berkeley, Calif.: University of California Press.

Parker, R. J. (1990). The relationship between dogmatism, orthodox Christian beliefs, and ethical judgment, *Counseling and Values,* 34(3), 213–216.

Patterson, P. & Wilkins, L. (1991). *Media ethics: Issues and cases.* Madison, Wisc.: Brown.

Perry, W. G. (1970). *Forms of intellectual and ethical development in the college years: A scheme.* New York: Holt, Rinehart and Winston.

Piaget, J. (1965). *The moral judgment of the child.* New York: The Free Press.

Rao, S. & Lee, S. T. (2005). Globalizing media ethics: An assessment of universal ethics among international political journalists, *Journal of Mass Media Ethics,* 20 (2 & 3), 99–120.

Rawls, J. (1971). *A theory of justice.* Cambridge, Mass.: Belknap Press of Harvard University Press.

Rest, J. R. (1979). *Development in judging moral issues.* Minneapolis, Minn.: University of Minnesota Press.

Rest, J. R. (1983). Morality. In P. H. Mussen, (ed.), *Handbook of child psychology, Vol. III, cognitive development* (pp. 556–629). New York: John Wiley & Sons.

Rest, J. R. (1986). *Moral development: Advances in research and theory.* New York: Praeger.

Rest, J. R. (1993). Research on moral judgment in college students. In A. Garrod, (ed.), *Approaches to moral development: New research and emerging themes.* (pp. 176–195). New York: Teacher's College Press.

Rest, J. R., & Narvaez, D. (eds.). (1994). *Moral development in the professions: Psychology and applied ethics.* Hillsdale, N.J.: Lawrence Erlbaum Associates.

Rest, J. R., Narvaez, D., Bebeau, M. J., & Thoma, S. J. (1999). *Postconventional moral thinking: A neo-Kohlbergian approach.* Mahwah, N.J.: Lawrence Erlbaum Associates.

Rest, J. R., Narvaez, D., Thoma, S., & Bebeau, M. J. (1999). DIT2: Devising and testing a revised instrument of moral judgment, *Journal of Educational Psychology,* 91(4), 644–459.

Rest, J. R., Thoma, S., Moon, Y. L., & Getz, I. (1986). Different cultures, sexes, and religions. In J. R. Rest, (ed.), *Moral development: Advances in research and theory* (pp. 89–132). New York: Praeger.

Tancredi, L. (2005). *Hardwired behavior: What neuroscience reveals about morality.* Cambridge: Cambridge University Press.

Thoma, S. (1986). Estimating gender differences in the comprehension and preference of moral issues, *Developmental Review,* 6(2), 165–180.

Steiner, L, and Okrusch, C. (2006). Care as a virtue for journalists, *Journal of Mass Media Ethics,* 21(2 & 3), 99–101.

Ward, S. (2004). *The invention of journalism ethics.* Montreal & Kingston: McGill-Queen's University Press.

Wilkins, L. & Coleman, R. (2005). *The moral media: How journalists reason about ethics.* Mahwah, N. J.: Lawrence Erlbaum.

Wilson, J. Q. (1993). *The moral sense.* Cambridge: Cambridge University Press.

3 A Theory of Patriotism for Journalism

Stephen J. A. Ward

1. Introduction

This chapter outlines a philosophical theory of patriotism for journalism in a global age. Patriotism – an attachment to the interests of specific countries – challenges global media ethics. Patriotism seems out of place in a world where journalism needs to consider issues from a global perspective. A journalistic and patriotic commitment to one's country seems not only outdated and parochial, but also opposed to a global journalism that strives to interpret events from a larger perspective.

In this chapter, I explore to what extent the attitude of patriotism can be accommodated within ethical journalism, domestic and global. I construct a theory to help journalists understand how they can be patriotic citizens yet not violate principles of responsible public journalism. It does so by setting ethical limits on the love of country and by identifying a distinct and appropriate 'object' of patriotism for democracy and democratic journalism.

I construct two forms of patriotism. In the first half of the paper, I recommend a 'moderate patriotism for democratic community', a rational and ethically restrained form of patriotism compatible with the ethical norms of democratic journalism. The second part of the paper argues that the development of global journalism requires that we transform this domestic idea of patriotism into a global patriotism for humanity. This global patriotism is more appropriate for an evolving cosmopolitan journalism. Nation-based forms of patriotism remain ethically permissible insofar as they do not conflict with the demands of global patriotism. The domestic version of patriotism is a temporary place-holder until we can articulate and implement global journalism ethics.

The outline is a response to the question: Can journalists be patriotic without compromising the principles of their profession? I deal with this question across several sections. In the first section I define patriotism and explicate the idea of moderate, democratic patriotism. In the second two, I explain how to evaluate claims of patriotism. In the third section, I discuss how a democratic patriotism is compatible with the tenets of ethical, democratic journalism. In the final section, I argue that the task is to construct a global journalism ethics devoted to global democratic community.

The chapter arrives at the following conclusion: Ethical journalists can be patriotic only under strict conditions – *if* patriotism is defined along moderate, democratic lines. Journalists can be patriots only if they are moderate, rationally constrained patriots serving their country and humanity by fulfilling their distinctive social role as critical informers of democratic citizens. They can be patriots only if they evaluate claims of patriotism according to the principles of inclusivity, rational restraint, and public scrutiny. When journalists serve a different form of patriotism, they violate their ethical role in an open democratic society

2. Forms of Patriotism

Patriotism is a contested value. Some people praise patriotism as a primary civic virtue that overrides other virtues. Critics reply that patriotism is aggressive and xenophobic. More than 100 million people were killed in patriotic wars during the last century. Tolstoy (1987) wrote: "Seas of blood have been shed over this passion (of patriotism) and will yet be shed for it, unless the people free themselves of this obsolete relic of antiquity" (p. 142). Therefore, is patriotism an unruly emotion or an essential civic attitude? Do appeals to patriotism carry ethical weight and, if so, how much? Patriotism is not a 'local' problem that fails to engage other issues. To evaluate patriotism we need a theory of partialities and a method of adjudication for conflicting loyalties. In dealing with patriotism, we encounter difficult questions about our obligations to others.

Patriotism is a problem for journalism ethics because patriotism entails duties of citizenship, and journalists *are* citizens. If patriotism demands that journalists not inform the public about a military mistake, does that violate the journalist's duty to report truthfully? Another source of trouble is that both patriotism and journalism ethics demand that journalists serve the public. What does 'serving the public' mean?

2.1 Political and Communal Patriotism

Historically, we can distinguish forms of patriotism as mainly communal or mainly political. Communal patriotism is love of a 'pre-political' community, a loyalty to one's tribe, one's land, or one's village, language, or customs. Communal patriotism is concrete, emotive, and folksy, based on direct personal ties to specific peoples and places. Communal patriotism is pre-political because it existed before the modern state with its complex political structures. Even if political association exists, the focus of communal patriotism is on non-political features such as language and custom. Political patriotism is love of one's country political values, structure, and ideals. Political patriotism is allegiance to one's country primarily because it exhibits a well-ordered and just structure of rights, freedoms, institutions, and laws. Political patriotism is loyalty to a constitution, to the rule of law, to the rights and freedoms of citizenship.

Forms of patriotism are communal or political depending on which aspect receives the greatest emphasis. Pure forms of political or communal patriotism are rare. Communal patriots usually favour certain political structures; and political patriots praise the constitution *and* the beauty of their country and its traditions. Cold War patriotism, Western or Soviet, was more than a communal love of one's land. It was a patriotism fired by political ideology. Even in Western democracies with a strong constitutional tradition, such as the United States or France, patriotism is not purely political but contains communal love of land and people.

The history of patriotism shows how these two forms of patriotic attachment have evolved and mingled.[1] In antiquity, the patriotism of the Athenian city-state or Roman republic joined a communal love of *terra patria* (land of the fathers) with a political patriotism directed at *republica* which secured common liberty and the common good. In the Middle Ages, *patria* becomes *patria paradisii* – a celestial polity that commands allegiance and the martyr's sacrifice, a higher love than our earthly love of parents and country. In the Italian city-states of the Renaissance, writers, from Bruni to Machiavelli, revived the idea of political patriotism as an attachment to polities that secure 'sweet liberty' and the civic good. In Europe, from the seventeenth century onward, a communal sense of patriotism, interpreted as a loyalty to the person of the king, vied with the political patriotism of reformers who sought a 'commonwealth'. Robert Filmer provided ideological support for the English king by developing a monarchical patriotism in his *Patriarca* of 1680, which Locke attacked in his *Two Treaties*. In the eighteenth century, in Diderot's *Encyclopaedia, patria* was defined, not as a place of birth, but as a 'free state' whose laws protect liberty and happiness, and allow citizens to participate in public life. A century later, Mill warned that the "principle of nationality" did not mean "a senseless antipathy to foreigners; or a cherishing of absurd peculiarities because they are national."[2] As humanity hurtled towards two world wars, patriotism was captured by politically conservative forces and then by an extreme communal nationalism based on populist appeals to racial superiority or, as Lukacs (2005) calls it, the "myth of a people" (p. 36). Loyalty to one's nation meant unity and purification through the expulsion of Jews and ethnic minorities. After the Second World War and the Holocaust, writers like Habermas argued that only a non-communal, political form of patriotism could be valid. It must be a "patriotism of the Constitution" based on universal political principles of liberty and democracy embodied in the constitution of the Federal Republic of Germany (Viroli, 1996, pp. 169–170).

2.2 Structure of Patriotism

To clarify this complex topic, we need to identify the structure of all forms of patriotism, and the structure of an ethical theory of patriotism. Patriotism is a group loyalty that involves an attitude directed, in varying strengths and in various ways, at a valued object. Therefore, an *ethical* theory of patriotism is a normative theory with three elements: (1) a description of what that attitude should be, (2) a description of what the object of patriotism should be, and (3) criteria for evaluating claims of patriotism in specific situations. One's normative theory will depend on one's ideals, such as freedom and democracy. *My* interest is in constructing a normative theory of patriotism for democratic journalism.

Nathanson (1993) provided a useful analysis of patriotism as an attitude. All forms of patriotism have a "positive commitment to act on one's country's behalf in ways that one would not normally act for other countries" (p. 34). Nathanson defines patriotism as "a special affection for, identification with, and a concern for one's own nation and a willingness to act on its behalf" (p. 38). The attitude of patriotic loyalty differs across several dimensions, such as the object of loyalty, the strength and scope of the loyalty, the basis for the loyalty, and the attitude toward other loyalties. Nathanson (1993, p. 110) uses these dimensions to distinguish moderate and fanatical loyalty. Fanatical loyalty focuses exclusively on one object as a supreme duty that always overrides other loyalties. Fanaticism, as Kekes (1990) has said, is "the ruthless pursuit of some goal" (pp. 77–79). Fanatical loyalty takes an intolerant view of other loyalties.

We can conceptualise these distinctions as occupying a continuum with extreme patriotism on one end and a rejection of patriotism (or weak patriotism) on the other end. Moderate patriotism lies between these extremes. Extreme patriotism includes: (1) a special affection for one's country as superior to others, (2) an exclusive concern for one's country's well-being and few constraints on the pursuit of one's country's interests, and (3) automatic or uncritical support for one's country's actions. Extreme patriotism prepares the ground for extreme nationalism. In contrast, moderate patriotism consists in: (1) a special affection for one's country, (2) a desire that one's country flourishes and prospers, (3) a special but not exclusive concern for one's country, (4) support for a morally constrained pursuit of national goals, and (5) conditional and critical support of one's country's actions (Nathanson, 1993, pp. 37, 38, 55). Moderate patriotism is moderate loyalty to one's country. For moderate patriots, their country is one of several objects of loyalty. This loyalty is limited, presumptive, and subject to scrutiny. Moderate patriotism is 'moderate' because it acknowledges limits to patriotic partiality. It eschews exaggerating the uniqueness and superiority of one's country as a basis for aggressive attitudes. It respects the interests of people in other countries.

Moderate patriotism is the basis for my concept of democratic patriotism. Democratic patriotism is a form of moderate patriotism. It shares with moderate patriotism a moderate attitude towards the object of its loyalty – one's country. However, democratic patriotism is distinguished by adopting a more specific object or goal for patriotism. It provides a political interpretation of 'love of country'. The object of democratic loyalty is an ideal political association that is republican in its stress on liberty and democratic in its egalitarian stress on civic participation and equality. Democratic loyalty is republican in being a love of the republic as an association of free citizens motivated by the public good. Democratic loyalty is democratic in being a love of the republic as a 'democratic community'. A community is democratic if its political principles are practised and embedded in everyday life, in law, in social practices, and in the operation of institutions.

The society exhibits democratic forms of human association across the entire society. Democracy, in this view, is not simply the right to vote, or majority rule, or the belief that the 'many' should govern. Democracy is free, equal, and respectful participation in social and political life. Democracy is a way of relating to others, of carrying out projects, of designing institutions, of educating, of persuading and deciding. In education, democracy means perfecting the critical powers of citizens so they can make meaningful choices and participate in a democracy defined not solely by competing interests but also by deliberation on the common good. For this, as Putnam (1992) has argued, we need liberal values and the unimpeded flow of information and the freedom to offer and to criticise a hypothesis in politics, science, or journalism. Democratic patriotism will be a weak loyalty if it consists only in the intellectual understanding of abstract principles. Democratic patriotism cannot thrive without opportunities for citizens to participate meaningfully in democratic community.

With Dewey, I see democracy as the richest kind of communal life. It is the precondition for full human flourishing and the application of intelligence to social problems. Democracy is needed to allow humans in society to see 'what we are capable of' and to have the freedom to engage in what Mill (2006) called "experiments of living" (p. 65). Democratic well-being is defined collectively as a society where citizens thrive within supportive structures of political association. To aim at democratic community is to aim at what Rawls calls a "well-ordered constitutional democracy" where the exercise of freedoms and the pursuit of goods are constrained by justice. The patriot is attached to inclusive liberal institutions that allow to flourish what Rawls (1991, p. 36) calls a "reasonable pluralism" of philosophies of life. Patriotism to democratic community combines communal experiences – the experiences of enriching civic life – with an attachment to the principles and institutions that make civic life possible.

In one sense, democratic patriotism is an 'artificial' passion created by certain historically contingent social structures. In another sense, it is a passion rooted in the human capacity for a sense of justice and goodness. Democratic life provides principles of solidarity among citizens that go beyond their shared language and location. Solidarity is based on principles of common human rights, capacities, and aspirations. If democratic community is the goal, what type of patriotism promotes this ideal? It is a moderate patriotism that asks a country to live up to democratic criteria that define and restrain patriotic emotion.

My theory of democratic patriotism is a political form of patriotism that emphasises rational principle and ethical ideal. A purely emotive, communal love of one's country is a potentially dangerous loyalty, vulnerable to excess and the rhetoric of demagogues. However, my theory recognises the psychological and historical importance of communal factors in the 'special affection' of patriotism. It is not possible (or necessary) to deny personal affection for one's country. The goal is to develop a strongly supported (and well understood) moderate discourse of patriotism that prevents extreme patriotism from claiming to be the 'real' patriotism. The theoretical task is to develop a framework which allows us to systematically integrate these communal values with ethical and political principles. The social challenge is to develop a civic culture that transforms communal loyalties to group or neighbourhood into a more encompassing, ethical loyalty to the common good, and ultimately all of humanity. This encompassing loyalty is a love of one's country as a democratic political community, which is part of a human community.

3. Evaluating Patriotism

I have sketched a notion of democratic patriotism that restrains patriotism in general. But how should we evaluate claims of patriotism in specific circumstances? To evaluate patriotism in the concrete is an example of a larger ethical task – to consistently evaluate our many conflicting partialities. In this section, I suggest an approach to evaluating partialities like patriotism.

We begin with the fact that partialities can be good or bad. Partialities can motivate ethical action, such as acting generously towards a friend. Partiality can prompt a father to dive into deep water to save his drowning child. Cottingham (1986, pp. 366–368) has argued that agent-related partialism and philophilic partialism are ethically valuable. Agent-related partialism is a preference for one's goals and a proper concern for one's welfare and enrichment. Philophilic partialism is a partiality to loved ones or friends. Some partialities express special relationships that entail duties, such as the duty of parent to child. In deciding whether to promote the interests of persons x, I assign a certain ethical weight to the fact that x is my loved one.

However, there are questionable forms of partiality. An extreme loyalty to Canada may cause me to be callous towards the AIDS epidemic in Africa. Oldenquist (1982) argues that group affection and loyalties bind people together into "moral communities" (p. 177). Not always. Blind loyalty to a tyrant or ethnic group can lead to genocide. A 'committed person' sounds admirable, but I may be a committed neo-Nazi. Royce (1928) said loyalty to a cause gives individuals a unifying identity. But loyalty should be to a good cause.

In evaluating partialities, we should adopt what I call the attitude of "mitigated impartialism" (Ward, 2007). Mitigated impartiality recognises the presumptive ethical weight of partialities. Mitigated impartialism stands mid-way between two incorrect views about partialities: impartialism and partialism. Impartialism is the claim that ethics requires us to allocate our time and resources without preference to our own goals, and without displaying favouritism to those people near to us. Partialism is the thesis that 'it is (not merely psychologically understandable but) morally correct to favour one's own'. Partialism runs into problems, such as how to select good partialities from bad. Impartialism struggles to recognise legitimate claims of partiality, such as a parent's love for his or her child. As Cottingham (1986, pp. 357–58) argues, in deciding between x and y, impartialists are wrong to say, "I should assign no weight to the fact that x is 'my own'." Mitigated impartialism recognises that partialities may have ethical weight. However, their ethical weight is determined by systematic evaluation.

We systematically evaluate partialities, such as patriotism, by applying the attitude of mitigated impartiality combined with a framework of restraining principles. Our framework can be expressed as a series of questions: We consider the dimensions of the patriotism being advanced. Is it fanatical or immoderate? Does it violate ethical principles? What are the consequences of being patriotic or loyal to x in situation y? Does honouring this partiality entail (or violate) rights and duties? What primacy should this claim of patriotism have vis-à-vis other partialities and other values? Does this claim of patriotism violate the ethical standards for some public office or public practice? What is the 'object' of this patriotism, e.g. the wishes of a charismatic leader or democratic community? Moreover, we ask whether the claim of patriotism is compatible with general principles of rational and ethical behaviour. On this analysis, a claim of patriotism upon citizens is reasonable and has *prima facie* ethical weight if and only if:

1. *The claim of patriotism is inclusive*: It respects the rights and freedoms of all citizens within a nation. Patriotism has no moral force when it supports actions that favour a sub-section of citizens or the repression of a sub-section of citizens.
2. *The claim of patriotism is restrained*: It is not xenophobic towards other peoples and it lacks the aggressiveness often associated with nationalism and extreme forms of patriotism. The policy must be consistent with fair relations among countries and not violate principles of international law and human rights.
3. *The claim of patriotism must survive sustained public scrutiny and investigation*. Patriotism should be what Scanlon (1998, p. 20) calls a "judgment-sensitive attitude" that is open to the force of reasons and facts. Such evaluation can only be made in a public sphere that is open, and informed by an impartial free press.

This approach identifies several methods for evaluating the ethical weight of patriotism with respect to journalism. Again, we can ask: Does the claim of patriotism ask journalists to be uncritical or extreme in their patriotism? Does it ask journalists to violate general ethical principles, right or duties, or to violate a principle of the profession of journalism? Does it ask journalists to promote a just liberal society, the political 'object' of democratic journalism? Is the claim of patriotism compatible with the stated principles of inclusivity, rational restraint and public scrutiny? By adopting this holistic form of evaluation, journalists would erect a critical, ethical 'barrier' against the emotive pressure of extreme claims of patriotism. Neither journalists nor citizens in general are required ethically to respond to the claims of patriotism if they fail to satisfy the criteria embodied in these methods of evaluation.

4. Patriotism and Journalism

4.1 The Compatibility Problem

Assume that, as a citizen, I commit myself to democratic patriotism, its restraining principles and methods of evaluation. Also assume that I am a journalist committed to ethical standards and democracy. How compatible are these commitments?

I contend that moderate democratic patriotism is largely compatible with (and supportive of) the aims of democratic, ethical journalism.

This assumes, of course, that we value a democratic, public journalism. Journalism should be, as Carey (2000) said, a "particular kind of democratic practice" (p. 22). Democratic journalism is a primary adherence to the long-term common interests of the public as a whole, not the interests of individuals, parochial interests, or lobby groups. The ultimate aim of public journalism is the democratic well-being of the public. The public is a political category. It refers to all individuals in a society who, alone or in groups, are able to act as citizens. The public is all members of the body politic. To act as a citizen is to be engaged with issues of the common good, justice, and the direction of the commonwealth. I do not act as a citizen (or a member of the public) simply by consuming goods, running a business, or enjoying a private moment with my family. To belong to the public is to belong to society's broadest political association, which concerns itself with how citizens govern and are governed. The public consists of all individuals that are part of society's cooperative political enterprise which aims at human flourishing within an increasing democratisation of society. Public journalism is the organised, socially recognised activity of communicating *to the public for the public,* from the impartial perspective of the public good, democratically understood. Journalists should speak to the public in a manner different from partisan communicators such as the social advocate, the lobbyist, or public relations expert. Berger (2000) has said that public journalism amounts to "journalism communication done on behalf of the public interest, by people who are relatively independent of special interest" (p. 81).

Ethically speaking, the primary duty of public journalism is not to provide a service to the people as consumers of goods, or as sports fans, or as people interested in entertainment or tomorrow's weather. The core function of public journalism is providing communication that creates, maintains, and empowers citizens, as a political whole. It serves citizens primarily by inquiring into the principles, institutions, and essential processes of liberal democratic society, or by assisting the democratisation of non-liberal societies. Journalism's main public duties are protecting basic liberties and human rights, monitoring political institutions and representative officials, promoting rational deliberation, and publishing important truths. Their duty is to provide objective information and critical analysis for democratic deliberation. That is what it means for a journalist to be patriotic and to serve the public.

Journalism ethics, like ethics in general, leaves room for partialities and special relationships that entail presumptive duties and have *prima facie* weight. Journalists are constantly embedded in relationships with sources, story subjects and other parties, which result in promises and feelings of loyalty. The task of journalism ethics is to systematically weigh these partialities with the broader public duties of journalism. Where the partial and public good conflict, the latter takes precedence. For example, a journalist might come to sympathise with aboriginals as she probes into a nation's mistreatment of these people. She may even hope that her journalism will help correct problems. But such attachments should not cause the journalist to violate the duty to report impartially and completely to the public. She should not become so emotionally close to groups of aboriginals that she does not report 'inconvenient' or negative facts about these groups. These are facts the public should know.

Service to democracy can be interpreted as journalism's social contract. As Klaidman and Beauchamp (1987) argue, journalism provides public benefits in return for freedom. Journalists have professional duties because, as a group, they have a cumulative and systematic impact on society. Power and influence entail responsibilities, and legitimate public expectations.[3] Journalists have a duty to improve the informational and deliberative health of citizens in the same way as public health officers are responsible for the physical health of citizens. Journalists support the public's 'informational' health by carrying out five democratic functions: (a) provide essential news for the public in an independent, accurate and comprehensive fashion; (b) act as a watchdog on abuse of power, and as a voice for the less powerful; (c) create a forum for the deliberation of public policy from a variety of views; (d) fairly represent groups and minorities, as befits a pluralistic society; and (e) write stories in a manner that encourages citizens to engage in the issues and to avoid a passive or cynical attitude.

We can now approach the question of compatibility. My model assumes that the journalist has a democratic role that is different and more specific in its duties than that of the citizen. The rights and duties of a democratic citizen *per se* are very general. All citizens have the right to vote, to influence public policy, to engage in political activity, to live under the rule of law, etc. However, in addition, democracy needs certain types of citizens – public persons – to fulfill various democratic duties, such as politicians, judges, heads of institutions, and journalists. The role of journalists is to ensure that an open democratic society is maintained by fulfilling its five functions through independent reporting.

Given these principles – a commitment to moderate patriotism, deliberative democracy and impartial journalism – we can draw two substantial conclusions about journalism and patriotism. One, the principles of democratic journalism are largely compatible with the principles of democratic patriotism because both share the goal of democratic community. An individual can be both a democratic journalist and a patriot to democratic community, although the journalist may serve democratic community in distinct ways. Democratic journalism and democratic patriotism share a substantial overlap of values such as freedom, openness, and tolerance. The democratic patriot and the democratic journalist will be on the same side of a number of public issues. Both will support accurate, unbiased information, free speech, a critical news media, and a public sphere with diverse perspectives. Both will favour the protection of liberties, transparency in public affairs, and the evaluation of appeals to patriotism.

Second, extreme patriotism is largely incompatible with democratic journalism because it tends to support editorial limits on the press, or it exerts pressure on journalists to be uncritical, partisan, or economical with the truth. Journalism's commitment to moderate democratic patriotism implies that journalists must reject pressure to depart from that role from demands to practise a more guarded, narrowly patriotic journalism. Journalism's democratic values come under severe test when a country decides to go to war, to deny civil liberties for 'security' reasons, or to ignore the constitution in order to quell domestic unrest. The duty of journalists to critique a country's president may be very unpopular among some citizens in times of war. The publication of human and civil rights abuses by government may lead to accusations that the press is aiding the 'enemy'.[4] Nevertheless, the public journalist is still duty-bound to resist such pressures and not fear social condemnation. Even in times of uncertainty, journalists have a duty to continue to provide news, investigations, controversial analysis, and multiple perspectives. They should not mute their criticisms and they should maintain skepticism toward all sources. Journalists need to unearth and explain the roots of their country's problems, and coolly assess alleged threats. If journalists abandon their democratic role, they will fail to help the public rationally assess public policy. The journalist's well-meaning desire to be patriotic may, in fact, assist the manipulation of public opinion by not questioning the powerful emotions of patriotism.

4.2 Whom does Journalism Serve?

The democratic idea that journalists serve society is easily confused with other conceptions. The cultural diversity of the countries served by journalism makes it inevitable that other cultures will have different models of good journalism and different notions of how journalists serve society. A communist or authoritarian model of the press will interpret how journalists serve society differently from liberal or 'social responsibility' theories.[5] In my model, serving the public is serving the democratic life of the public, not serving the state, a government policy, or an institution, such as the military. Media outlets do not serve the public by pleasing their own audiences with jingoistic messages. Serving the public is about creating a media system, or media space, that encourages a critical, open public sphere of diverse, often unpopular, views. To serve the public is to help a reasonable, informed public to exist.

The idea that journalists serve society can be interpreted in ways that encourage the silencing of critical voices. For example, in Southeast Asia and other areas, the developmental journalism paradigm began among journalists in the late 1960s. Developmentalism (Murthy, 2001) was to be an authentic expression of indigenous culture and protection against manipulation by former colonial masters. Developmental journalism was contrasted with a Western liberal press model, with its principles of independence, objectivity, and neutrality. On the face of it, developmental journalism has noble goals: to use media to develop countries with weak economies and serious social problems; to build social solidarity and allow people to take control of their lives. However, in the 1980s and 1990s, leaders of Southeast Asian countries, such as Indonesia, Malaysia, and Singapore, attempted to harness the media for their own interests, in the name of nation building and economic development. Serving the nation through 'developmental journalism' meant pointing out corruption among minor provincial officials but not corruption in the highest places. It meant downplaying or ignoring government mistakes in economic or social planning; it meant not damaging social solidarity with 'embarrassing' reports of inadequate health services, or violations of human rights. It meant editors taking 'advice' from political leaders on what coverage was in the 'national interest'. These problems continue. For example, the role of news media in post-apartheid South Africa has been a subject of debate. President Thabo Mbeki has attacked the news media (De Beer and Wasserman, 2004) as 'fishers of corrupt men,' whose criticisms of government are tantamount to working against the 'national interest'. Therefore, we need to avoid simplistic interpretations of 'non-Western' ideals for journalism. In this book, Fourier warns against the misuse of indigenous concepts, such as the African notion of *ubuntu* in journalism ethics.

For public journalism, the problem is not with the goals of development, or social solidarity. The problem is how those goals are interpreted and how the press is expected to serve them. To 'serve the public' according to democratic journalism, three elements must be present: (a) a notion of 'serving the public' that is *not* reducible to the interests of the current government or special interests, (b) the adoption of an independent, impartial stance by journalists, which creates a critical distance between reporter and story, and between reporter and state official, and (c) the use of the press to create a critical, deliberative, public sphere. Without these factors, 'serving the public' is reduced to the rhetoric of uncritical patriotism. The idea of media-supported social solidarity becomes the idea of not challenging the status quo. Public journalism insists that, in the long-run, social goals are best pursued by allowing the media to construct a critical and open public space for deliberation. This belief fits nicely with the idea of moderate, democratic patriotism.

5. Global Journalism and Patriotism

My analysis has found substantial compatibility between a certain conception of journalism, democratic journalism, and a certain conception of patriotism, moderate patriotism. The analysis assumes nation-based concepts. I have presumed, up to this point, that patriotism is loyalty to a country or nation, and journalism's duty is to serve the democratic community of that country. But is a nation-based notion of patriotism still adequate in a global world with global media? In the rest of this paper I suggest that the answer is no. Journalism ethics needs to construct new aims and principles from a cosmopolitan perspective. Part of that construction includes the embrace of a new 'object' for patriotism – a global patriotism to humanity or the human good.

5.1 Why a Global Journalism Ethics?

Historically, journalism and journalism ethics have been parochial. Journalism ethics was developed for a journalism of limited reach, whose public duties were assumed to stop at the border. As a result, in times of conflict, patriotism as love of nation trumped other journalistic values such as critical truth-telling. The sufficiency of this parochial ethics has been undermined by the globalisation of news media and the global connectedness of all regions of the world. The facts are familiar. Media corporations are increasingly global enterprises. Technology gives journalists the ability to gather information from around the world. News reports, via satellite or the internet, reach distant countries.

With global impact comes global responsibilities. The violence that rippled around the world after the publication of the cartoons of Mohammed in a Danish newspaper is one example of global impact. As Ali Mohamed's analysis of the cartoons show, our world is not a cozy McLuhan village.

My proposal is that we construct a *global journalism ethics* by using a cosmopolitan ethics to reinterpret the aims of journalism.[6]

5.2 Cosmopolitan Ethics

Cosmopolitan ethics, expressed long ago in the writings of Stoics, Christian humanists and Kant, asserts the equal value and dignity of all people, as members of a common humanity. As Brock and Brighouse (2005) write: "Each human being has equal moral worth and that equal moral worth generates certain moral responsibilities that have universal scope" (p. 4). Our primary allegiance should be to a borderless, moral community of humankind. This principle rules out assigning ultimate ethical value to collective entities such as states or nations. It rules out positions that accord no value to some types of people, or establish a moral hierarchy where some people count for more than others. The nationality, ethnicity, religion, class, race, or gender of a person is morally irrelevant to whether an individual is a member of humanity. Cosmopolitanism grounds universal principles of respect and freedom on this recognition of our common humanity. The claim of humanity is not the cognition of an abstract principle. It is the ability to perceive and value our common humanity in the situations of life. It is respect for mankind's rational and moral capacities wherever and however they are manifest. It is in our concrete dealings with others that we recognise humanity's common aspirations, vulnerabilities and capacities, as well as its potential for suffering.

Cosmopolitanism is a thesis about identity and responsibility. Cosmopolitans regard themselves as primarily defined by the common needs and aspirations that they share with other humans. This cosmopolitan identity is more important to their sense of self and 'ethical identity' than facts about their place of birth, social class, or nationality. In terms of responsibility, cosmopolitanism, according to Brock and Brighouse (2005) "highlights the obligations we have to those whom we do not know, and with whom we are not intimate, but whose lives touch ours sufficiently that what we do can affect them" (p. 3).

Cosmopolitanism has received increasing attention because of the debate over the role of the nation-state in a global world. But there are varieties of cosmopolitanism and it is difficult to formulate precisely what cosmopolitanism requires. Does equal moral worth entail that everyone should have an equal share of the land? As Fishkin (1982) asks: "Are comfortable North Americans morally bound to contribute to foreign aid to the point of damaging their ability to provide for their children's university education?" Despite these uncertainties, there is a growing consensus among cosmopolitans that, at the least, people everywhere should be able to meet their basic needs and develop their capacities.

The issue that engages cosmopolitanisms and their critics is not the option between a completely partial ethics and a completely impartial ethics. Most cosmopolitans do not dispute that we have special relationships with friends and family. The central issue is the obligation of citizens to nations, and the obligations of nations to other nations, especially underdeveloped states. What do citizens owe to their fellow compatriots and what do they owe to non-compatriots? One answer is weak cosmopolitanism: There are *some* extra-national obligations. Another is strong cosmopolitanism: Our obligations are always global. Our fellow nationals have no claim on us and we have no right to use nationality (in contrast to friendship or familial love) to guide our discretionary behaviour. Today, most of the interesting cosmopolitan debate concerns how to find a position between weak and strong cosmopolitanism.[7] These attempts to integrate national partiality into a cosmopolitan attitude are similar in form to my attempt to integrate partialities into ethics, to walk between partialism and impartialism.

In my view, the cosmopolitan attitude does not deny or devalue cultural diversity or legitimate partialities. The cosmopolitan thinker is under no illusion that people will stop loving their family and country. The cosmopolitan attitude does not deny that particular cultures and traditions are valuable. Instead, the cosmopolitan attitude is concerned with the *priority* and *limits* of our attachments. To say that our primary allegiance is to humanity is to say that more partial concerns have a *prima facie* right to be recognised, but may be trumped by broader concerns. The claim of humanity acknowledges the stoic view that we live simultaneously in two communities: the local community of our birth, and a community of common human aspirations. It insists only that, in negotiating our way between these two communities, we should not allow local attachments to override fundamental human rights and duties. When there is no conflict with fundamental principles, life can continue to be lived according to partial principles. However, there are situations, such as military intervention in a foreign country or the establishment of a fair world trading system, where we need to assess actions from a perspective of global justice and reasonableness. The cosmopolitan attitude limits our parochial attachments by drawing a ring of broader ethical principles around them.

Cosmopolitanism does not deny that people can have legitimate feelings of concern toward their country or compatriots. But it also insists that moderate patriotism be evaluated from a cosmopolitan perspective. This accommodating view goes further than some, like Nussbaum, seem prepared to accept. Nussbaum (1996) associates patriotism with a strong patriotic pride that is "both morally dangerous and, ultimately subversive of some of the worthy goals patriotism sets out to serve" (p. 4), such as national unity in devotion to justice and equality. Cosmopolitanism, for Nussbaum (1996), provides an alternative to extreme patriotism or a divisive "politics of difference" (p. 4). Kwame Anthony Appiah (2006), however, leaves more room for patriotism in his cosmopolitanism. He advances the idea of "cosmopolitan patriots," and of "partial cosmopolitanism" as a cosmopolitanism "that celebrates cultural differences while ruling out extreme nationalism" (pp. xvi–xvii). He argues that living in parochial communities narrower than the species is better than living under a world-state. Appiah (1996) believes that cosmopolitans should defend the right of others to live in "democratic states with rich possibilities of association within and across their borders" (p. 29). Similarly, Coutrie and Nielsen (2005, p. 180) have argued for a "rooted cosmopolitanism" which holds that patriotic sentiment is ethically permissible and valuable. These writers are trying to articulate a framework in which we can recognise the ineliminable impulse in humans to value both the partial and the impartial, to be attached to both the universal and the particular.

Conclusion

If we adopt a cosmopolitan attitude in journalism, we change the aims and principles of journalism ethics, and we alter our conception of democratic journalism. The object of democratic journalism becomes not only the promotion of national democratic community but also global democratic community. Cosmopolitan journalists are 'global patriots' with a special affection for humanity and its flourishing. The claim of humanity extends the journalist's loyalty from the public of her hometown and country to humanity at large.

The promotion of a global democratic community contains two goals.[8] One is the use of journalism to promote and protect basic human capacities and needs, to raise the level of global social justice. The other is the more 'political' quest of advancing democratic community through the promotion and protection of basic rights and the ability of citizens to participate in political processes. Both goals promote the 'human good' as the material, social and political goods of a dignified and flourishing life.

To borrow an analogy from music, a cosmopolitan ethic transposes the discussion of serving the public good into a new 'key' where familiar terms take on new meanings. Journalism's social contract to a society becomes a 'multi-society' contract. The journalist becomes a trans-national public communicator. Journalistic credibility for a local public becomes credibility for a global audience. Journalistic independence comes to include independence from the pressures and biases of one's own nation. Objectivity becomes the ideal of informing impartially from an international stance. Global journalism seeks to facilitate rational deliberation in a global public sphere and facilitate understanding among groups.

The cosmopolitan attitude does not imply that news organisations should ignore local issues or regional audiences. It does not mean that every story involves global issues or requires a cosmopolitan attitude. What is at issue is a gradual widening of basic editorial attitudes and standards – a widening of journalists' vision of their responsibilities and a reinterpretation of the standards used to evaluate stories.

The following three imperatives state the essential components of a cosmopolitan perspective in journalism:

Act as global agents

Journalists should see themselves as agents of a global public sphere. The goal of their collective actions is a well-informed, diverse and tolerant global 'info-sphere' that challenges the distortions of tyrants, the abuse of human rights and the manipulation of information by special interests.

Serve the citizens of the world

The global journalist's primary loyalty is to the information needs of world citizens. Journalists should refuse to define themselves as attached primarily to factions, regions or even countries. Serving the public means serving more than one's local readership or audience, or even the public of one's country.

Promote non-parochial understandings

The global journalist frames issues broadly and uses a diversity of sources and perspectives to promote a nuanced understanding of issues from an international perspective. Journalism should work against a narrow ethnocentrism or patriotism.

The phrase 'journalists as world citizens' denotes an ethical ideal and a gradual shift in practices and perspective. Journalists as world citizens reject narrow perspectives steeped in ethnocentrism, extreme patriotism and partisanship. The phrase refers, optimistically, to a hoped-for evolution in the ethical identity of journalists.

Notes

1   For a history of how communal and political patriotism evolved, see Viroli (1995) and (2002). On republicanism, see Skinner (1978) and Honohan (2002).
2   Mill, *A System of Logic*, Book VI. 10.5, cited in Viroli (1996, p. 29).
3   See Kovach and Rosenstiel (2001).
4   For example, in late 2005 and into 2006, the US administration characterised journalists and citizens who had exposed a secret programme of surveillance of the communications of American citizens as enemies of America.
5   See Christians & Nordenstreng (2004).
6   For global media ethics see Black & Barney (2002) & Ward (2005).
7   Held (2005, p. 18) argues for a "layered cosmopolitanism" that provides a framework of principles that allow for argument and negotiation of "particular spheres of value" in which national and regional affiliations are weighed. Tan argues that if we establish a just structure of global institutions, it is permissible to favour one's compatriots. Tan (2005, p. 164).
8   For an exposition of a "cosmopolitan democracy" see Held (2005, pp. 267–286), and Held (2000).

References

Aboulafia, M. (2001). *The cosmopolitan self: George Herbert Mead and continental philosophy*. Urbana, Ill: Illinois University Press.

Appiah, K.A. (1996). Cosmopolitan patriots, In J. Cohen, (ed.), *For love of country: Debating the limits of patriotism: Martha C. Nussbaum with respondents* (pp. 21–29). Boston: Beacon Press.

Appiah, K.A. (2006). *Cosmopolitanism: Ethics in a world of strangers*. New York: Norton.

Berger, G. (2000). Grave new world? Democratic journalism enters the global twenty-first century, *Journalism Studies*, 1(1), 81–99.

Black, J. & and Barney, R. (eds.). (2002). Search for a global media ethic, [Special issue] *Journal of Mass Media Ethics*, 17(4).

Brock, G. & Brighouse, H. (eds.). (2005). *The political philosophy of cosmopolitanism*. Cambridge: Cambridge University Press.

Carey, J.W. (2000). Some personal notes on US journalism education, *Journalism: Theory, practice and criticism*, 1(1), 12–23.

Christians, C. & Nordenstreng, K. (2004). Social responsibility worldwide, *Journal of Mass Media Ethics*, 19(1), 3–28.

Cohen, J. (ed.). (1996). *For love of country: Debating the limits of patriotism: Martha C. Nussbaum with respondents*. Boston: Beacon Press.

Cottingham, J. (1986). Favouritism and morality, *Philosophical Quarterly*, 36(144), 357–373.

Coutrie, J. & Nielsen, K. (2005). Cosmopolitanism and the compatriot priority principle. In G. Brock & H. Brighouse, (eds.), *The political philosophy of cosmopolitanism* (pp. 180–195). Cambridge: Cambridge University Press.

De Beer, A. & and Wasserman, H. A fragile affair: The relationship between the mainstream media and government in post-apartheid South Africa. Paper presented to University of Missouri School of Journalism, April 9, 2004, Columbia, Miss.

Fishkin, J. S. (1982). *The limits of obligation*. New Haven, N.J.: Yale University Press.

Hartle, A. (1989). *Moral issues in military decision making*. Lawrence: University of Kansas Press.

Held, D. (1995). *Democracy and the global order: From the modern state to cosmopolitan governance*. Cambridge: Polity Press.

Held, D. (2000). The changing contours of political community: Rethinking democracy in the context of globalization. In Barry Holden, (ed.), *Global democracy: Key debates* (pp. 17–31). London: Routledge.

Held, D. (2005). Principles of cosmopolitan order. In G. Brock & H. Brighouse (eds.), *The political philosophy of cosmopolitanism* (pp. 10–27). Cambridge: Cambridge University Press.

Honohan, I. (2002). *Civic republicanism*. London: Routledge.

Kant, I. (1964). *Groundwork of the metaphysic of morals*. (H.J. Paton, Trans.) New York: Harper and Row.

Kant, I. (1996). *The metaphysics of morals*. (Mary Gregor, Trans.) Cambridge: Cambridge University Press.

Kant, I. (1998). *Religion within the bounds of mere reason*. (A. Wood & G. Giovanni, Trans.) Cambridge: Cambridge University Press.

Kekes, J. (1990). *Facing evil*. Princeton, N.J.: Princeton University Press.

Klaidman, S. & Beauchamp, T. (1987). *The virtuous journalist*. Oxford: Oxford University Press.

Kovach, B. & Rosenstiel, T. (2001). *The elements of journalism*. New York: Crown Publishers.

Lukacs, J. (2005). *Democracy and populism*, New Haven, N.J.: Yale University Press.

Mill, J. S. (2006). *On liberty and the subjection of women*. London: Penguin.

Murthy, D. (2001). *Developmental journalism*. New Delhi: Dominant Publishers.

Nathanson, S. (1993). *Patriotism, morality and peace*. Lanham, MD: Rowman and Littlefield.

Nussbaum, M. C. (1996). Patriotism and cosmopolitanism. In J. Cohen, (ed.), *For love of country: Debating the limits of patriotism: Martha C. Nussbaum with respondents* (pp. 3–17). Boston: Beacon Press.

Nussbaum, M. C. (2006). *Frontiers of justice*. Cambridge, Mass.: Belknap Press.

Oldenquist, A. (1982). Loyalties, *The Journal of Philosophy*, 79(4), 173–193.

Putnam, H. (1992). "A reconsideration of Deweyan democracy," *Renewing philosophy*. Cambridge, Mass.: Harvard University Press.

Rawls, J. (1992). *A theory of justice*. Oxford: Oxford University Press.

Rawls, J. (1993). *Political liberalism*. New York: Columbia University Press.

Rawls, J. (2002). *The law of peoples*. Cambridge, Mass: Harvard University Press.

Royce, J. (1928). *The philosophy of loyalty*. New York: Macmillan.

Scanlon, T. (1998). *What we owe to each other*. Cambridge, Mass.: Harvard University Press.

Skinner, Q. (1978). *The foundations of modern political thought.* 2 vols. Cambridge: Cambridge University Press.

Tan, Kok-Chor. (2005). The demands of justice and national allegiances. In G. Brock & H. Brighouse, (eds.), *The political philosophy of cosmopolitanism* (pp. 164–179). Cambridge: Cambridge University Press.

Tolstoy, L. (1987). *Writings on civil disobedience and nonviolence.* Philadelphia, Pa: New Society.

Viroli, M. (1995). *For love of country: An essay on patriotism and nationalism.* Oxford: Clarendon Press.

Viroli, M. (2002). *Republicanism.* (A. Shugaar, Trans.) New York: Hill and Wang.

Ward, S. J. A. (2007). Utility and Impartiality: Being Impartial in a Partial World, *Journal of Mass Media Ethics,* 22(2 & 3), 151–167.

Ward, S. J. A. (2005). *The invention of journalism ethics: The path to objectivity and beyond.* Montreal, Que.: McGill-Queen's University Press.

Ward, S. J. A. (2005). "Philosophical foundations for global journalism ethics," *Journal of Mass Media Ethics,* 20(1), 3–21.

4 Media Ethics: Towards a Framework for Media Producers and Media Consumers

Nick Couldry

1. Introduction

Media are an inescapable part of daily life. Yet media consumption has until recently been an act performed by audiences at a distance from processes of media production. Perhaps this is why journalistic codes of 'media ethics' are formulated exclusively from the point of view of media professionals, not media audiences, and why issues of media ethics are not generally thought of as the subject of legitimate intervention by members of the public, even, as Onora O'Neill noted in her 2002 BBC Reith Lectures (O'Neill, 2003), in societies that claim to be democracies. This needs to change in an era when via the internet at least some aspects of information and image production/circulation are being decentred. If the old "division of labour in democratic discourse" (Bohman, 2000) between media producers and media consumers is now open to challenge, then our understanding of media ethics also needs to change, with considerable implications for the broader ethics of consumption in today's media-saturated societies.

Suppose we adopt a different starting point: that media are a matter of central concern for *all* citizens, whether media producers, consumers or hybrid producer-consumers, and that therefore we must build within an *inclusive* framework of media ethics that can address the ethical concerns and ambitions of anyone involved in, or affected by, the media process. Such a broader framework for media ethics could contribute to the wider critique of 'mere' consumerism and to generating new models of pleasurable and empowered consumption, and the obligations it entails.

An immediate obstacle, however, is that we lack a philosophically grounded framework within which media producers and media consumers can, as citizens, debate whether the media we have are ethical. This chapter explores how we might build at least the foundations of such a framework from within the tradition of ethical thought that derives originally from the 4th century BC Greek philosopher, Aristotle. Justifying this starting point will involve navigating through some difficult philosophical choices, but little or no philosophical background will be assumed in what follows.

Before I proceed further, let me make clear the main problematic that guides my approach to media ethics and explain how it links to the wider aim of this book. Whatever philosophical tradition we draw upon, media ethics will, I propose, be of little use unless it has a global dimension: in that sense, it must be 'beyond borders'. Since media unquestionably do help shape actions and worldviews on a global scale, we cannot exclude the global from our reflections: a media ethics must in scale and scope be a global media ethics, or it is nothing at all. This however does not mean seeking to impose from a particular standpoint one normative framework on the rest of the world (a criticism frequently made of uses of the term 'global'). On the contrary, the emphasis must be on contributing, through our formulations as media academics and media professionals, to the conditions of broader dialogue and through that dialogue an emerging (and so not yet visible) consensus.

This has major implications for the way we approach the philosophical choices that, inevitably, will feed into our particular formulations of media ethics. If media ethics must from the start aspire to an application 'beyond borders', it must take account of the *lack* of value consensus (whether on moral values, or on understandings of rationality or history or the status of science) on a global scale. A global media ethics cannot legislate such diversity and disagreement away; instead, it should acknowledge such diversity, by starting from premises that are normatively minimal. It should, I suggest, draw as little as possible on assumptions about what specifically is to be valued: its account of value should at the start at least be "thin", and not "thick" (in Clifford Geertz's [1971] famous term). A global media ethics requires, in other words a pragmatic eclecticism, if it is to address the challenge of simultaneity across difference with which a mediated world confronts us. Bruno Latour (2004) formulates that challenge well in a series of questions:

> An entirely new set of questions has now emerged [on the political stage]: "Can we cohabitate with you?" "Is there a way for all of us to survive together while none of our contradictory claims, interests and passions can be eliminated?". . . "What should now be simultaneously present?" (p. 40).

This vision – of the need to ask new questions in the face of the global simultaneity that media make possible, indeed now make compulsory – fits well, I suggest, with the project of global media ethics, even if it is formulated in other terms.[1]

From this perspective, the approach to media ethics I will propose deliberately does not start out from detailed values or principles of duty; if it did, it could not be the basis of consensus, since huge differences of worldview (religious, political, cultural) between media professionals and consumers across the world would quickly emerge. Instead, the approach I propose aims to build consensus from minimal premises – the premises necessary for answering clearly and systematically how, given our profound and mutually obvious differences, all of us who share the earth's surface can, with media's help, live well together. For reasons explained later, I believe those minimal premises can best be built from the resources that have come down to us from the Aristotelian tradition.

2. Philosophical Choices

There are many types of normative positions that people take up in relation to media. One type looks at media's organisation and, in the form of 'public sphere' theory, asks whether media's current organisation helps or hinders democracy. This often involves large-scale arguments about public service and market provision, and addresses the organisational structures through which media gets made: it does not make judgements about what particular media actors do on particular occasions. By contrast, the type of normative position which I call 'media ethics' (in the broad sense) is concerned primarily with the specifics of what media do and what we do with media. Not that it is limited to the 'micro' level of media practice, for the long-term and long-distance consequences of media also have ethical consequences; it is now commonplace to talk of media as an 'environment' or 'ecology', and the practical and ecological aspects of media ethics are inseparable from each other.

An advantage of media ethics is that, instead of struggling right away with huge questions about the organisation of late modern polities – what, for example, should be the state's and corporate power's relationship to media resources? – media ethics asks directly of the journalist or news source: should you have done what you did? Are the types of things you do (doorstepping a celebrity to get a picture for a celebrity magazine, for example) something that contributes to a good life for yourself or for anyone else? Is it ethical for me to accept payment for a story I supply to a newspaper? Media ethics asks such questions of any media operation, any media source, anywhere, *regardless* of the political system in which they are situated. It asks such questions not from a technocratic point of view – does your rulebook or manual allow you to do what you did? – but from a broader ethical or moral standpoint whose authority does not derive from media's day-to-day operations.

Of course, detailed journalistic codes exist in almost every country (see Bertrand, 2000, for a useful international review), but they are not what I mean by 'media ethics'. Media ethics in the broad sense should ask two questions: first, what are the ethical or moral standards by which any of us should judge what media organisations and media professionals – indeed anyone who contributes to the media process – do? And, second, how do such standards of media ethics relate to our general ethical frameworks for judging how people act?

The specific approach I am proposing follows the route of neo-Aristotelian virtue ethics. Of course this is not the only possible starting point for a framework of media ethics. Arguably, there are four other major alternatives within 'Western' philosophical traditions and no doubt many more within non-Western traditions. Christian humanism, Deleuzian or Foucauldian 'nomadism', a Kantian deontology and a Levinasian ethics of communication. Because of the constraints of my own philosophical knowledge, I must limit my discussion here to Western alternatives, but my arguments, as already noted for preferring neo-Aristotelian approaches in some form, are based on the degree to which they *do not* depend on specific norms and values tied exclusively with the 'West', while at the same time retaining rigour and clarity. I discuss Christian humanism and 'nomadism' only briefly since they can generate at most specific value-positions on media and communications, not broad frameworks in which new moral or ethical questions about media can be posed. The Christian humanist tradition of media ethics developed in the US in the 1980s and 1990s by Clifford Christians (Christians, Ferré and Fackler, 1993) is based on the specific values of 'dialogue' and 'global human community'; for all its insights, a philosophical framework so tied to specific religious values is, I argue elsewhere (cf. Couldry, 2006, p. 106 ff.), of limited use in developing a media ethics for a *global* context where consensus over such values is impossible because of the multiplicity of religious and secular traditions that must come together. As to Deleuzian "nomadism" (Braidotti, 2006), I am not aware of its application to the evaluation of media and communication, but I will say little about it because I am highly sceptical about its claims to have transcended universal values. Charles Taylor's (1985) sympathetic but effective demolition of Foucault's claims to have escaped reliance on universal values is equally relevant to Deleuze. In any case, I do not believe that 'nomadism' can provide a coherent or clear basis for dialogue about media ethics *between* philosophical traditions. Levinasian approaches (Pinchevski, 2005; Silverstone, 2006) are much more fruitful, but unfortunately there is no space to discuss them here.

So the key choice on which I want to concentrate is between deontological frameworks deriving from the Enlightenment philosopher Immanuel Kant (Kant, 1997) and the ethical tradition deriving ultimately from Aristotle (Aristotle, 1976). The distinction between approaches based on notions of 'the good' (that is, ethics which specifies virtue) and those based on a notion of the 'right' (that is, deontology which specifies duty) has been a fundamental fault-line in the last two centuries of moral philosophy. (I leave out here the until recently dominant alternative to deontology, utilitarianism, because I believe that ethics necessarily starts out from broadly social considerations which utilitarianism as a framework based exclusively in the optimisation of individual good cannot by definition provide.) The key fault-line here can be summed up historically in the difference between Aristotle's question "what is the good life for human beings?" and Kant's question "what actions are the duty of any rational being?" Aristotle's approach remains specific to the form of life called human, whereas Kant's approach addresses *any* rational being. This is a crucial difference, because Kant's 'transcendental idealism' aims to stand above the things that human beings might from time to time agree upon as good, and as a consequence, I would argue, stand above exactly the historically contingent practices out of which a media ethics might be built.

The word 'ethics', not 'morality', is usually associated with the Aristotelian or neo-Aristotelian historical tradition (Williams, 1985, p. 1); however, the difference of terms is pure convention, since both 'ethics' and 'morality' have their origins in classical terms for custom, one Greek and the other Latin, but let's leave that point to one side. The 'ethics' tradition is sometimes referred to as 'teleological', because Aristotle's ethics was based on the search for principles that best enacted the 'end' (in Greek, 'telos') of human life; by contrast, the tradition of prioritising the analyses of obligation and duty rather than the good flowing from Kant is often called 'deontological' (coming from the Greek word for obligation). The 'ethics' approach is, initially, aimed more generally at how we should live, whereas deontology is concerned, quite specifically, with what I am in a specific situation rationally required to do.

There are of course complications: it is possible to follow in the tradition of 'ethics' without believing in Aristotle's teleology; there are forms of deontology that are not Kantian (for example the work of Emmanuel Levinas); while some philosophers now argue that it is the *compatibilities* between the ethical and deontological traditions that are important (O'Neill, 1996). But the basic distinction between ethics and morality/deontology is important in guiding our choice of frameworks for what I called media ethics in the broad sense. It represents the difference between, on the one hand, searching for some open-ended and quite general principles (not a comprehensive system) for evaluating media practice, on which human beings at a particular place and time *might* come to agree; and, on the other hand, searching for a comprehensive and systematic specification of moral rules for media practice that any rational being anywhere *must* find compelling. My clear preference is for the former approach over the latter.

Why? *First*, I am highly sceptical about the possibility or desirability of developing morality, including a media-related morality, as a complete system of rules, judged for its ability to compel any rational person's acceptance (for example, Rawls' "theory of justice"). *Second*, I believe that the starting-point of deontology – the question of right or duty – is secondary to the starting-point of ethics, the question of what is good. As Paul Ricoeur points out, Rawls' attempt to downplay 'the good' in his theory of justice fails and 'the good' in the form of virtue is obstinately there in the first sentence of *A Theory of Justice*: "Justice is the first virtue of social institutions, as truth is of systems of thought" (Ricoeur, 1992, p. 197, discussing Rawls, 1972, p. 1). In prioritising the question, 'what type of life is good?' over the question, 'what type of action is required by duty?', I am following Hegel's position in his controversial response to Kant in the early 19th century. Hegel (1991) responded to Kant's abstract system of rational duty for the 'good will' in the following terms:

> However essential it may be to emphasise the pure and unconditional self-determination of the will as the root of duty ... to cling on to a merely moral point of view without making the transition to the concept of ethics reduces this gain to an empty formalism, and moral science to an empty rhetoric of duty for duty's sake (p. 162).

While developing a full framework of media ethics at a sufficient level of detail to guide action in specific cases is beyond the scope of this article (I return to this apparent limitation in my conclusion), my aim here is at least to establish some starting principles, and for these principles to be more than merely abstract or formal. To do this we need, as Hegel said, to "make the transition" from formal duty to "the concept of ethics", that is, to a consideration of what might count as a good life in the conditions of mediated societies.

Third, the greater flexibility inherent to questions about the 'good' as opposed to questions about 'right' or 'duty' is needed if media ethics is to be genuinely global in its scope. No common ground exists, on a global scale, for building agreement on questions of right or duty: how can we possibly hope to find agreement between Christian, Islamic, and secular traditions, for example, on what we are rationally required to do in relation to media, when each tradition has different traditions for thinking not only about obligation but also about rationality itself (cf. MacIntyre, 1988, chapters 18–20)? Suitably adjusted and developed, the neo-Aristotelian tradition of virtue ethics whose roots predate Christian and Islamic traditions *does* provide tools for developing consensus about how to evaluate what media do. The reason is that virtue ethics prioritises questions of the good – not the good in an abstract sense ('good' for any rational being), but the good 'for man'. I am not saying that such a consensus about the good in relation to media already exists, but that only the neo-Aristotelian tradition poses the key questions in such a way that we can begin to imagine in broad terms how such a consensus might emerge.

Within the neo-Aristotelian tradition there are, I believe, substantive things we can plausibly say about 'the good' for man in relation to media that do not rest on tradition-specific values (such as Christian humanists' value of 'human community') but derive instead from our orientation, as human beings, to certain shared questions and shared facts, including the unavoidable fact of global media.

3. What would a Neo-Aristotelian Approach to Media Ethics Involve?

We can get a good sense of how neo-Aristotelian media ethics might proceed from the philosopher Warren Quinn (1995):

> (O)ne tries to determine what, given the circumstances, would be good or bad in itself to do or to aim at. These questions are referred to larger ones: what kind of life it would be best to lead and what kind of person it would be best to be. The sense of 'good' and 'best' presupposed in this noncalculative form of practical thought is very general (p. 186).

Let me make this more specific, although in the space available I will have to be quite schematic. (For more detail on what distinguishes Aristotelian approaches, see Crisp, 1996; Hursthouse, 1999, and for a useful discussion of how Aristotelian approaches apply to the parallel case of medical ethics, see Oakley and Cocking, 2001.)

4. The Questions of Virtue Ethics

An important advantage of the Aristotelian ethical tradition (whether in its original 4th century BC or recent, neo-Aristotelian form) lies in the simplicity of the questions it asks. Two questions are fundamental:

1. How should I live?
2. Following on from (1), how should each of us conduct our life so that it is a life any of us should live?

    Question (1) is the question reputedly posed by Socrates in ancient Athens, and its usefulness derives from its openness.

    From questions (1) and (2) follow automatically a further question:

3. How we should live *together*? (Since if we live, we have no choice but to attempt to live together drawing on shared resources.)

    Note that in this further question no assumption is made about the 'community' (if any) to which questioner and respondent belong: they could be any two individuals anywhere. This is important, if we apply the Aristotelian questions to a contemporary world where people interact on a far larger scale, and, as a result, experience far more complex value disagreements, than could be imagined in ancient Greece (Williams, 1985, pp. 48, 53).

    Media ethics, I suggest, can develop questions (2) and (3) into a specific media-related question:

4. How should any of us (whether media professionals or not) act ethically in relation to media?

    Or, a little more precisely:

    4 a. How should we act in relation to media and available media resources, so that media processes contribute to lives that, both individually and together, we should live?

But this is just the most basic skeleton of the neo-Aristotelian virtue ethics approach. What differentiates it from other normative frameworks and what differentiates the various types of virtue ethics from each other is how they conceive of 'the good' by reference to which such questions are answered.

In Aristotle's original virtue ethics, the reference point was a view of 'human nature' that very few if anyone would now accept because of its offensive features (women as 'naturally' inferior to men, 'barbarian' others as naturally inferior, slaves as 'naturally' second-class humans); clearly, such features must be discarded from any workable neo-Aristotelianism today. But, unless we *deny* that there is such a thing as human nature, Aristotle's questions remain a useful starting-point (Foot, 2000) even if they may not yield all we need to know about how to act in particular media-related situations.

Important here is recent work by neo-Aristotelian philosophers who insist on a *flexible* naturalism in ethics. Such an approach can allow for a continuous rediscovery of what constitutes human 'nature': after all, why assume human 'nature' is fixed for all time? Indeed we can argue that human nature encompasses precisely the ability to live not only by certain fixed principles distinctive of the species (what we might call our 'first nature') but also "within a reflexively *and historically adjustable* set of principles"; "it is natural to us to participate in a history that is *more than merely* natural" (Lovibond, 2002, pp. 25, 63, adjusted emphasis). This "second nature" (MacDowell, 1994, p. 84) involves reflection on our history and also on our first ("fixed") nature.

This move is crucial because *media* ethics automatically confronts a global space, not a neat world segment (such as the nation- or city-state): our world involves conditions of human interaction radically different from those Aristotle knew. There is an analogy here with an important argument two decades ago by Hans Jonas. Jonas pointed out that modern ethics faced a new type of problem from classical ethics, namely the long-term effects of human technology on the environment; as a result, he argued, human "nature" itself must be rethought, since the scale of human action is not only local or national, but increasingly global (Jonas, 1984, p. 1).

It is similarly implausible now to exclude from virtue ethics *media's* consequences for a world audience who, we must remember, may share very few moral principles with the producers of those messages. The "imperative of responsibility" (in Jonas' (1984) phrase) for media ethics must address the need to live in a mediated world and in spite of what may be fundamental value *dis*agreements with those others who similarly must live in that mediated world. Even more obvious, contemporary ethics must adjust to the fact of media itself; it must adjust to the way, as Roger Silverstone so eloquently argued, media bring a 'world' of experience and potential interaction into being. The very idea of *media* ethics already entails a major adjustment to the starting conditions of traditional ethical thought, yet we have no choice but to make it. Virtue ethics is, after all, pragmatic and factually focused: it asks "how shall we live together?" – so there is nothing strange about taking into account the (factual) conditions for living that obtain between us in mediated societies and a mediated world.

There is another basic step in virtue ethics which must be emphasised. It routes all normative questions through models of what type of person each of us should be. Virtue ethics asks what stable dispositions (or 'virtues') each of us need to have in order to live well together. Admittedly, there is a dispute in interpreting Aristotle about whether he specifies 'virtues' in terms of what will help us live well together, or whether he draws his list of virtues from another source, from conventional thought about how people should act (Swanton, 2003, pp. 9, 87). But since Aristotle is quite explicit that his ethics is not grounded in isolation from everyday thought, but rather seeks to clarify everyday thought's foundations, this point may be of secondary importance. Neo-Aristotelian virtue ethics (by contrast with other types of virtue ethics) takes as its reference point the degree to which virtuous dispositions will contribute to 'human flourishing', that is, a good life individually and together. 'Virtues' are the means by which stable dispositions to act well are specified, but the reference points by which virtues are specified are not particular 'values', but precisely those facts about shared human life on which potentially we can come to agree.

5. Communicative Virtues

But how can we convert the intuitive advantages of virtue ethics into something more specific for the media case? A crucial if simple starting point is that at every stage of their history humans have had an interest in "gathering correct information about their environment" (Lovibond, 2002, p. 77), which requires them to be able to rely on what others tell them about that environment. From here Sabina Lovibond develops a useful notion of communicative virtue:

> If information about deliberatively relevant circumstances is (so far as it goes) a natural good, the lack of such information is equally a natural evil and the benefit or harm we can incur from these sources brings communicative behaviour within the scope of ethics (p. 78).

Can we make the notion of 'communicative virtue' more specific? By far the most detailed treatment is provided by Bernard Williams in his book *Truth and Truthfulness* (2002). In a complex argument, Williams suggests two basic "virtues of truth" or truthfulness (Williams, 2002, p. 44): *accuracy* and *sincerity*. The subtlety of Williams' argument lies in insisting on the non-negotiable importance of these virtues for all human social life, while rejecting any assumption that particular embodiments and articulations of those virtues have an absolute and obligatory status for all historical periods. It has never, Williams argues, been enough for people to *pretend* to care about telling the truth, since if that was all they did, we would never have a stable basis for trusting them to tell the truth. It is only therefore if truth-telling is stabilised as a virtue – a disposition that humans can rely upon, because it is regarded as a characteristic of virtuous people – that truth-telling contributes to the good collective life.

The *second* way of making more specific the notion of communicative virtue for media is to consider the specific features of media as a type of human practice. Alisdair MacIntyre's proposal to tie virtue ethics closely to the evaluation of particular practices is useful here. Media constitute a "practice" in MacIntyre's sense (1981, p. 175), that is, a coherent and complex form of cooperative human activity whose internal goods involve distinctive standards of excellence, which, if achieved, extend our notion of human excellence. Media is a practice with very general implications; media practice *matters* for how humans flourish overall in an era where we are dependent on the exchange of vast amounts of socially relevant information, very often through media. Not only does media practice matter to all of us, the media production process potentially involves all of us. As Susan Sontag (Sontag, 2004) was one of the first to point out, the digital media environment is one in which all of us have ethical responsibilities: with our computers, mobile phones, and digital cameras, we are all in principle now able to 'input' the media process. Equally, how can we say that our comments on a YouTube discussion thread about an unknown person's mash-up of recent television clips are *not* part of media culture? Yet discussion as to the appropriate ethical framework for thinking about what non-media professionals do, outside of institutional pressures and supports, when they blog, send in celebrity spottings to a magazine, post photos and videos onto YouTube, rework clips, comment on other peoples' clips and mash-ups, and so on, has barely started. Such a debate can only develop if we recognise the preliminary point that none of us should be exempt from the media-related virtues that we regard as relevant to media professionals.

6. The Ends of Media Practice

This requires us to be more specific about the aims (or 'ends') of media practice. Lovibond's notion of communicative virtue is, admittedly, rather generalised, while Williams' account of the virtues of truthfulness did little to make our sense of journalistic virtue more specific. There are, however, two "regulative ideals" (Oakley and Cocking, 2001), which can plausibly be seen as internal to the practice of journalism on a global scale. They need to be separated, even if I realise I ran them together in an earlier discussion (Couldry, 2006, p. 130 ff.).

The first aim which orients media values is *to circulate information that contributes to the successful individual and collective life of the territory to which they transmit.* Everywhere there will be differing views about whether media institutions currently fulfil this standard. That this is an *aim* of the media process, however, is 'non-negotiable' since information on all scales up to the global is necessary for the successful conduct of collective human life.

The second aim is: *through not just the circulation of fact but by providing opportunities for the expression of opinion and voice, to help us sustain a peaceable life together in spite of our conflicting values, interests and understandings.* This second aim is not to be understood as based on some supposedly consensual value of global 'community' and dialogue – we don't need to make that implausible assumption. It is based, more plausibly, on the *necessity*, if we are to live peaceably together for people, individually or through groups with which they identify, to believe that they are visible, not invisible, to each other. This applies particularly when it comes to discussing how common resources are shared; and the necessity for some degree of mutual understanding to be achieved across major differences of value, tradition and belief.

Let me say a little more about how we should understand these aims in detail. The point of media – its intrinsic aims as a practice – is the sustainability of a successful individual and collective life. This necessarily involves both the circulation of important facts, but also the sustaining of a space where, through media, we can recognise each other as valid agents, notwithstanding our differences. Insofar as our media cultures *undermine* either mutual recognition or shared recognition of the facts our collective life must address, then media ethics would encourage us to put those media cultures into question. If, as I have argued, today's media cultures inevitably involve much more than the hermetically sealed practices of media professionals – then all of us, whether we have the official status of media producers or are 'mere' consumers who contribute to the media process more occasionally and less directly, need to reflect on the aims of media as a human practice. Such reflections can contribute to our wider reflections on what is a good life for us and for those with whom we have no choice but to interact, including through media. It follows that to hive off media 'consumption' from the domain of media ethics – as do the old textbook approaches to journalistic codes – ignores the ethical challenges which an age of media saturation poses. This in turn will contribute to the broadening of our framework of global media ethics in a way that better recognises the challenges of a digital media world without borders.

It is open to journalists – indeed any citizens – to say they don't care about such necessities, but if so they must produce plausible reasons. These two aims of media practice interact at all scales from the local to the global in helping to define what living by the communicative virtues might mean for all those involved in, or around, the practice of media.

Conclusion

You might by now have two objections: first, that the aims just specified of media practice are far removed from media consumption as traditionally conceived; and, second, that, even if we link the above discussion to the contemporary media consumer, we remain a long way from resolving what choices a news editor, for example, should make when faced with the decision of publishing an image or opinion from a war zone. By way of conclusion, let me deal with each of those objections in turn.

The everyday circumstances of media consumption are shaped by a long history of separating media producers from media consumers. While this separation feels different depending on whether we are talking about a small neighbourhood newspaper or website – where, in principle, we might feel we could influence the editor or reporter – or a global media organisation where we have no chance of that, the basic fact of "social separation" between media producers and media consumers has been fundamental to modern media since the start (Baudrillard, 1981). And yet that separation is being destabilised by the diffusion online of certain possibilities for producing and circulating images, information and opinion. Ethically, what matters most is the shift from a situation where media production and circulation was generally something done by 'others' – 'the media' – to a situation where making or circulating an image, opinion or testimony enters the repertoire of imaginable actions for the average media *consumer*. It is not that media consumption (watching the news or a film at home, picking up a free newspaper on the way to work, glancing at the headlines on a web portal during your lunch break) carries exactly the same ethical responsibilities as professional media production – that ignores the very different possibilities for *acting on* information that still separate those inside and outside large media organisations (cf. Couldry, Livingstone and Markham, 2007, chapter 9). My underlying premise is that, because in limited ways production and consumption are becoming part of the same continuum of *experiencing* media, media ethics can no longer operate purely as an internal debate for the media industry closed to the people we will still for a long time no doubt call 'media consumers'. As a result, both the scope and the fundamental principles of media ethics need recasting for an age when all of us have a stake in, at times a direct responsibility for, the way our world (and that of others) is represented through media.

But we cannot expect this transformation of media ethics to take place quickly. At issue, after all, is the broadening of media ethics into a conversation that involves all citizens and is reflexively connected by citizens to their diverse experience of media, whether production, circulation or consumption. Specialist media professionals will of course not disappear: so this expanded media ethics must involve both more reflection by media consumers on the very particular conditions under which media professionals now have to work, and at the same time more reflection by media professionals on the legitimate stake that media consumers as citizens have in media professionals' productions. Clearly, this will require a long period of debate and mutual listening, quite apart from the philosophical questions that have to be resolved if a coherent and clear framework of media ethics is to be established.

That is why I have aimed in this chapter only to set out some modest signposts at the start of the long path ahead. We are obviously some way off formulating satisfactorily the detailed questions – to be posed to media producers and consumers alike – that must follow from the first principles of media ethics set out here. Claiming otherwise – claiming that we should already be able to specify in detail the consequences of media ethics for the future practice of, say tabloid journalism or the reporting of distant disasters – is misleading because premature. What matters now – yet this is already a major shift in the orientation of public debates about media – is to be headed in the direction of a broader media ethics and with the right equipment for the journey.

"Without news", as Jean Seaton beautifully puts it, "that is *careful of us*, how can we judge our situation, and know where we are?" (Seaton, 2005, p. xxiii, added emphasis). Media ethics is about developing our shared understanding of what that care might involve, since each of us are involved, regularly or occasionally, in the media process; enacting that care is a necessary part of responsible, reflexive consumption in worlds that are unavoidably mediated, and mediated in ways that crucially affect our possibilities of living sustainably together. As Roger Silverstone argued, media, if not our total environment, are an essential contrapuntal element in the world we now inhabit (Silverstone, 2006, p. 54). So too Tocqueville noted of early 19th century America that "if there were no newspapers, there would be no common activity" (Tocqueville, 1864, p. 135). But if so, why should those involved in media – which, in various ways, means all of us – be accountable by any *lesser* standards than the virtues that we agree are inherent to the practice of media? How can any of us claim that the ethical issues and debates that arise from this realisation can be resolved on any scale smaller than the global? How can we contribute to such resolution without taking seriously the conditions – of normative uncertainty – within which any such dialogue must start?

Notes

As to whether Latour's questions are adequate for a global politics, I cannot comment here. I understand global media ethics as operating on a broader scale than politics, in the sense, that an ethical global media would act to sustain the stage for a better global politics. It may be that Latour's questions are more useful pointed in relation to ethics than to politics, and that the separation between the two remains important.

Acknowledgement

For an earlier version of these ideas, and for more background on these debates, see Couldry (2006, chapter 7). [Thanks to Paradigm Press for permission to reproduce some material from that chapter.]

References

Aristotle. (1976). *Nicomachean ethics*. (J. Thomson, Trans.). Harmondsworth, U.K.: Penguin.

Baudrillard, J. (1981). *For a critique of the political economy of the sign*. St. Louis: Telos Press.

Bohman, J. (2000). The division of labour in democratic discourse. In S. Chambers and A. Costain (eds.) *Deliberation, democracy and the media* (pp. 47–64), Lanham, Md.: Rowman and Littlefield.

Braidotti, R. (2006). *Transpositions*. Cambridge: Polity Press.

Christians, C., Ferré, J. and Fackler, M. (1993). *Good news: Social ethics and the press*. New York: Longman.

Couldry, N. (2006). *Listening beyond the echoes: Media, ethics and agency in an uncertain World*. Boulder, Col.: Paradigm Books.

Couldry, N., Livingstone, S. and Markham, T. (2007). *Media consumption and public engagement: Beyond the presumption of attention*. Basingstoke: Palgrave Macmillan.

Crisp, R. (1996). Modern moral philosophy and the virtues. In R. Crisp (ed.) *How should one live?* (pp. 1–18) Oxford: Oxford University Press.

Foot, P. (2001). *Natural goodness*. Oxford: Oxford University Press.

Geertz, C. (1971). *The interpretation of cultures*. Chicago, Ill.: Chicago University Press.

Hegel, F. von (1991). *Elements of the philosophy of right*. (H. Nisbet, Trans.). Cambridge: Cambridge University Press. Original work published 1821.

Hursthouse, R. (1999). *Virtue ethics*. Oxford: Oxford University Press.

Jonas, H. (1984). *The imperative of responsibility*. Chicago, Ill.: Chicago University Press.

Kant, I. (1997). *Groundwork of the metaphysic of morals*. (M. Gregor, Trans.). Cambridge: Cambridge University Press. Original work published 1785.

Latour, B. (2004). From realpolitik to dingpolitik, or how to make things public. In B. Latour and P. Weibul (eds.) *Making things public: Atmospheres of democracy*, (pp. 14–43) Cambridge, Mass: MIT Press.

Lovibond, S. (2002). *Ethical formation*. Cambridge, Mass.: Harvard University Press.

MacIntyre, A. (1981). *After virtue*. London: Duckworth.

MacIntyre, A. (1988). *Whose justice? Which rationality?* Notre Dame: University of Notre Dame Press.

McDowell, J. (1994). *Mind and world*. Cambridge, Mass.: Harvard University Press.

Oakley, J. and Cocking, M. (2001). *Virtue ethics and professional roles*. Cambridge: Cambridge University Press.

O'Neill, O. (1996). *Towards justice and virtue*. Cambridge: Cambridge University Press.

O'Neill, O. (2000). Distant strangers, moral standing and porous boundaries. In *Bounds of justice*, (pp. 186–202). Cambridge: Cambridge University Press.

O'Neill, O. (2003). *A question of trust*. Cambridge: Cambridge University Press.

Pinchevski, A. (2005). *By way of interruption: Levinas and the ethics of communication*. Pittsburgh, Pa.: Duquesne University Press.

Quinn, W. (1995). Putting rationality in its place. In R. Hursthouse, G. Lawrence & W. Quinn (eds.) *Virtues and reasons: Philippa Foot and moral theory* (pp. 181–208). Oxford University Press.

Rawls, J. (1972). *A Theory of Justice*. Oxford: Oxford University Press.

Ricoeur, P. (1992). *Oneself as another*. Chicago, Ill.: Chicago University Press.

Seaton, J. (2005). *Carnage and the Media*. Harmondsworth, U.K.: Penguin.

Silverstone, R. (2006). *Media and morality: On the rise of the mediapolis*. Cambridge: Polity Press.

Sontag, S. (2004, May 24). What have we done? *Guardian*.

Swanton, C. (2003). *Virtue ethics*. Oxford: Oxford University Press.

Taylor, C. (1985). *Philosophy and the human sciences, Philosophical Papers*, vol 2 . Cambridge: Cambridge University Press.

Tocqueville, A. (1864). *Democracy in America*. (H. Reeve, Trans.). vol 2. Cambridge: Sever and Francis.

Williams, B. (1985). *Ethics and the limits of philosophy*. London: Fontana/Collins.

Williams, B. (2002). *Truth and truthfulness: An essay in genealogy*. Princeton: Princeton University Press.

SECTION 2

Global, Local, and Critical Theory

ie invasion of Iraq, the pri
iantanamo bay, and the w
est Bank, make it seem ab
e can talk about the empi
atiotemporal way as 'po
iving moved beyond. In th
e continuing effects of imp
e project of postcolonia
hich makes visible the lon
colonialism, empire, those w
posed it, and contempor
resistance seem more urg
ir. In the past decade pos
eory has generated e
is generated extensive disc
scussions in varied di
varied disciplines rangli
nging from anthropology
hropology, history, ge
ography, political science
iical science, and art, to i
literary, film, gender,
n, gender, cultural, psychoana
ychoanalytical, and queer

5 Media Ethics and Human Dignity in the Postcolony

Herman Wasserman

1. Introduction

The global and the local, the stubborn reminders of South Africa's apartheid past and the seductive promise of a postmodern future meet each other at Cape Town International Airport. Since South Africa emerged from apartheid, the city has become a popular tourist destination for travellers forming part of what Appadurai (1996) has called the "ethnoscape" of globalisation. But not all mobility is voluntary or leisurely – South Africa also receives thousands of refugee applications per year as a result of forced migration (South Africa Yearbook, 2006, p. 345). This city has always been a place where histories meet, and often clash violently. The legacy of colonialism and apartheid in South Africa can still be seen in the city's urban geography. Tourists making their way past the glitzy, modernised airport to the lush vineyards of the grand wine farms, originally planted there by Dutch settlers and French Huguenots and from where wine is now exported to the corners of the globe, are confronted with a sea of corrugated iron shacks crouching close to the road. In parts of this sprawling township, there is no electricity, not a single tree in sight, people use communal taps and live an hour's walk from the nearest toilet (Joubert, 2007). This is the South African landscape that John Pilger (1998, p. 597) has referred to as "beauty out of one eye, a slum out of the other". In this landscape, people's basic struggle for food, shelter, health and safety is a struggle to be counted as humans. It is a struggle for human dignity.

South Africa, as one of the most unequal countries of the world, is a microcosm of the ongoing struggle on the continent and the globe, where billions suffer from lack of nutrition, education, shelter and health care that others take for granted as part of the global logic of capitalism (Pilger, 1998, p. 608). World poverty puts us before an ethical choice. Our common humanity demands that as global citizens we see the lot of the world's poor as an urgent collective task (Sparks, 2007, p.1). We are faced with an ethical imperative in this regard also in our roles as consumers and producers of global media. Increasingly these roles are merging to that of mutually involved 'participants'. The media is "deeply implicated" (McQuail cited in Ang, 1998, p. 87) in global social conditions because of its "enhanced role in the organisation of national and global society". The problem of world poverty is therefore also a problem for global media – especially if we take the ethical implications of our actions in this realm seriously.

How then should we think about global media ethics from the perspective of the lived realities in localities? The example of South Africa reminds us that the global cannot be thought without the local, nor the present without the past, especially in countries in transition. The disastrous effect that colonialism and apartheid had on human dignity in South Africa extends further than the material dimension. The history of racial segregation and discrimination still reverberates through a society where the psychological scars of institutionalised racism lie very close to the surface and manifest itself in continued violence, racism and suspicion. These historical contestations also impact on the role and ethical imperatives of the media. Conceiving of the media's moral duties as somehow having global relevance cannot therefore gloss over the particularities of the local context. A global media ethics would have to be located in relation to local histories of cultural, political and social struggle, as well as the power relations underlying contemporary global-local exchanges.

It has been suggested (Christians & Nordenstreng, 2004, p. 21) that the concept of human dignity has universal validity and as such can form the cornerstone of a global media ethic. In this paper I would like to explore this concept in more detail from the perspective of the media in the postcolony. A question to be addressed is how a concept such as human dignity translates from its supposedly global validity to local contexts. In this regard I will take the South African example as a point of departure, not only because of the country's contemporary condition as alluded to above, but also because historically the concept of human dignity has been a central concept in the struggle against apartheid, as Koopman (2007) reminds us with reference to the work of Archbishop Denis Hurley (e.g. Hurley, 1966). The concept of human dignity continues to resonate in post-apartheid South Africa, for instance in a proposed pledge for school children based on "universal values that you would want any human being to attach themselves to", according to the Education Minister Naledi Pandor (*Sunday Times*, 2008). Yet in the pledge this supposedly universal concept of dignity is explicitly linked to a recognition of the specific "injustices of our past" (*Sunday Times*, 2008), reminding us that concepts are given content within specific histories and relationships. Although my discussion of human dignity takes its point of departure from the South African situation, the implications of my argument should have broader relevance for the relationship between the global and the local in media ethics. I will draw on postcolonial criticism as a potential theoretical framework that could enrich our understanding of how the ethical value of human dignity might be interpreted within local contexts. The aim is to contribute to a theoretical framework that could situate the norm of human dignity within historical and contemporary geopolitical formations.

2. Human Dignity and the Search for Global Media Ethics

The search for global media ethics forms part of an ongoing project to develop a framework that would be "explicitly cross-cultural" and "universal within the splendid variety of human life" (Christians & Traber, 1997, p. viii). It has been argued (Christians & Nordenstreng, 2004, p. 21) that the concepts of human dignity, truth and non-violence could serve as universal ethical concepts within a social responsibility framework. According to these authors, "respect for another person's dignity is one ethical principle on which various cultures rest" (2004, p. 21). They explain the concept as respect for the "sacred status" of human beings, and an acknowledgement of the "interconnectedness among all living forms so that we live in solidarity with others as equal constituents in the web of life" (2004, p. 21).

The concept of human dignity does indeed feature in various intellectual traditions, but is "very differently constructed" in them (May, 2006, p. 52). The imperative to treat humans as having intrinsic, equal and unqualified value in themselves underlies the Kantian tradition (Dean, 2006, p. 3; Donaldson, 1992, pp. 137–138), although Kant's use of the term "is deceptively obscure" (Dean, 2006, p. 4). Elements of Kant's ethical philosophy have been combined with elements of the social contract tradition in John Rawls' theory of justice. The emphasis on human dignity and development has been used as a basis for the capability approach of Martha Nussbaum and Amartya Sen (Nussbaum, 2000; 2006; Nussbaum & Faralli, 2007; Sen, 1999). This approach defines human dignity as the fulfillment of a set of key criteria for a decent human life and human flourishing. Applied ethics in areas such as bio-ethics, global public health, and contemporary global human rights theories have drawn on the Kantian doctrine that all rational humans are members of a single moral order (Dean, 2006, p. 3; Donaldson, 1992, pp. 144, 150; Horton, 2004). Consequently, the enhancement of human dignity is a cornerstone of international humanitarian law (Veuthey, 2005) and of liberal democratic theory. It is as such that human dignity is listed as a democratic value next to equality and freedom in the South African Constitution (South African Government, 1996). The Kantian principle of treating others as ends in themselves rather than as means is seen by Donagan (1977; see Donaldson, 1992, p. 151) as fundamental to the Hebrew-Christian tradition. Yet some Reformed-Christian (Vorster, 2007) and Jewish (Shultziner, 2006) scholars have pointed to tensions between the secular-liberal and theological uses of the term. In contemporary Christian theological anthropology the dignity of the most vulnerable is especially acknowledged (Koopman, 2007). Within such an approach human dignity is seen as that which is "violated where the basic needs of humans are not met", and its restoration seems to occur in terms of interdependence and care (Koopman, 2007). Human dignity is a concept also found in non-Western contexts like Buddhism (May, 2006, p. 51) and Chinese philosophy (Zhang, 2007). Where African traditions are invoked, human dignity has taken on a communitarian aspect, bringing it in confrontation with what is seen as Western individualism (Rao & Wasserman, 2007). This has been the case in South Africa, where normative media frameworks based on individual freedom and media independence have been challenged by Africanist demands for the incorporation of indigenous cultural values and recognition of past injustices and racial discrimination. (See Fourie in this volume for a critique of this discourse.) From the above examples it seems that while human dignity apparently has broad resonance across various ethical traditions, this broad theoretical spectrum also results in considerable differences in interpretation of the concept.

I want to argue for a critical approach to the concept of human dignity, one that situates the term within a historical and political context, and across both a material and a symbolic axis. My argument is based on the assumption that for millions of people around the globe, human dignity might be an inalienable moral right that they theoretically can lay claim to, but that this right can only be realised – can only come to *mean* something in their lives – if radical social change is brought about. Harvey (2005, pp. 35, 37) convincingly argues that media have been part and parcel of the globalisation of neo-liberalism. Big media conglomerates have wielded such hegemonic influence over media discourses that the idea of freedom has come to be understood narrowly as inextricably linked to free enterprise and the search for new markets (in which these media giants themselves are leading participants). This process has led to the deepening of the ideals of freedom and human dignity only for an elite, while increasing the misery of the rest (Harvey, 2005, pp. 37–38).

If the media professes to be guided by the principles of freedom and human dignity, it should be held accountable to those principles. A normative counter-perspective is needed that would foreground the failure of global modernity to bring about freedom and human dignity on an equal basis, and appeal to the media's moral responsibility to contribute to a process where these values could be realised. This critical perspective would resonate with the work of Nussbaum and Sen to the extent that it also sees human dignity as the outcome of a contestation within "large asymmetries of power" (Nussbaum & Faralli, 2007, p. 147), and the realisation of certain entitlements and capabilities (Nussbaum 2006, pp. 76–77). However, I want to draw on postcolonial theory in an attempt to situate this demand for a critical perspective on human dignity within the historical framework of colonialism and its continued global effects. In doing so, I hope to highlight the need for a global media ethics that recognises contextual specificity at the same time as it takes account of the power relations underlying media globalisation.

Postulating human dignity as a potential universal concept for communication ethics as Christians and Nordenstreng (2004, p. 21) have done, is ostensibly supported by the use of the term in various religious, cultural and scholarly traditions. Its interpretation in the field of global media ethics is unlikely to be any less contested than in other fields of applied ethics. It can be argued that since global media are implicated in global power relations on a social, political and economic level, a theory of human dignity would have to situate this value concept accordingly. Human dignity as an ethical concept for global media would therefore have to be defined in terms of geopolitical formations, both historical and contemporary. In the subsequent discussion I would like to explore whether postcolonial criticism can make a contribution to such a definition.

The notion of human dignity is implicit in postcolonial criticism, as this field of inquiry is directed critically against the long history of colonialism and its contemporary articulations, in which significant sections of the global human population were systematically denied rights and freedom. Postcolonial theory has been criticised for homogenising these diverse local colonial experiences around the single global temporality of European history. It has also been seen as an overly culturalist approach, to the expense of a critique of material relationships and political power (Dirlik, 2005, p. 576). To avoid these pitfalls, it needs to be noted from the outset that the notion of human dignity needs to be viewed not only in its symbolic and cultural dimensions, but also as integrally linked to persisting global material inequalities. Postcolonial theory is useful in understanding not only geopolitical relationships in the era of global capitalism, but also the "replications in societies internally of inequalities and discrepancies once associated with colonial differences" (Dirlik, 2005, p. 579). The relationship between global modernity and postcolonialism pertains both to cultural and epistemological issues, but also to social and political formations (Dirlik, 2005, p. 580):

> Postcoloniality represents a response to a genuine need, the need to overcome a crisis of understanding produced by the inability of old categories to account for the world. The metanarrative of progress that underlies two centuries of thinking is in deep crisis. Not only have we lost faith in progress but also progress has had actual disintegrative effects.

Postcoloniality addresses issues that have far-reaching effects for human dignity in global society, issues in which the media have a role to play. These issues include (Dirlik, 2005, p. 583): the relationship between eurocentrism and capitalism; the relevance of modernity to a "postmodern, postsocialist, post-Third World situation"; the place of the nation, the relationship between the local and the global; the transgression of borders and boundaries; and hybridity in subjectivities and epistemologies.

In our search for global media ethical values, we should not only be motivated by what Gikandi (2005, p. 609) refers to as the celebratory narrative of globalisation, but also by its counternarrative, namely that of crisis. Just as global media facilitates increased mobility across borders, the shrinking of the world and cultural hybridity, it also forms part of – and contributes to – a world that is starkly divided between those that benefit from globalisation and those that remain on its margins. If human dignity is to serve as an ethical value for global media, its measure should be the extent to which dignity is afforded to the vulnerable in global society – those "hidden voices and faces" that John Pilger (1998, p. 3) refers to as "unpeople". It could be argued that the global poor are less concerned with cultural hybridisation brought about by globalisation, than with the "material experiences of everyday life and survival" (Gikandi, 2005, p. 612). Postcolonial theory has contemporary relevance for these global subjects, because "like the legendary subalterns of colonial culture, the majority of the postcolonial subjects who live through the experience of globalisation cannot speak" (Gikandi, 2005, p. 622).

A global ethic founded upon a historical and political understanding of the factors that have obscured these "unpeople" from the attention and compassion of the media, can bring hope to those on the margins. To return to a South African example: Alistair Sparks (1990, p. 341; also quoted in Pilger, 1998, p. 13), recalls how the presence of foreign media at funeral rallies during the liberation struggle in South Africa turned individuals into a community and reaffirmed their human dignity in the face of brutal oppression:

> Here the anonymous individuals of a humiliated community seemed to draw strength from the crowd, gaining from it the larger identity of the occasion and an affirmation of their human worth. Their daily lives might seem meaningless, but here on these occasions the world turned out, with its reporters and its television cameras, to tell them it was not so, that their lives mattered, that humanity cared, that their cause was just; and when they clenched their fists and chanted their defiant slogans, they could feel that they were proclaiming their equality and that their strength of spirit could overwhelm the guns and armoured vehicles waiting outside.

3. Human Dignity between the Global and the Local

While the ethical norm of human dignity can be identified in several religious, cultural and philosophical frameworks around the world, it has to be interpreted within local contexts in order to provide a norm for media to guide their actions. This question of how the global relates to the local is the central problematic of the search for global media ethics.

The notion of universal values in itself is problematic. Intercontextual normative concepts such as truth, arrived at through a rational knowledge of reality, have become suspect in a complex, diverse postmodern age wherein Western culture and epistemology have been experiencing a crisis (Ang, 1998, p. 81). As Christians (1997, p. 4) has shown, the "paradigm of immutable and universal morality" has become generally discredited as belonging to the dominant gender and class (Christians, 1997, p. 4; cf. Assiter, 2003, p. 7). Especially pertinent is the realisation that notions of universality can mask power relations. It could be argued that the use of the media for "development" in Africa within the modernisation paradigm, devised as a "mechanical series of steps Africa could take in order to resemble the West in its political and economic behaviour (Bourgault, 1995, p. 228), was underpinned by such a notion of universality. This mimicking of Western economic and social organisation benefited the elite class of citizens, who were "content to share the spoils of the patronage (colonial) system and to parrot the value of the modernity model for their countries". In the process, the rural masses and the urban proletariat have been economically largely disenfranchised (Bourgault, 1995, p. 227). Even as the emphasis has subsequently shifted to a communitarian theory of interdependence and participatory development (Bourgault, 1995, p. 238), some critics (e.g. Nyamnjoh, 2005; Ebo, 1994) have illustrated how media theory inherited from discourses of modernisation and liberal democracy remain dominant even if they are unsuitable for the lived reality of journalists and media workers in African contexts. It would therefore be important that a concept like human dignity should be explored in a participatory manner if it were to have relevance for global media ethics. The danger that Clifford (1988, pp. 200–211) points out regarding the incorporation of ideas and concepts from localities into an overarching narrative claiming to be universal, is that these concepts and values become divorced from the dynamic processes in which they obtain their meaning. If a value such as human dignity is to become a dynamic rather than static concept for media in local contexts, the concept should be interpreted critically within the power relations and material conditions within which media operate in such contexts. A theoretical approach that would make such an interpretation possible has to be found.

4. Human Dignity and Postcolonialism: The Potential

The interpretation of a supposedly universal concept like human dignity within local contexts would need to take account of its meaning within specific histories, cultural dynamics and social struggles. Postcolonial criticism can provide the critical vocabulary needed to situate a normative value like human dignity in terms of history and power relations (May, 2006, p. 56).

To approach the search for universal ethical values from the point of view of postcolonial theory might seem strange at first glance, since "postcolonial criticism repudiates all master narratives" (Dirlik, 2005, p. 565). Postcolonial criticism is marked by a "politics of location" rather than one informed by fixed categories, and "local interactions take priority over global structures" in the formulation of the relationship between "First" and "Third" World (Dirlik, 2005, p. 567). However, postcolonial criticism does have an ethical dimension, one that is concerned with global conditions and relations. McMillin (2007, p. 57) points to the "activist and ethical component" of postcolonial studies that "questions the violence that occurs in imperial domination", and contains a "rethinking of peoples and cultures by the experiences that bind them, not just by ethnicity or nationality". One such shared experience among large sections of the world is the aftermath of colonialism and its lingering effects. The role of media in the reproduction of imperial power structures is not a recent phenomenon (McMillin, 2007, p. 66) but the renewed focus on media's role in processes of globalisation has brought increased attention to the way in which contemporary global power relations show similarities to those of colonialism (McMillin, 2007, p. 55).

Although it could be argued that all normative theories of media have political implications, in the case of postcolonial theory these implications are overt rather than implied or obscured. Postcolonial theory is an approach explicitly committed to intervention and therefore is "highly political" (Shome & Hegde, 2002, p. 250). Postcolonial studies seek to address issues emerging from past and contemporary contexts of modernity, making visible how present global processes of domination and resistance are related to colonial power relations; the nature of knowledge and the links between power and knowledge; the mutual implication of history, geography, geopolitics and the international division of labour; and providing historical and international depth to the understanding of cultural power (Shome & Hegde, 2002). Since postcolonial criticism is also concerned with the revision of existing frameworks of knowledge, it could provide a critique of prevailing normative media frameworks and the traditions from which they derive. If postcolonial criticism is brought to bear on normative media theory as a system of knowledge, it would see normative theory transformed "from static disciplinary competence to activist intervention" (Shome & Hegde, 2002, pp. 250–251).

A postcolonial approach to global media ethics would therefore be concerned with the origins of current media ethical thought, but would also have as its aim the search for hidden knowledge, that which is left out (see Venn, 2006, pp. 12, 13). As far as the interpretation of a concept like human dignity is concerned, this would mean seeking out alternative and perhaps competing interpretations of what such a normative concept might mean in different contexts.

Postcolonial criticism is an inherently ethical enterprise, since it seeks to "speak to western paradigms in the voice of otherness" (McEwan, 2003, p. 9). In other words, such criticism is inherently ethical because it seeks to bring to the fore those voices that have been marginalised, and opposes theoretical frameworks that contribute to such exclusion and inequality. As a "strategic response to contemporary globalisation" (Ahluwalia, 2001, pp. 5–6), postcolonial theory can contribute to a media ethics that will acknowledge interconnectedness between people worldwide but also interrogate the terms upon which these connections rest.

Postcolonial theory's concern with hybridity (e.g. Bhabha, 1994) could likewise provide a critical edge to the analysis of global media. The notion of hybridity in media has received renewed attention as global media formats are localised for domestic markets (McMillin, 2007, p. 112). Such analyses of media hybridity are, however, not always critical of the power imbalances attending upon exchanges between the local and the global. The process of "glocalisation" has also been noted in terms of media ethics (Wasserman & Rao, 2008). A postcolonial approach to glocalisation in media ethics will open the way for understanding ethical values as concepts that are always situated and negotiated contextually, between the local and the global.

Postcolonial theory could, in the light of the above, be useful as a critical perspective on global media ethics, as it brings into focus a range of questions and highlights hidden assumptions. As a critical approach, its use could primarily be to enhance global media ethics by posing critical questions and interrogating the basis upon which central concepts (like, in the context of this paper, human dignity) rest. This is not to say, however, that postcolonial theory is the only alternative way to approach global media ethics, or even that it could stand on its own as an ethical theory. The limits of this approach should also be acknowledged.

5. Human Dignity and Postcolonialism: The Pitfalls

There are, however, certain pitfalls of using postcolonial theory to develop a global media ethic. Firstly, care should be taken not to assume that postcoloniality refers only to a specific period in history. Clearly countries such as South Africa are in many ways not yet past the colonial moment in terms of its continued effects and legacies. Postcoloniality as a critical concept in media studies is therefore useful in the sense that it provides a critical perspective of the ongoing relations of domination and resistance in which global media are implicated.

A postcolonial approach to global media ethics will take local interpretations of values like human dignity seriously, and seek to understand how such concepts would be understood in indigenous knowledge systems. Yet such an exploration of local knowledge could lead to what one could call the pitfall of authenticity. This entails the romantic idealisation of a supposedly pristine postcolonial situation, where local values and epistemologies existed free of outside influence. It could be argued that such an isolated and pure state never existed. But even if it did, it would be naïve to assume that it could be excavated from the past and unproblematically reinstated in the present. Crude invocations of postcolonial values and attempts to impose 'indigenous values' on media can create new forms of exclusion. This might entail the view that only certain sections of the postcolonial society have the right to criticise the government, for example, or that certain subjects are considered taboo, that open and frank debate belongs to a foreign culture or that there is only one valid and essential postcolonial cultural identity (for critiques of these positions see Tomaselli, 2003; Fourie, 2007, and Fourie in this volume).

In the light of these criticisms, attempts to reposition media ethics scholarship within an African context (e.g. Rønning & Kasoma, 2002, see also Banda in this volume) or to find similarities between African ethical concepts such as *ubuntu* and the Western ethical tradition of communitarianism (Christians, 2004) would therefore have to be made circumspectly. The call for a validation of local knowledge and indigenous ethical theories is not the same as an appeal to some precolonial essence or the supposition that cultural traditions can emerge unscathed by history. The key difference between a postcolonial approach that dialectically positions local cultural knowledge in relation to inherited frameworks from elsewhere, and an essentialist return to nativism, would be that the former is rooted in the evolving and dynamic *lived experience* of colonised subjects, rather than the fixed and idealised notion of tradition or culture. Furthermore a postcolonial attention to hybridity would be interested in the overlaps, interstices and contestations between the local and the global instead of pitting them against each other in an idealised, simplistic fashion.

For instance: a key norm in liberal-democratic media ethical frameworks is editorial independence. In practical terms this can translate into a proscription against reporters taking bribes. In many African contexts, however, the low salaries and insecure conditions of employment of journalists have resulted in journalists accepting payment from news sources in return for coverage (Ndangam, 2006). Instead of labeling this practice as 'bribery' and simply condemning it (therefore applying the Western ethical framework uncritically to the African context), or doing the inverse by relativistically viewing this as a 'local' or 'cultural' practice Western ethical frameworks have nothing to say about, a judgement could be reached by applying a hybrid ethical framework. This could mean an acknowledgement of the ways in which African journalists have to negotiate their professional conduct and identities in such a way as to cope with the material conditions of their work while retaining the ethical imperative of providing credible and fair news reports. Such an approach would incorporate ('global') ethical notions of fairness, credibility and truth-telling into a framework that acknowledges the ('local') socio-economic conditions under which such notions are lived out. Such a hybrid, glocal media ethics would have been made possible by the overarching postcolonial perspective that the current socio-economic conditions under which African journalists operate are at least in part rooted in a history of exploitation and oppression and contemporary global imbalances in economic power. Ethical norms would therefore be constructed with due cognisance of the current conditions under which journalists in postcolonial contexts work. Ethical ideals would be based upon expectations of 'the good' within such contexts without assuming that the interpretations of ethical norms are the same across dissimilar settings. Ethical ideals themselves would be understood as situated within epistemological histories that cannot be divorced from power relations. The fact that certain ethical norms have become dominant globally would be viewed with skepticism based on a critical perspective of globalisation itself. This is because postcolonial criticism makes us aware of the "historicity of the present" (Venn, 2006, p. 12) and engages with globalisation in a more critical way than market-based theories that accept "the benign nature of capitalism" (Sparks, 2007, p. 14). As Grossberg (2002, p. 369) remarks: "It is sometimes said that the recent concern for globalisation has put postcoloniality on the agenda. I think it is perhaps more accurate to say that postcolonial studies helped to put globalisation on the agenda (although sometimes I fear that globalisation is conceptualised in ways that erase issues of colonialism and its continuing legacies and effects)."

6. Implications for Journalism and Media

A postcolonial understanding of the media ethical value of human dignity would situate the concept historically and within continued global asymmetries of power. This would entail a critical view of how ethical theories come to acquire dominance in global epistemologies, and an insistence on the specificity of local interpretations of ethical concepts. In a postcolonial context, this interpretation would be shaped by the systemic denial of human dignity during colonialism (and in the South African case, apartheid) as well as its enduring material and symbolic legacies. As an interventionist approach, a postcolonial media ethics would include the imperative for media to contribute to the redress of past injustices, with human dignity as a positive value towards which the media should actively strive. In other words, media would be given positive duties to help create the conditions under which people can regain and sustain their dignity.

Such a critical postcolonial approach should not be mistaken for a "developmental model" for the media (McQuail, 2005, p. 178), which entails the possibility of restrictions on press freedom by government in order for media to contribute to developmental goals. A postcolonial approach would in fact remain attentive to new forms of domination that may arise in the postcolony, and resist new imperialisms whether they be internal to a country or from the outside. This is not to say that the language of postcolonialism cannot be misappropriated by a ruling elite to serve politically expedient goals. Such has been the criticism leveled against the post-apartheid African National Congress (ANC) government's proposal to establish a Media Appeals Tribunal that would replace the current self-regulatory system in South Africa. The tribunal would "be accountable to Parliament and (...) would adjudicate the balance between media freedom and individual rights to privacy and dignity" (Boyle, 2007).

The current chapter does not allow for an evaluation of the success or otherwise of the South African self-regulatory system or the lack of self-criticism on the part of the media (see Wasserman, 2006a; 2006b for related discussions). It is worth noting however that dignity in this formulation is constructed in terms of individual rights rather than in terms of communities. The use of the term here therefore suggests a liberal definition similar to that of the Constitution noted above. As such it does not contribute to an understanding of dignity as a value that has to be restored to a group which has been discriminated against under colonialism and apartheid, but instead opens the way for individuals (like government ministers or public officials) who feel aggrieved by legitimate adversarial media coverage to initiate litigation. This could then pit the right to dignity against the right to free speech (Berger, 2007).

But viewing human dignity as a group rather than an individual right can also become extremely problematic, especially in a racially diverse postcolonial society such as South Africa. The South African public broadcaster, the South African Broadcasting Corporation (SABC), lists the *"Restoration of Human Dignity"* as one of its core editorial values (SABC). In his attack on the South African National Editors' Forum (Sanef) for tolerating the publication of the private health records of the country's Minister of Health by the *Sunday Times* newspaper, the SABC's group CEO and Editor-in-Chief Dali Mpofu interprets dignity in racial terms, pertaining to the majority of South Africans (i.e. blacks) whose dignity was stripped away under apartheid (Mpofu, 2007). There is an argument to be made in support of Mpofu's outrage at what was an ethically dubious instance of muckraking reporting. However, that this type of interpretation can become overtly exclusionary to the detriment of open debate in the country, is suggested by the fact that the SABC's political editor, Abbey Makoe, in his capacity as chair of the steering committee of a new Forum of Black Journalists (FBJ), secured an off-the-record address by the new ANC chairman, Jacob Zuma exclusively for black journalists (*The Times*, 2008).

Clearly crude appropriations of the postcolonial lexicon to justify new systems of exclusion or privilege for a postcolonial elite should be distinguished from attempts to create a new society where dignity is restored for the formerly oppressed in a broad-based way. The latter approach to human dignity would not be a façade behind which corrupt public officials can hide from the criticism of the public that elected them. Instead, human dignity as a norm would rather encourage the media to give more voice to exactly those sections of the public who are too often lost from the media's view – the poor and marginalised who still bear the brunt of the legacies of colonialism and apartheid. Setting human dignity as a normative ideal for media in a postcolonial context might extend to a questioning of news values and practices that privilege an elite perspective. In post-apartheid South Africa the prominent news discourse on crime provides an example of how conventional news values (such as reference to elite people, in Galtung and Ruge's famous taxonomy, critically revisited by Fowler, 1991) articulate with social hierarchies inherited from colonialism and apartheid. When a prominent white historian, David Rattray, was murdered in KwaZulu-Natal, his death led to a sustained media outrage[1] for weeks, culminating in an advertising campaign by a bank (later withdrawn, allegedly under pressure from government) that would have had newspaper readers mailing letters to President Thabo Mbeki, demanding tougher action against crime. Yet, as the editor of a Cape Town tabloid, the *Daily Voice* has remarked (Brophy, 2007), on the same day as Rattray was killed, eight murders took place on the Cape Flats (an area designated for 'coloureds' under apartheid, who were forcibly removed from areas reserved for whites). None of the mainstream commercial media, the tabloids excluded, were as interested in these eight people. Nor, of course, were big financial institutions interested. A postcolonial media ethic concerned with human dignity as a central value would be concerned about the news mechanisms, routines and norms that continue to exclude or obscure the fate of historically marginalised groups from the mediated public sphere.

The media can facilitate the restoration of dignity on a symbolic level by equitable representation of marginalised groups, but also by changing the perspective from which they choose to represent social reality. What would this mean for media? For journalists, who often display "a level of ethnocentrism long held unacceptable in other fields" (Alia, 2004, p. 22), it requires a commitment to social change, which in turn presupposes an understanding of other socio-political and cultural contexts. This might require a willingness to "abandon the rules of conventional training" to follow a more ethnographic approach. Crucially, such an ethnographic approach would not only study "other" cultures, but be used for a critical interrogation of one's own assumptions (Alia, 2004, pp. 23, 26). An ethnographic approach to journalism is one that "starts with an attitude of complete ignorance and is 'based on the principle of *learning from people,* rather than *studying people*'" (Alia, 2004, p. 26). Especially in a postcolonial context like South Africa, where racial and ethnic polarisation has caused widespread ignorance of the 'other', a journalism of dignity would have to entail such a learning attitude.

To treat people with dignity also means providing them with a space from where they could exercise agency in engaging with global forces that shape their lives. This would mean investigative work to uncover and clarify the connections between the local and the global that often go unseen, so that space is created for media audiences to engage with these forces. Alia (2004, p. 43) describes these connections as "from policy to practice, country to country, government to corporation, business to labour, profit to health and safety, and so on". It would call on journalists – to paraphrase John Pilger (1998, p. 4) – to question "political vocabularies" and the "prevailing politico-economic orthodoxy", to reveal the true nature of power, explore its contours and identify its goals and targets. A critical postcolonial perspective would mean shattering the myths of modernity and progress and pierce the "fog surrounding globalisation" (Parameswaran, 2002).

Affording human dignity to people in the first instance means paying attention to them. An ethic that would redirect its focus to those on the margins as people worthy of respect and dignity, would compel news media to question its orthodox news values, to focus media attention on peoples and issues that would otherwise (if the hidden interconnections between the local and the global remain obscured) seem remote. Such attention to 'other people' would show similarities to other ethical approaches such as communitarianism where a reciprocal relationship between members of the community is recognised. This would mean a significant departure from the status quo for the global media, where "other nations do not exist unless they are useful to 'us'" (Pilger, 1998, p. 2). Attention to others in this sense is completely different from the voyeuristic gaze bestowed on them in colonial discourse or in the conventional type of journalism where journalists are "professional, specialised tourists", spectators of "calamities taking place in another country" (Sontag, 2003, p. 16). The inverse relationship between dignity denied to objects of media attention and their proximity to the content producer and media audience is one that has often been noted in critical scholarship. As Sontag (2003, p. 65) observes on war photography:

> Generally, the grievously injured bodies shown in published photographs are from Asia or Africa. The journalistic custom inherits the centuries-old practice of exhibiting exotic – that is, colonised – human beings: Africans and denizens of remote Asian countries were displayed like zoo animals in ethnological exhibitions mounted in London, Paris and other European capitals from the sixteenth until the early twentieth century.

Conclusion

If human dignity is to serve as a universal value to be strived for by media globally, it would have to be interpreted and applied within local contexts, but in relation to a global set of power relations within which media producers, audiences and participants are mutually interdependent. Such a global picture would have to be enriched with a complex understanding of cultural, economic and social factors that have impacted on how human dignity is understood in various contexts. This demands an approach to global media ethics that is reciprocal, participatory and inclusive of various perspectives, yet retains a critical edge that allows for political intervention. This chapter has argued that postcolonial theory could contribute analytical tools for such a critical understanding. Postcolonial theory has limits and flaws, and should be seen as a critical mode of inquiry that could provide a new perspective on the search for global media ethics, rather than as an exhaustive and comprehensive ethical framework in itself. In this regard the chapter has sought to indicate how a postcolonial approach to media ethics could find links with other traditions like communitarian ethics or the capability approach to human dignity.

The shared experience of colonialism worldwide, its aftermath and its replication in new manifestations of global inequality, can produce a complex and textured understanding of the value of human dignity as it pertains to global media. The interpretation of this value will always be specific to the different contexts within which it is evoked, yet when approached through the shared history of global relations of dominance and resistance, can obtain global resonance. Appiah (who has also been critical of postcolonial theory), has intimated this when he described postcolonialism's resistance to power as "grounded in an appeal to an ethical universal" (1991, p. 348). Seen this way, postcolonial criticism becomes a rebellion against the negation of human dignity, "an appeal to a certain simple respect for human suffering, a fundamental revolt against (…) endless misery (…)" (Appiah, 1991, p. 353).

Notes

1   Coverage of the Rattray murder extended to overseas media. The UK newspaper, the *Daily Telegraph* launched an essay prize in memory of Rattray, who they describe as being murdered by "Zulus, the very people Rattray had for so long championed" (*Daily Telegraph*, 2008).

References

Ahluwalia, P. (2001). *Politics and post-colonial theory: African inflections*. London: Routledge.
Alia, V. (2004). *Media ethics and social change*. Edinburgh: Edinburgh University Press
Ang, I. (1998). The performance of the sponge: Mass communication theory enters the Postmodern World. In Brants, K.; J. Hermes; L. van Zoonen, (eds.), *The Media in Question: Popular Cultures and Public Interests* (pp. 77–88). London: Sage.
Appadurai, A. (1996). *Modernity at large: Cultural dimensions of globalization*. Minneapolis, Minn.: University of Minnesota Press.
Appiah, K.A. (1991). Is the Post- in Postmodernism the Post- in Postcolonial? *Critical Inquiry*, 17 (Winter), 336–357.
Appiah, K.A. (2005). *The ethics of identity*. Princeton, N.J.: Princeton University Press.
Assiter, A. (2003). *Revisiting Universalism*. Hampshire: Palgrave Macmillan.
Berger, G. (2007). Media dignitaries debating dignity. Retrieved 21 February, 2008, from http://www.thoughtleader. co.za/guyberger/2007/10/22/media-dignitaries-debating-dignity/.
Bhabha, H.K. (1994). *The location of culture*. London: Routledge.
Bourgault, L. (1995). *Mass media in Sub-Saharan Africa*. Bloomington, Ind.: Indiana University Press.
Boyle, B. (2007). Press freedom under threat. *Sunday Times*, 22 December. Retrieved 21 February 2008 from http://www.thetimes.co.za/PrintEdition/News/Article.aspx?id=667328.
Brophy, K. (2007). Remarks as part of panel on tabloids, "Are we true to the public trust?" South African National Editors' Forum Council Meeting, Cape Town, 9 February.
Christians, C. (1997). The Ethics of being in a communications Context. In Christians, C. & Traber, M., (eds.), *Communication ethics and universal ethics* (pp. 3–23). London: Sage.
Christians, C. (2004). Ubuntu and communitarianism in media ethics, *Ecquid Novi*, 25(2), 235–256.
Christians, C. & Traber, M. (1997). Introduction. In Chrisitians, C. & Traber, M., (eds.), *Communication ethics and universal ethics* (pp. viii–xvi). London: Sage.
Daily Telegraph, (2008). David Rattray: A man with a gift of storytelling and a vision for the future. Retrieved 21 February 2008 from http://www.telegraph.co.uk/portal/main.jhtml?view=DETAILS&grid=&xml=/portal/2008/01/ 31/ftrattray131.xml.
Dean, R. (2006). *The value of humanity in Kant's moral theory*. Oxford: Oxford University Press.

Dirlik, A. (2005). The postcolonial aura: Third world criticism in the age of global capitalism. In Desai, G. & Nair, S., (eds.), *Postcolonialisms* (pp. 561–588). Oxford: Berg.

Donagan, A. (1977). *The theory of morality*. Chicago, Ill.: University of Chicago Press.

Donaldson, T. (1992). Kant's global rationalism. In Nardin, T. & Mapel, D.R., (eds.), *Traditions of International Ethics* (pp. 136–157). Cambridge: Cambridge University Press.

Ebo, B.L. (1994). The ethical dilemma of African journalists: A Nigerian perspective, *Journal of Mass Media Ethics*, 9(2), 84–93.

Fourie, P.J. (2007). Moral philosophy as a threat to freedom of expression: from Christian-Nationalism to *ubuntuism* as a normative framework for media regulation and practice in South Africa, *Communications-European Journal of Communication Research*, 32 (2007), 1–29.

Fowler, R. (2001). *Language in the news: Discourse and ideology in the press*. London: Routledge.

Gikandi, S. (2005). Globalization and the claims of postcoloniality. In Desai, G. & Nair, S., (eds.), *Postcolonialisms* (pp. 608–634). Oxford: Berg.

Grossberg, L. (2002). Postscript, *Communication Theory*, 12(3), 367–370.

Harvey, D. (2005). *A brief history of neoliberalism*. Oxford: Oxford University Press.

Horton, R. (2004). Rediscovering human dignity, *The Lancet*, 364 (9439), 1081–1085.

Hurley, D. (1966). *Human dignity and race relations*. Johannesburg: South African Institute of Race Relations.

Joubert, P. (2007, 9–15 February). "I eat with robbed money". *Mail & Guardian*, p. 13.

Koopman, N. (2007). Some theological and anthropological perspectives on human dignity and human rights, *Scriptura*, 95(2), 177–185.

May, J.D. (2006). Human dignity, human rights, and religious pluralism: Buddhist and Christian perspectives, *Buddhist-Christian Studies*, 26 (2006), 51–60.

McEwan, C. (2003). Material geographies and postcolonialism, *Singapore Journal of Tropical Geography*, 24(3), 340–355.

McMillin, D.C. (2007). *International media studies*. Malden, Mass.: Blackwell.

McQuail, D. (2005). *McQuail's mass communication theory*. London: Sage.

Mpofu, D. (2007). Termination of SABC/SANEF Association. *Mail & Guardian Online*. Retrieved 21 February 2008 from http://www.mg.co.za/ContentImages/318523/sabc_letter.pdf.

Ndangam, L.N. (2006). "Gombo": Bribery and the corruption of journalism ethics in Cameroon, *Ecquid Novi: African Journalism Studies*, 27(2), 179–199.

Nussbaum, M.C. (2000). *Women and human development: The capabilities approach*. Cambridge: Cambridge University Press.

Nussbaum, M.C. (2006). *Frontiers of justice: Disability, nationality, species membership*. Cambridge, Mass.: Harvard University Press.

Nussbaum, M.C. & Faralli, C. (2007). On the new Frontiers of Justice. A dialogue, *Ratio Juris*, 20(2), 145–161.

Nyamnjoh, F.B. (2005). *Africa's media – democracy & the politics of belonging*. Pretoria: Unisa Press/London & New York: Zed Books.

Parameswaran, R. (2002). Local culture in global media: Excavating colonial and material discourses in National Geographic, *Communication Theory*, 12(3), 287–315.

Pilger, J. (1998). *Hidden agendas*. London: Vintage

Rao, S. & Wasserman, H. (2007). Global journalism ethics revisited: A postcolonial critique, *Global Media and Communication*, 3(1), 29–50.

SABC. (N.d.). Editorial code of practice. Retrieved 27 February 2007 from http://www.sabc.co.za/portal/site/sabc/me nuitem.7ddb6388f2d6e524bc5194f0064daeb9/.

Schultziner, D. (2006). A Jewish conception of human dignity, *Journal of Religious Ethics*, 34(4), 663–683.

Sen, A. (1999). *Development as freedom*. New York: Knopf.

Shome, R. & Hegde, R.S. (2002). Postcolonial approaches to communications: Charting the terrain, engaging the intersections, *Communication theory*, 12(3), 249–270.

Sontag, S. (2004). *Regarding the pain of others*. London: Penguin.

South African Government. (1996). Constitution of the Republic of South Africa. *South African Government Information*. Retrieved 21 February 2008 from http://www.info.gov.za/documents/constitution/index.htm.

South Africa Yearbook. (2006). Auckland Park: GCIS.

Sparks, C. (2007). *Globalization, development and the mass media*. London: Sage.

Sunday Times. (2008). Pandor unveils school "pledge". Retrieved 21 February 2008 from http://www.thetimes.co.za/News/Article.aspx?id=704331.

The Times (2008). Zuma to address blacks-only forum. Retrieved 22 February 2008 from http://www.thetimes.co.za/News/Article.aspx?id=712137.

Tomaselli, K.G. (2003). 'Our culture' vs 'foreign culture'. An essay on ontological and professional issues in African journalism, *Gazette,* 65(6), 427–441.

Venn, C. (2006). *The postcolonial challenge – towards alternative worlds.* London: Sage.

Vorster, N. (2007). A theological evaluation of the South African constitutional value of human dignity, *Journal of Reformed Theology,* 1(3), 320–339.

Wasserman, H. (2006a). Globalised values and postcolonial responses: South African perspectives on normative media ethics, *The International Communication Gazette* 68(1), 71–91.

Wasserman, H. (2006b). Tackles and sidesteps: normative maintenance and paradigm repair in mainstream media reactions to tabloid journalism, *Communicare,* 25(1), 59–80.

Wasserman, H. & Rao, S. (2008). Globalization, glocalization and journalism ethics, *Journalism: Theory, Practice, Criticism,* 9(2), 163–181.

Zhang, Q. (2007). Human dignity in classical Chinese philosophy: Reinterpreting mohism, *Journal of Chinese Philosophy,* 34(2), 239–255.

6 Postcolonial Theory and Global Media Ethics: A Theoretical Intervention

Shakuntala Rao

1. Introduction

The invasion of Iraq, the prisoners of Guantanamo Bay, and the wall in the West Bank, make it seem absurd that we can talk in any spatiotemporal way as 'post' or as having moved beyond. In the face of the continuing effects of imperialism, the project of postcolonial studies which makes visible the long history of colonialism, empire, those who have opposed it, and contemporary sites of resistance, seem more urgent than ever. In the past decade postcolonial theory has generated extensive discussions in varied disciplines ranging from anthropology, history, geography, political science, and art, to literary, film, gender, cultural, psychoanalytical, and queer studies. Shome and Hegde (2002), in a special issue on postcolonial theory of the journal, *Communication Theory*, made a plea to communication scholars to "recognise the relevance of this interdisciplinary area and why engaging the postcolonial enables us to rethink communication through new visions and revisions, through new histories and geographies" (p. 249). Such a plea must now be integrated into the varied theoretical corners of the vast, often times shifting terrains, of the discipline. While Shome and Hegde began the dialogue on postcolonial theory and globalisation within the communication discipline, I take on the task forwarded by Shome and Hegde and focus our attention in this paper on one specific area of communication studies, namely media ethics.

In reality, discussion about media and journalism ethics and practices are taking on global dimensions as more and more journalists work in global media conglomerates and are required to keep track of economic and political issues which span transnational audience interests. Until now the debates in media ethics have been largely derived theoretically and historically from the West.

While globalisation has created a great deal of debate in economic and policy circles, many implications of the phenomenon remain virtual *terra incognita*. Media and journalism practices are at the centre of this uncharted continent. While scholars have concentrated on media and journalism ethics and ethics codes in media corporations in the West, little theoretical work from and about the non-West has entered the discussion.

This chapter hopes to add a fresh theoretical perspective to the discussion of global media ethics. The aim is to understand the possible ways that conversations in global media ethics can be enriched by postcolonial theory. I examine the possibilities of integrating the theoretical work of postcolonial thinkers to the literature of media ethics. I focus especially on the aspect of postcolonial theory which examines the place of non-Western indigenous theories in formulating ethical theories about media. Using the works of Dipesh Chakrabarty and Edward Said, two prominent postcolonial writers, I argue that to build a radically non-coercive and anti-imperialist vision of humanity, or to "decolonise universality" (De, 2002, p. 42), one should recognise the value and usefulness of local epistemologies. I contend that such an effort must engage non-Western indigenous theories which have evolved outside of (or parallel to) European Enlightenment philosophies by recognising them as epistemologically rich and key to how media practitioners make ethical decisions around the world.

Since the publication of Shome and Hegde's article, the geopolitics of the world has been even more radicalised (for example, with the ongoing wars in Iraq and Afghanistan, the re-emergence of a dictatorial regime in Russia, intensification of Iran's nuclear capabilities, and escalation of numerous civil wars in Africa, Asia, and Latin America) media continues to play a central discursive role in the way the international relations debates are conceptualised, framed, and resolved. The role of media in the reproduction of imperial power structures is not a recent phenomenon (McMillan, 2007) but the renewed focus on media's role in processes of globalisation has brought increased attention to this fact. When one studies local production and consumption patterns, global media has been both integrated and accommodated, as well as hybridised and resisted (Mattelart, 2002; Sinclair, 2004; Thomas, 2006). This intersection between the global and local, and the contestations ensuing from this encounter, have not yet received adequate attention in media ethics scholarship (Banda's article in this anthology is one such attempt). While several attempts have strived to provide a global perspective on media ethics, these perspectives have paid little attention to postcolonial thematics (Shome & Hegde, 2002, p. 251) such as hybridity, diaspora, subalternity, and transnationalism. Instead, media ethics scholarship has dealt with the relationship between the local, national, global, and transnational forces in a manner consistent with an upbeat image of a syncretic global village or the "neoliberal idea of a rising tide lifting all boats in the global economy" (Loomba, Kaul, Bunzl, Burton & Esty, 2005, p. 8). While scholars have collected and examined case-studies in media ethics from around the world to arrive at universal ethical values, such scholars have paid inadequate attention to epistemological differences and power relations between and among nations, cultures, and peoples. I argue that a study of media ethics in the age of globalisation needs to move 'back' to the study of history and of structures that have historically connected the globe rather than treating globalisation as a new or historically unique phenomenon. A postcolonial approach to communication – and global media ethics specifically – would demand closer attention to the intersections between the local and the global and interrogate them against the background of a colonial past. Hulme (2005, p. 46) sceptically asks if it is even possible to imagine the globe "without invoking imperial prospects and privileges, and that mere talking about the globe implies a level of planetary consciousness which is colonial by its very nature." Bhabha and Comaroff (2002) observe:

> The neoliberal triumphalist 'aura' that accompanies the boom-and-bust of economic globalisation while celebrating 'free markets' creates its own historical melancholias and political amnesias. It is as if the advance of science, technology, and dot.com consumerism will somehow transform the unequal world into a level playing field – but the favelas, ghettos, townships, and shantytowns have not turned into silicon valleys. Fifty years after independence, Indian literacy and poverty rates have hardly budged; the poverty lines in the US has barely shifted in this half-century while we delight in the accelerated connectivity between California and Bangalore (p. 40).

The proliferation of media, which ensures that even the remote towns and cities of the world can uplink into the integrated and interconnected world of satellite channels and globally formatted programming, has not led to equality among media production and distribution processes. Therefore, to swiftly abandon or ignore a theoretical understanding of the structural links between colonial and neocolonial forms of global hierarchy or epistemological and colonial conditions leading up to this particular moment in the history of global relations would be premature. The world systems that have shaped the planet's social and cultural spaces for centuries cannot be erased by superficial optimism or simplistic pessimism. The theoretical task regarding global media and postcolonial theory started by Shome and Hegde remains just as critical today as it did when *Communication Theory* published the special issue. The thematics which postcolonial studies introduced to the Western academy from its inception may take new meaning but retain old questions which are significant in our study of global media ethics: to understand the contemporary shape of neoliberal global institutions including transnational media structures and flows; critique the intellectual spectrum that produces the dominant discourses of globalisation; understand the shifting terrains of dominance and resistance and the significance of race, class, gender, and sexuality; and analyse the enduring ideal of nation and varied forms of nationalisms. Postcolonial theory can help media ethics scholars come to terms with what is really new about globalisation or to understand globalisation as a new epoch, nonetheless substantially organised by familiar structures of power and linkages (Loomba, Kaul, Bunzl, Burton & Esty, p. 16). While several chapters in this anthology address the aforementioned issues, this chapter delineates the theoretical contribution that non-Western epistemologies can make to global media ethics.

2. Globalisation and Media Ethics

Globalisation has created enormous anxiety in the academy, especially as intellectuals realise that the nation-state can no longer contain the world's future major predicaments and crises. While it is premature to announce the "death of the nation", its ability to control flow of information and culture is under threat (Shome, 2006). Nation-states themselves continue to regroup in fundamental ways on supranational lines, for example, the case of the EU which has adopted a single currency and less strict border controls (Gikandi, 2002). Even in the age of globalisation, patterns of belonging continue to inspire coherence and conflict and, hence, have ethical implications on media and communication. Nation-states have begun to acknowledge the shifting terrains of power impelled by transnational, non-governmental, and supranational forces. Paradoxically, globalisation has also led to the rise of local, regional, and sub-national interest groups.

Each discipline has privileged its own set of concerns in relation to globalisation. For media scholars, globalisation has come to denote the increased interconnectedness between peoples, cultures, and places generally "a world united by telecommunications, computer-generated information systems and the immediate and personalised forms of television" (Banerjee, 2002, p. 519). Until recently, media scholars working with global sensitivities had been limited to a broadly defined and loosely categorised sub-field called international communication. For a long time, international communication was defined by geography, media policy between nations, and by static definitions of nation-states. Ignored were roles that non-governmental agencies or non-state actors played within a nation or across national borders. Globalisation was often conflated with Americanisation and Americanisation, in turn, was not understood in local ways except for "Western domination" (Anokwa, Lin, & Salewan, 2003, p. 3). When discussed, transnationalism was understood only as a prerogative of multinational capital or of multilateral agencies such as the World Trade Organisation, International Monetary Fund, or International Telecommunication Union. International communication scholars did not consider anti-globalisation groups, such as the World Social Forum, as possible actors. Colonialism was an epoch which had either been long forgotten or required little critical examination in the increased global flow of persons, commodities, and ideas. Given the dynamic flow of information and images around the world, discussions of globalisation cannot ignore media's ethical practices or vice versa. Within media ethics theoretical literature, however, discussions of colonialism, globalisation, or transnationalism have largely been absent. As others in the communication discipline tackled the questions of media globalisation, scholars in media ethics continued to assume that the theoretical ethical analyses of the Western media could be universalised. The few times scholars discussed international media and journalism ethical practices, they assumed that, with the exception of a few culturally idiosyncratic practices, most journalists share a core worldview and a common set of values. Few textbooks, in and outside the West, have expanded the usual list of foundational theories in ethics such as Aristotle's Golden Mean, Kant's Categorical Imperatives, Humanism, and Utilitarianism to include non-

Western, indigenous ethical theories. Others have discussed media ethics along with issues of diversity and multiculturalism, a debate centred on inclusiveness, self-reflection, and openness to others (Wood, 1997). Such perspective began with the assumption that the Western culture had historically devalued and erased diversity, and that, if individuals would only address diversity with openness and change, ethics and attitudes towards differences will shift. This perspective failed to acknowledge that individual ethical frameworks are also shaped by history and location. Such premises also did not acknowledge that the relationship between individuals is not merely about friendship, but is comprised of a contentious and unequal history that exists between societies, which can play out both in the most minor of interpersonal conversations and in public policy debates among nations.

Only more recently, a set of critical theories of ethics such as Communitarianism, Neo-Aristotelian virtue ethics, and Feminism have been included in discussions of media ethics. Such theories have problematised the core assumptions of the Enlightenment legacy of a presumed humanism and an ideal, autonomous, and sovereign subject. Communitarianism, for instance, "focuses on the outcome of individual ethical decision, understood not as disconnected choices but analysed as the impact of the sum of the choices on society" (Patterson and Wilkins, 2005, p. 14). In Couldry's (2006, p. 112) neo-Aristotelian theory of media ethics, one is drawn to what he describes as "media's reflexive virtues which allows for more dialogical use of concepts such as truth, accountability, and privacy." These theorists have not shied away from questions of inequality and have been quick to challenge the hegemony of liberalism with its "atomistic view of the individual citizen" (Couldry, p. 107). It is beyond the scope of this chapter to provide an in-depth comparison between postcolonial theory and Communitarianism, Feminist ethics, et cetera, though such an analysis could be valuable for the future. Instead, I focus on the ways postcolonial critique gives us possibilities to expand on what we define as ethical theories and conceptual frameworks. Ultimately, it is an effort that Appiah (2006, p. 94) calls the acknowledgement and "respect for historically, socially, and politically authentic identities of others" to which I add the recognition and respect for theoretical identity of others.

3. Colonial Aftermath

The term 'postcolonial' has referred to a disparate group of cultural and other practices which, while emerging from individual colonial histories and national identities, have nevertheless been influenced by the various effects of European colonisation. What countries as vastly different as South Africa and India also irreducibly share is the multiple task of assessing the extent of the "injustices committed under their respective colonial subjugations" (Lopez, 2001, p. 21). The colonial aftermath, writes Gandhi (1998), is both a moment of liberation and imprisonment. On one hand, the end of colonialism is a time to celebrate freedom from centuries of oppression, and yet, it is a moment when newly independent colonial subjects realise the "psychologically tenacious hold of the colonial past and its continuing effects in the present" (Gandhi, p. 6). Nandy (1983), in his book, *The Intimate Enemy*, writes of two kinds of colonialism. The first kind, the more transparent and obvious in its effect, includes physical coercion, violence, oppression, and conquest. He argues it is the second kind of colonialism which is more insidious, and therefore, leads postcolonialism into intense crises. It was pioneered by "rationalists, modernists, and liberals who argued that colonialism was really the messianic harbinger of civilisation to the uncivilised world" (Gandhi, p. 15). This type of colonialism suppressed – within the West and outside it – any knowledge system that did not ascribe to models which evolved from the European debates of Enlightenment. This kind of systemic psychological and ideological violence, Nandy observes, effectively marginalised, and most damagingly emptied out the meaning of, the epistemology of the native. Such "minor knowledges", as Deleuze and Guattari (1986, p. 211) labeled them, had been violently deterritorialised within the academy as Western intellectual history had become universalised and canonised. For Bhabha and Comaroff (p. 40), colonialism wrote "the history of native entirely in the passive voice, or worse rendered that native mute and inert, a *tabula rasa* onto which Europe, equally reified, inscribed its desires, demands, and determinations."

When Kant responded to the question, "Was ist Aufklärung?" or "What is Enlightenment?" in a 1784 essay, he began the debate about subjectivity and philosophy which would have profound impact on the intellectual history of the world. Kant's concept of subject was one that was rational, autonomous, self-sufficient, and masculine. As this intellectual strand took hold of Western philosophy, it essentially universalised the rational subject of Enlightenment as the agent of the "entire history of humanity" (Venn, 2006, p. 9). Part of the project of postcolonial theory has been to understand and critique the teleological thrust to make the Enlightenment idea of the subject, through colonialism and in the form of modernisation (and globalisation as its most recent avatar), hegemonic. While Kant's subject was ready for encounters, he was only able to engage those who would have a "coherent political culture that functions within the European State-oriented political imaginary" (Campbell and Shapiro, 2005, p. xvi). This subject would also compete with religious and traditional narratives of those who have lived their lives outside of the linear history and teleology of Enlightenment thinking. In discussions of ethics, Enlightenment thought – whether manifested in the form of Kant's categorical imperatives or Bentham and Mill's utilitarianism – was able to masquerade as above history and religion. Grounding enlightenment ethics in exclusively secular modes changed the foundational discourses to the point that religion and religious ethics had to be excluded from discussions of ethics, although ethical theories often had religious roots and, in many cultures, a vocabulary taken from religion.

One task of the postcolonial theoretical project has been to recover the systems of knowledge which have been a priori considered outside of modernity but are deeply implicated in modernisation and the modern subject. Bhabha and Comaroff (2002, p. 25) astutely observe that, "(The) life world of postcolonialism is a way of surviving modernity." For Bhabha and Comaroff, the temporal march of progress, rationality, and the State became corrupted in the colonial and postcolonial conditions where they played "a double aporetic role: on one hand they made emancipatory claims, crucial to the definition of modern citizenship; however, as part of the power practices of the colonial state they created inequality, injustice, and indignity" (p. 23). Bhabha and Comaroff write, "from the interstices of this paradoxical situation, the postcolonial perspective emerges" (p. 24). The discourses and processes of modernity had been taken for granted and routinised in every existing social and institutional apparatuses of the non-West. Therefore, a critical engagement with the legacy of colonial modernity and the epistemic foundation of Western Enlightenment cannot be avoided if one is to understand globalisation. Surviving modernity is also a process of recovery where one does not remain "deadlocked in the decentering of rational subject positions but attempt to build a politico-epistemic future" (De, p. 43). Such an assessment proposed by De must recognise, measure, and reckon with the impact of colonialism on national cultures, its lingering influence in the modern cultural and political institutions, and help us begin to interrogate the present epistemological model of the world. An assessment is necessary as we begin a project of global media ethics where ethical theories form the epistemological foundations on which media practices around the world are to be judged as 'right' or 'wrong'.

4. Provincialising Europe

The epistemic violence perpetrated on non-Western indigenous knowledge is the subject matter of Chakrabarty's (2000) seminal book, *Provincialising Europe*. Chakrabarty is concerned not with European history or the epoch of European imperial dominance, but, rather with "decentering the imaginary universal and secularist vision of the human as an outcome of Western political modernity" (p. 2). The European coloniser of the 19th century both preached this Enlightenment humanist at the colonised and at the same time denied it in practice, writes Chakrabarty, "But the vision has been powerful in its effects" (p. 4). This negation of speech by practice demonstrably constructed the modern social sciences and humanities as emerging from only a European intellectual tradition which traced its roots back to the ancient Greeks. The task of provincialising Europe, for Chakrabarty, is not to dismantle all that is European or Western, or to engage in a cultural relativism that assigns reason or democracy as synonymous with or exclusively to Europe, but to grasp the cultural and spatio-temporal location of Enlightenment steeped in its own biases, possibilities, and conditions. Chakrabarty also hopes, simultaneously, to recuperate social and political theories of local, and non-Enlightenment traditions. Chakrabarty makes the following observation about South Asian history:

> Faced with the task of analysing developments or social practices in modern India, few if any Indian social scientists or social scientists of India would argue seriously with, say, the 13th century logician Gangesa or with the grammarian and linguistic philosopher Bartrihari, or with the 10th or 11th century aesthetician, Abhinavagupta.

Sad though it is, one result of European colonial rule is that the intellectual traditions once unbroken and alive in Sanskrit or Persian or Arabic are now only matters of historical research for most – perhaps all – modern social scientists in the region. They treat these traditions as truly dead, as history. And yet past European thinkers and their categories are never quite dead for us in the same way (pp. 5–6).

Chakrabarty thus encapsulates postcolonial theory's quarrel with social sciences, ethics, and humanities by provincialising the knowledge claims of Europe; he wants scholars to begin to cast a critical eye on the genealogy and formation of humanist knowledge. Provincialising Europe, therefore, provides a careful historical and philosophical method to retrieve epistemological foundations for and from the non-West. It is up to us, urges Chakrabarty, "to build an archive or repository of these other horizons so that we can use them to fabricate our theoretical lives" (Chakrabarty in Dube, 2002, p. 867).

5. Traveling Theory

Edward Said also takes on the task of decolonising universality, although in a different way to Chakrabarty. Since the publication of a trilogy of books, *Orientalism* (1978), followed by *The Question of Palestine* (1979) and *Covering Islam* (1981), Edward Said's profound intellectual impact has been well articulated by many scholars (McClintock, Mufti, and Shohat, 1998; Said and Vishwanathan, 2001; Williams and Chrisman, 1994). Undoubtedly one of the internationally most influential books, *Orientalism*, scholars argued, changed the course of humanities and is often credited with inventing the field of postcolonial studies. The dominant thrust of *Orientalism*, which aimed to establish a form of noncoercive knowledge and power in Western culture's representation of the East, examined an array of 19th century French and British writers, poets, philologists, travelers, and colonial administrators, such as Chateaubriand, Lamartine, Flaubert, Sylvestre de Sacy, Ernest Renan, Richard Burton, and others. Drawing from the works of Foucault, Adorno, and Gramsci, Said claimed that European scholars took a vast region, one that spreads across a myriad of cultures and countries including most of Asia as well as the Middle East, and constructed it as singular, the 'Orient', which can then be studied as a cohesive whole. Orientalism essentialised an image of a prototypical Oriental – a biological inferior who is culturally backward, peculiar, and unchanging. "The writings of these Europeans expressed a will not only to understand what [was] non-European, but also to control and manipulate what was manifestly different" (Said, 1978, p. 288).

While *Orientalism* is credited with the evolution of the 'new humanities' whose aim was to challenge the exclusions and elisions of marginalised knowledge from privileged and canonical knowledge systems, I focus our attention on one of Said's later essays, *Traveling Theory*. This essay was originally published in *Raritan Quarterly* in 1982 and later included in numerous anthologies. In this essay Said investigates what happens to ideas, conceptual frameworks, and theories when they "travel" from place to place, "What happens to it [theory] when, in different circumstances and for new reasons, it is used again and, in still more different circumstances, again?" (Said, 2001, p. 195). Using George Lukacs' theory of reification as an example, Said argues that theories develop in response to specific historical, material, and social conditions, but whenever they move from their points of origin or location in which they were conceived, the power and rebelliousness associated with them disappear and they become dehistoricised and assimilated into their new locations. The first time a human experience is recorded and then given theoretical formulation, Said writes, "its force comes from being directly connected to and organically provoked by real historical circumstances" (2001, p. 197). Later versions of these theories cannot have the same ethico-political impact as the original and "these theories are degraded and subdued and their insurrectionary force is tamed and domesticated" (2001, p. 215). Said followed this essay with the publication, 12 years later, of *Traveling Theory Reconsidered*, in which he revised his earlier claim to propose that a theory can travel as long as it is reinterpreted and reinvigorated in new political, social, and cultural locations. Particularly impressed with Lukacs' influence on Fanon, Said reconsiders the geographical dispersion of the theoretical motor and "its immense capabilities for radical change as opposed to facile universalism or over-general totalising" (2000, p. 452). Said writes that to "pull a theory from one sphere or region to another" (2000, p. 451) must be done with care and not with a sense of borrowing or adapting. One must fully understand the political and cultural affiliations of the theory from whence it originated, and the conditions of its creation and writing, before one can make it travel. To prevent a theory from becoming a relatively tame academic substitute for the real thing and to avoid such domestication, one must see the profound potential of theory to "move beyond its confinement, to emigrate" (2000, p. 451), as he argues Fanon does with the Lukacsian figure in his book *Wretched of the Earth*. In the following sections I show how Chakrabarty and Said's work contribute to the epistemic decolonisation of universality, and to a recuperation of indigenous theory, which can further enrich discussions of global media ethics.

6. Indigenous Theory

Before we embark on such a task, I must clarify my definition of indigenous theory. The word 'indigenous', especially in the context of theory and theorising, has often been either equated with native (and subsequently been defined as authentic, unchanging, pure, and autonomous) or as a label for original peoples (to a particular region) who had been colonised by European settlers. I reject any interpretation of the indigenous as purely a nativist project. Indeed, there have been native struggles by the colonised and nationalists that have used the rhetoric of exclusion and violence with the same force as the coloniser, thus, nullifying the moral ground on which their own rhetoric was built. Instead, my use of indigenous theory is borrowed from Pillai who writes that all theories are indigenous, which means that "all theories are historically, culturally, and politically specific" (1993,

p. 133). To reclaim indigenity as an open and reflexive category, for Pillai, is a task that requires a recognition that every theory has a set of historical, cultural, and political conditions that informed its making, writing, and constituting. The problem arises when theories "built themselves on their ability to forget their own conditions of emergence and distribute themselves universally" (Pillai, p. 136) based on a turn towards forgetfulness. Pillai (p. 134) explains:

> ... the project of rethinking indigenity is not a question of searching for the original or the authentic, but a persistent return to the local which is open to definition and redefinition. To argue that all theories are indigenous then, is simply to emphasise their cultural conditions of emergence. Theories become imperialist when they masquerade as universals by suppressing their particularity and indigenity.

By acknowledging that all theories are indigenous, I acknowledge that every moment of theorising depends upon the particular and the local context within which the theorising takes place. Recognition of the particularity or local is not an end in itself, but a moment "of reflexivity [and] assumes localisation as a significant constitutive moment of all theorising" (Pillai, p. 135).

One task of colonialism was to destroy "every last remnant of alternative ways of knowing and living, to obliterate collective identities and memories and to impose a new order on the colonised" (Smith, 2002, p. 69). An effect of colonisation has been that non-Western theories have scarcely been recognised as theories, thus, they are either relegated to evidentiary status, or worse, rejected as religious and dogmatic.

My advocacy of indigenous theory is neither an attack or rejection of Western theories, nor in Gandhi's (p. 1) words a form of "postcolonial revenge"; instead, it is a way to seek epistemic respect for non-Western theories and to recognise the 'Other as Theory' in the debates around universalisation and globalisation. In the next section I will briefly discuss my point that Chakrabarty and Said's ideas of Provincialising Europe and Traveling Theory can inform literature of global media ethics. I will also provide some examples of scholarly efforts that have integrated non-Western indigenous theories to show how they can enrich the discussion of global media ethics.

7. Postcolonial Theory and Global Media Ethics: Point of Intervention

In many contemporary societies, media pervade both the public and private sphere where experiences are profoundly mediated. Satellites, direct broadcasting services, and digital technology have allowed global media institutions to enter living rooms in a vast array of cultures and nations. While the consumption, reception, and distribution of images go global, the study of contemporary media ethics continues to centre on ideas of objectivity, freedom, and responsibility, which take as their unit of moral measurement the autonomous and reasonable individual free of cultural and political affiliations. For example, when a journalist's choice of moral and acceptable action is often measured outside of his or her religious life (Mohamed's chapter in this anthology critiques such an assumption). The global media landscape will require radical rethinking of the individual moral being. The study of global media ethics, therefore, will require a careful theoretical (re)grounding. To accomplish such revision, Said's concept of Traveling Theory and Chakrabarty's Provincialising Europe can provide theoretical possibilities for media ethics scholars.

The relevance of Said's Traveling Theory to the media ethics scholarly literature can be best judged by asking a series of intervening questions: 'What happens to theories often used in media ethics literature, such as Social Responsibility, Deontological, or Utilitarianism, when they are used to study media practices in, say, China?'; 'Do they get superimposed on other pre-existing theories of religion and life, such as those derived from Confucianism, Daoism, Buddhism, Yao, or many other philosophical and cultural traditions that have existed in China for centuries?'; 'Do these theories get indigenised in specific cultural, social, and political locations?'; 'Do these theories produce any meaning in a media existing under a version of Communism, a political and economic model exported from the West and, yet, integrated to local traditions?'; 'What, then, would be the model of a good journalist in China given that Confucianism, according to Byun and Lee (2002), is premised on a set of values of consensus and individuality different from those in the West?' For Shohat and Stam (1994, p. 15), "unthinking eurocentrism" is seeing the West and non-West as two worlds that constantly "interpenetrate in an unstable space of creolisation" where theories mingle, change, and take new meaning. Writing about the influence of social responsibility theory in Japan, for instance, Tsukamoto (2006, p. 59) observes, that the canons of journalism adopted by the post-World War II Japanese media which were guided by social responsibility theory which emphasises impartiality, tolerance, guidance, responsibility, pride, and decency, changed the way the Japanese media viewed the importance of press freedom and its obligations to society. He also notes, however, that the social responsibility doctrines in Japan have worked radically differently from those in the US. Japanese journalists stress freedom less and restraint more than do their US counterparts. Said's plea to scholars is to become acutely cognisant of the content of theory when it travels, what that theory does, and what happens to it in the act of traveling. The cumbersome task of decolonising universality, Chakrabarty (p. 8) believes, must begin with scholars' abandoning the supremacy of one theoretical skeleton and formulating ethical theories that can help explain various ethical practices around the world. He urges us to seek a space for multiple knowledge systems which work either to counter or harmonise with Enlightenment philosophical approaches, and which can be immeasurably useful in our analysis of the local and global nexus.

Scholars have already made several attempts to integrate non-Western indigenous theories to media studies but not much of this has taken place in the specific field of media ethics. Pillai's work with *rasa*, a theory from *Natyashashtra*, an Indian classic text written in the 11th century, about Indian aesthetics and its interpretative role in Indian films, for instance, has shown us the ways in which local theories can influence media consumption and production. For Pillai (p. 154), explanatory frameworks like *rasa* are often demoted from a structuring role to the level of evidence and are taken merely to "signify cultural difference", but are not used at conceptual or theoretical levels. If scholars relegate structural frameworks like *rasa* to mere cultural data, they can further justify the argument that 'legitimate' structuring principles about aesthetics and media need to come from elsewhere. By giving us an account of *rasa*, Pillai suggests that it is possible to "construct indigenous theories without being reductive" (p. 154) or romantic. Juluri (2005), another critic who attempts to recuperate and apply indigenous theory, aims to centralise Gandhi's syncretic philosophy of *ahimsa* to the intellectual foundation of communication and media theories. Juluri applies Gandhi's view of *ahimsa* to studies of media violence. He suggests that communication and media scholars move away from the "antiquated rational/emotional binary in Western philosophy" (p. 197), which naturalises the inevitability of violence, to understand *ahimsa* as a potential universal and eternal value. "The immense sweep of violence that has seized the world, first as colonialism, and now as globalisation," writes Juluri, makes it imperative that we no longer marginalise *ahimsa* and nonviolence by depending unthinkingly upon "decades of intellectual saturation in the ideologies of violence" (p. 212). Scholars need to make ahimsa, Juluri argues, a central epistemological condition to theorising media violence. Gunaratne (2006), another scholar attempting to recover and use indigenous theory, recently critiqued Habermas's theory of communicative action; he challenges the universalisation of Habermasian theory. Gunaratne provincialises Habermas within a specific European historical context, and writes that Habermas's theory "does not match the ontological, epistemological, and historical reservoir of the non-West" (p. 95). "Habermasian theory [of communicative action and the public sphere]," writes Gunaratne (p. 109), "is clearly a product of eurocentric verticality, for it sees no positives in the historical development of non-Western societies or non-Western epistemologies." Using Buddhist and Chinese philosophies, Gunaratne argues that Habermas (like his predecessor Max Weber) ignores much in non-Western and Eastern philosophies akin to communicative rationality. Both Buddhist and Chinese philosophy recognise the validity claim of rightness (conventional truth) derived through social consensus, writes Gunaratne (p. 139). The provincialising of the theory of communicative action along these lines would make the theory more appealing to non-Europe and help bring non-Western theories back to visibility in the global academy.

There exists little scholarly work in media ethics which addresses the essentials of non-Western theories and uses them as epistemology akin to the scholarship of Pillai, Juluri, and Gunaratne. Although hardly exhaustive, my work with Wasserman is a starting point. In our analysis of ubuntu and ahimsa as ethical theories, we have shown that non-Western indigenous theories and complexities of postcolonial identities need to be integrated into a discussion of global media ethics (Rao & Wasserman, 2007). We argue that one cannot fit theories like ubuntu or ahimsa neatly into any global media ethics framework without acknowledging these indigenous theories as fundamental conceptual frameworks which people use to make meaning of their lives and practices, as ways they understand and consume media products, and to think through behaviours they consider ethical or unethical among media practitioners.

An ethical issue such as the invasion of privacy, for example, has radically different meaning and implications in varied cultural locations. Privacy is inherently connected to how one conceptualises the private sphere, individual space, and one's relationship to others. In India, graphic photographs of dead bodies are routinely published and broadcast on media. According to Vedantic Hindu philosophy death is a form of *moksha*, the highest state of liberation, and a public exhibition of a dead body is not a matter of privacy for the individual or his or her family. Death is a moment of celebration where one celebrates the passing of one life to another. Most branches of Hindu philosophy advance the idea of reincarnation in conjunction with *niskamakarma* (O'Flaherty & Derrett, 1978). *Niskamakarma* is the belief that people live their lives and perform ethical actions with a sense of non-attachment to the material world. Teachings of *Bhagwat-Gita*, the classic text on Indian ethics from the epic, *Mahabharata*, emphasise how one is expected to lead an ethical life. According to the Gita, it is death that takes us to a greater good beyond immediate perceptual experiences (Buch, 2003). The immense belief in religion and pantheon of gods in India, even among the poorest, is driven by a moral understanding that one must continue to be *niskamakarmic* even if one suffers great humiliation, defeat, or pain, for one is expected to do good in this life to have his or her virtuous actions be rewarded in the next. Expectations of privacy in one's death would seem unnecessary if death is the freedom of the *atman* (soul) from attachments of *artha* (materials) and *kama* (desire).

Niskamakarma, a belief organically connected to the philosophies of *samsara* (the cycle of birth and death) and *purusarthas* (the ethical duties of men), cannot merely be understood as 'cultural difference' but as an epistemological foundation around which Hindu life revolves. Protecting one's privacy or invasion of privacy may have limited meaning in such a context where individual space and identity is conceived differently. As one journalist says, "People in India do not understand and interpret harm in the same way as those in the West. For [Indians] the publication of the photograph of a dead body of someone in their family is a public event, not a private one, since death itself is public." The epistemological and religious foundations of such ethical practices have spanned thousands of years and cannot simply be discarded as immoral. If we are to understand how global media works and to develop global media ethics, we must expand the conceptual frameworks to theorise about ethics. To have a global ethics is to produce, create, and resurrect knowledge – often non-institutionalised knowledge – that must go beyond narrow disciplinary legacies and rigid norms of citations validated by groups of experts.

Media's ethical practices around the world differ significantly. To understand why these differences exist or to find common ethical principles, requires decolonising universality. One way of decolonising universality, I have argued in this essay, is to recognise – academically and institutionally – non-Western indigenous theories as being equally exhaustive and profound in their implications to understand global media ethics as Western Enlightenment theories have been considered to be.

8. Conclusion

Postcolonial theory addresses the multiple and interlocked hierarchies of a postimperial world and also takes into account how people mobilise against separatism by working through critiques of ethic divisiveness to negotiate a common human ground. This must be done with a sense of epistemic syncretism where media practitioners can adopt both a Western theory of media ethics (for instance social responsibility) as well as theories from local traditions and religious life. The point is not to pitch one against the other as opposites: Western versus indigenous or global versus local, but to bear the local upon the universal in a non-coercive way so as not to reject non-Western and indigenous as non-theoretical but to accept them as theory and equally capable of analysing media's ethical practices. A careful grounding in the specifics of the local does not impose a regime or 'tyranny of the local', but shows that such an ethics might disclose a layered full-spectrum of social, cultural, historical, and political contexts in which people produce and consume media. We must learn to evolve away from what Sinclair, Jacka, and Cunningham (1996, p. 22) call "peripheral vision" wherein the 'West' is presumed to be the centre which dominates the peripheral 'Rest' by producing outward flow of media products, journalism styles, and media ethics and move towards the appreciation of both Western and non-Western ethical theories of media. Any efforts to develop an inclusive global media ethics platform will rest in its ability to be cognisant of history and to integrate multiple systems of knowledge.

Acknowledgement

The author wishes to thank Erin Mitchell, Herman Wasserman, and Lee Wilkins for their comments.

References

Anokwa, K., Lin, C. A., and Salewan, M. B. (2003). International mass communication from the tower of babel to the babel fish. In K. Anokwa, C. Lin, and M. Salewan (eds.), *International communication: Concepts and cases* (pp. 1–4). New York: Wadsworth. Appiah, A. (2006). *Cosmopolitanism: Ethics in a world of strangers.* New York: W. W. Norton.

Banerjee, I. (2002). The local strikes back? Media globalisation and localisation in the new Asian television landscape. *Gazette: The International Journal for Communication Studies,* 64(6), 517–535.

Bhabha, H. and Comaroff, J. (2002). Speaking of postcoloniality, in the continuous present: A conversation with Homi Bhabha. In T. A. Goldbert and A. Quayson (eds.), *Relocating postcolonialism* (pp. 46–55). New York: Blackwell.

Buch, M. A. (2003). *The principles of Hindu ethics.* Delhi: Bharatiya Kala Kendra Prakashan.

Byun, D., and Lee, K. (2002). Confucian values, ethics, and legacies in history. In S. Bracci and C. Christians (eds.), *Moral engagement in public life* (pp. 73–96). New York: Peter Lang.

Campbell, D., and Shapiro, M. (2005). Introduction: From ethical theory to ethical relations. In D. Campbell and M. Shapiro (eds.), *Moral spaces: Rethinking ethics and world politics* (pp. i–xv). Minneapolis, Minn.: University of Minnesota Press.

Chakrabarty, D. (2000). *Provincialsing Europe.* Chicago: University of Chicago Press.

Couldry, N. (2006). *Listening beyond the echoes: Media, ethics, and agency in an uncertain world.* Boulder, Col: Paradigm.

De, E. N. (2002). Decolonising universality: Postcolonial theory and the quandary of ethical agency, *Diacritics*, 32(2), 42–59.

Deleuze, G., and Guttari, F. (1986). *Kafka: Toward a minor literature* (D. Polan, Trans.). Minneapolis, Minn.: University of Minnesota Press.

Dube, S. (2002). Presence of Europe: An interview with Dipesh Chakrabarty. *The South Atlantic Quarterly*, 101(4), 859–68.

Gandhi, L. (1998). *Postcolonial Theory: A critical introduction*. New York: Columbia University Press.

Gikandi, S. (2002). Globalisation and the claims of postcoloniality, *The South Atlantic Quarterly*, 100(3), 628–58.

Gunaratne, S. A. (2006). Public sphere and communicative rationality: Interrogating Habermas's eurocentrism, *Journalism and Communication Mongraphs*, 8(2), 94–156.

Hulme, P. (2005). Beyond the straits: Postcolonial allegories of the globe. In A. Loomba, et al. (eds.), *Postcolonial Studies and beyond* (pp. 42–61). Durham, N.C.: Duke University Press.

Juluri, V. (2005). Nonviolence and media studies, *Communication Theory*, 15(2), 196–215.

Loomba, A., Kaul, S., Bunzl, M, Burton, A., and Esty, J. (2005). Beyond what? An introduction. In A. Loomba, et al. (eds.), *Postcolonial studies and beyond* (pp. 1–38). Durham, N.C.: Duke University Press.

Lopez, A. J. (2001). *Posts and pasts: A theory of postcolonialism*. Albany, N.Y.: State University of New York Press.

Mattelart, A. (2002). An archeology of the global era: Constructing a belief, *Media, Culture, and Society*, 24, 591–612.

McClintock, A., Mufti, A., and Shohat, E. (1997). *Dangerous liaisons: Gender, nation and postcolonial perspectives*. Minneapolis, Minn.: University of Minnesota Press.

McMillan, D. (2007). *International media studies*. London: Blackwell.

Nandy, A. (1983). *The intimate enemy: The loss and recovery of self under colonialism*. Delhi: Oxford University Press.

O'Flaherty, W. D., and Derrett, J. D. (1978). *The concept of duty in South Asia*. New Delhi: Vikas Publishing House.

Patterson, P. and Wilkins, L. (2005). 5th ed. *Media ethics: Issues and cases*. Boston, Mass.: McGraw Hill.

Pillai, P. (1993). *Reinterpreting the Margins of Theory*. Unpublished doctoral dissertation, University of Massachusetts-Amherst, USA.

Rao, S., and Wasserman, H. (2007). Global media ethics revisited: A postcolonial critique. *Global Media and Communication*, 3, 29–50.

Said, E. (1978). *Orientalism*. New York: Pantheon.

Said, E. (2001). Traveling Theory. In M. Bayoumi and A. Rubin (eds.), *The Edward Said reader* (pp. 197–295). New York: Vintage.

Said, E., and Vishwanathan, G. (2001). *Power, politics and culture: Interviews with Edward Said*. New York: Pantheon.

Shohat, E., and Stam, R. (1994). *Unthinking eurocentrism: Multiculturalism and the media*. New York: Routledge.

Shome, R. (2006). Interdisciplinary research and globalisation. *Communication Review*, 9(1), 1–36.

Shome, R., and Hegde, R. (2002). Postcolonial approaches to communication: Charting the terrain, engaging the intersections, *Communication Theory*, 12(3), 249–270.

Sinclair, J. (2004). *Contemporary world television*. London: BFI.

Sinclair, J., Jacka, E., and Cunningham, S. (1996). *New patterns in global television: Peripheral vision*. New York: Oxford University Press.

Smith, L.T. (2002). *Decolonizing methodologies: Research and indigenous peoples*. London: Zed Books.

Thomas, A. O. (2006). *Transnational media and contoured markets: Redefining Asian television and advertising*. New Delhi: Sage.

Tsukamoto, S. (2006). Social responsibility theory and the study of journalism ethics in Japan, *Journal of Mass Media Ethics*, 21(1), 55–69.

Williams, P., and Chrisman, L. (1994). *Colonial discourse and postcolonial theory: A reader*. New York: Columbia University Press.

Wood, J. T. (1997). Diversity in dialogue: Commonalities and differences between friends. In J. M. Makau and R. C. Arnett (eds.), *Communication ethics in an age of diversity* (pp. 5–26). Urbana, Ill.: University of Illinois Press.

Venn, C. (2006). *The postcolonial challenge: Towards alternative worlds*. London: Sage.

7

African *Ubuntuism* as a Framework for Media Ethics: Questions and Criticism

Pieter J. Fourie

1. Introduction

The rethinking of media ethics has been going on for a number of decades. The chapters it this book indicate how such rethinking is being done from a number of theoretical, philosophical and research perspectives. Probably the main impetus for rethinking media ethics is the impact of globalisation on the media and the impact of the media on globalisation, turning the world into a small place. Closely linked to the processes of globalisation is the development of information and communication technology (ICT). ICT has created far-reaching effects on how people communicate through and with media and on how they use media. New technology has created a new media environment with new media practices demanding new ways of thinking, also about media ethics.

In comparative media research (see, for instance, Hallin and Mancini, 2004) there is almost consensus that the old "theories of the press" or "old" normative media theory on which media ethics are usually based are no longer adequate for an understanding of the ways in which the media perform in a new world. This is the world called by some the post-modern world, by others late modernity. Whatever the case may be, it is increasingly difficult to underwrite or defend a media ethics that is mainly Western-inspired and biased and/or inspired from the perspectives of Western Christianity. We need to acknowledge other philosophies, religions, and world and life views (see in this regard, for instance, Gunaratne, 2005).

In South Africa, one of these 'other' world and life views is called *ubuntuism*[1] (see point 3 for an explanation of what *ubuntuism* means) which is, from time to time, seen as a possible African framework for media ethics and as an African contribution to the rethinking of media ethics and normative media theory.

The purpose of this chapter[2] is to take a closer look at *ubuntuism*. What is *ubuntuism*? Can it be applied to the media? Can it work as an ethical framework for media practice and performance?

After a brief explanation of what *ubuntuism is* and its possible application to media practice, questions are raised about the feasibility of *ubuntuism* as an ethical framework for media practice. The questions are related to and asked in the context of (i) changed African cultural values, (ii) the distinctiveness of *ubuntuism* as an African moral philosophy, (iii) the vulnerability of moral philosophy to political misuse, (iv) the implications of *ubuntuism* for journalism practice, and (v) *ubuntuism* in the context of globalisation and a new (commercialised and technologically driven) media environment.

For a better understanding of this chapter, and to conclude this introduction, three remarks about the background and context of the *ubuntu* discourse are necessary. From the onset, it must be emphasised that at this stage the *ubuntu* discourse cannot be described as a focused effort to develop a comprehensive theory on the basis of which media performance could be ethically judged from 'an African perspective'. It should rather be seen as an intellectual quest to rediscover and re-establish *idealised values of traditional* African culture(s) and of *traditional* African communities. Yet, given South Africa's history of apartheid in which Christian nationalism was misused as a moral philosophy to mobilise a 'patriotic' media in the service of *volk* ('nation') and *vaderland* ('homeland'/'fatherland'), it is important to raise critical questions about *ubuntuism* as a possible framework for normative media theory or media ethics.

Furthermore, the *ubuntu* discourse should be seen in the context of South African politics. Since the beginning of the 1990s, South Africa has been exposed to fundamental political, economic, social and cultural change. It is a society in transition from a semi-authoritarian to a democratic order in line with Western principles of democracy. In this transition the South African media has not been left intact. There is an ongoing process of changing the racial composition of the South African media from predominantly white to black (in terms of regulation, ownership, and workforce), and of instituting and revising new regulatory policies in line with international policy trends and developments. In terms of skills, products, and technology, the country today hosts what is probably the most advanced media sector on the African continent. As such, the South African media sector is under the same pressure and faces the same challenges and opportunities as the media in Western societies, where trends such as liberalisation, privatisation, commercialisation, convergence, and globalisation dictate a move away from the media as primarily a cultural institution to a market-driven one.

Yet, and despite going along with these (post)modern trends and producing (post)modern media, the new and increasingly black generation of media owners and practitioners are also expected to honour African traditions, to *serve* and not only represent their communities, to represent and reflect reality from an African perspective, and to reinterpret freedom of expression and concepts such as public interest in an indigenous way.

The discourse about *ubuntu* as an ethical framework should thus also be seen as part of this expectation to rediscover and honour the traditional and the indigenous while at the same time pursuing modern trends (see 4.2). It can also be seen as another example of the paradoxes characterising South African society – a society with a first but also a third world economy and with great divides between rich and poor, literate and illiterate, healthy and ill, and so on.

2. The Revision of Normative Media Theory

South African media theorists and researchers are confronted with the same kind of theoretical and research questions as those debated by scholars in the West. This includes the question whether or not 'old' normative media theory based on Siebert, Peterson and Schramm's *Four Theories of the Press* (1956) and later adaptations thereof, are still applicable. However, and for the purpose of this article, two perspectives closely related to those in favour of modern media and media practices and those in favour of a more traditionalist approach, can be identified.

The modern perspective is adopted by those in support of the free market. They substantiate their arguments with some of the main premises of post-modern normative media theory which, inter alia, advocates pluralism and diversity as a cornerstone of media policy, as the only safeguard for freedom of expression, and as a foundation for *a* media ethics. The traditionalists argue that pro-diversity and pluralism arguments seldom take non-Western interpretations based on non-Western worldviews of social responsibility and freedom of expression into account. Consequently, they base their arguments on some of the main premises of postcolonial and comparative media theory which, amongst other things, provides the foundation for the project of investigating *ubuntuism* as a framework for media ethics. See Fourie (2007) for a more in-depth discussion of the main premises of the post-modern and postcolonial critique of normative media theory.

However, although the consideration of *ubuntuism* as an Afrocentric framework may be based on the premises of postcolonial media theory, it is nevertheless difficult to describe the *ubuntu* discourse as a focused academic and research-oriented project to develop an African normative theory on the basis of which media practice and performance could be measured. Rather, the discourse mainly consists of sporadic articles in which *ubuntuism* is raised as an option for the establishment of an African approach to media ethics. (See in this regard, for instance, the regular articles about the media in the online newsletter of the African National Congress, *ANC Today*, available at http://www.anc.org.za.)

The need for an African approach to media practice and ethics is usually expressed in attacks on the present media system by those who perceive it as an unwanted remnant of Western colonialism. The criticism is then that, although the racial composition and ownership of the South African media may be changing, the media still 'think' and 'perform' in terms of Western news values and professional practices (see, for example, Kasoma, 1996; Blankenberg, 1999; Kamwangamalu, 1999). Moreover, much of what is being written about *ubuntu* and the media, and much of what is being perceived to be the meaning and essence of *ubuntuism* for the media, derives from an intellectual quest to rediscover and re-establish the *idealised values of traditional* African culture(s) and *traditional* African communities. As Popper (1966) has shown, such a search for and idealisation of the traditional is characteristic of thinkers and their societies during times of social, cultural and political transformation (as South Africa is experiencing). (See 4.2.)

But what is *ubuntuism*?

3. What is *Ubuntuism*?

Explaining the essence of *ubuntuism* as a unique African moral philosophy, is a daunting task. It demands a sound knowledge of the ontology and epistemology of traditional African culture, philosophy and ethics. Without such knowledge and understanding, any explanation of *ubuntuism* runs the risk of being a reduced account of a rich system of values. It is sometimes also argued that only a (black) African can fully understand *ubuntuism* (cf. Ramose, 2002). In what follows, this research is thus conscious of the risk of oversimplifying, misrepresenting, and not grasping the true meaning of *ubuntuism*. For the following brief overview of some of the main characteristics of *ubuntuism*, I mainly rely on the work of Louw (2004), Blankenberg (1999), Ramose (2002), Shutte (2001), Christians (2004), Hamminga (2005), and Nussbaum (2003).

Ubuntuism can be understood as a social philosophy, a collective African consciousness, a way of being, a code of ethics and behaviour deeply embedded in African culture. It is the capacity in African culture to express compassion, reciprocity, dignity, harmony and humanity in the interest of building and maintaining a community with justice and mutual caring (see Nussbaum, 2003, p. 1).

The term *ubuntu* is derived from the Zulu maxim *umuntu ngumuntu ngabantu*, meaning 'a person is a person through other persons' or 'I am because of others'.

This maxim is also interpreted by different African cultures and in different African countries and languages, to mean, 'a person is defined with reference to the community', ' I am because we are, and since we are, therefore I am', 'it is through others that one attains selfhood', 'a person is born for the other', and, in the words of the West African politician-poet-philosopher, Leopold Senghor, "I feel the other, I dance the other, and therefore I am" (Nussbaum, 2003, p. 1).

With regard to the consequences of *ubuntuism* for mass communication, an outstanding characteristic of *ubuntuism* is its emphasis on *community*[3] and *collectivity*. *Ubuntuism* moves beyond an emphasis on the individual and individual rights, and places the emphasis on *sharing* and on individual *participation in a collective life*. Community is the context in which personhood is defined. As such, it differs from the emphasis on the *self* in mainstream eurocentric philosophies. The essence of being is participation with other humans. Whereas Western individualistic democracy insists on freedom of the self from intrusion by others, a person's freedom in *ubuntuism* depends for its exercise and fulfilment on personal relationships with others. A person is first and foremost a participatory being dependent on others for his/her development. *Ubuntuism* therefore places a high premium on negotiation, inclusiveness, transparency, and tolerance.

The emphasis on collectivism should, however, not been seen as collectivism in the sense of communism or First World socialism in which the individual is only part of the community (see Shutte, 2001, pp. 8–9). 'Community' in *ubuntuism* is not opposed to the individual nor does it simply swallow the individual up. Rather, it understands the individual to become a *unique centre* of shared life (see Blankenberg, 1999, p. 43). Christians (2004, p. 245), in interpreting Louw (2004), formulates it as follows:

> Since the self cannot be conceived without necessarily conceiving of others, *ubuntu* adds a universal and compelling voice against the Enlightenment's atomistic individuals who exist prior to and independently of their social order. In the West, where "individualism often translates into an impetuous competitiveness", the cooperation entailed by *ubuntu*'s "plurality of personalities" in a "multiplicity of relationships" is an attractive, though overwhelming concept. The modernist concept of individuality "now has to move from solitary to solidarity, from independence to interdependence, from individuality vis-à-vis community to individuality à la community".

Formulated differently, *ubuntuism* acknowledges individuality not in the service of the self, but in the service of others and the community. Hamminga (2005, p. 2) explains the African experience of collectivity as follows:

> A part of a tree does not choose an individual existence. No part of a body, and by "body" the community to which you belong is meant, can meaningfully survive cut off from the rest. And everything you do, serves the purpose of enhancing the vital energy, the procreation of the community. It is all about *togetherness and caring for each other within the community (tribe)*. What the individual does solely for own benefit is worse than dying: he will never be a root of the tree. Therefore, for the "classic" African, Western society, with its emphasis on individuality, is a very lonely place. To the African it seems difficult to be an individual in the West, because in Western society individuals do not see a group (a tree) in which to be an individual.

From this emphasis on community and the role of the individual in service of the community, stems what can be described as a general *ubuntu* morality or a general framework of moral values.

3.1 *Ubuntuism* and the Media

What are the possible implications of *ubuntuism*'s emphasis on collectivism for an African normative media theory?

Taking *ubuntuism*'s emphasis on the community as point of departure, authors such as Blankenberg (1999), Christians (2004), Okigbo (1996), Shutte (2001), and Wasserman and De Beer (2004) show how an *ubuntu* normative framework would require a media and journalism whose primary role would be to provide a space for the concerns, ideas, and opinions of the community. The overall purpose of the media would be to play a developmental role in the sense of stimulating citizen participation, community participation, and consensus based on widespread consultation with the community. In the context of the needs of developing countries, it would encourage action towards civic transformation and community renewal. In this process, the media would need to ensure the well-being of the collective, rather than the protection of individual rights. The media would be seen as a catalyst for moral agency and as such contribute to moral literacy.

Insofar as freedom of expression is concerned, an *ubuntu* approach may be that the interest of the individual and individual rights to freedom of expression are intertwined with that of the community. Freedom of expression therefore means the *freedom of the community* to articulate its opinions, questions, concerns, and needs, and not necessarily the freedom of an individual (for example a journalist) or a specific group (for instance a newspaper or a political party) to articulate an opinion or criticise someone or an opinion. The value of freedom of expression is measured in terms of its relevancy to the well-being of the/a community and to the well-being of the individual.

As far as the question of 'public interest' is concerned, the same emphasis would be placed on the community. The public's right to know would be assessed in terms of the potential harm the information could do to a particular community. How the media should play this role is not based on a prescribed set of professional codes, but rather on a deep-seated general morality that requires the journalist to act in harmony with the morality of the community. As Christians (2004, pp. 250–251) sees it:

> *Ubuntu* morality does not construct an apparatus of professional ethics. Rather, it works and provides an ethic of general morality. It does not develop rules for professionals, but urges a sensitivity and preoccupation with the moral dimensions of everyday life. The moral domain is understood to be intrinsic to human beings, not as a system of rules, norms and ideals external to society and culture. Professionals occupy the same social and moral space as the citizens they report on. How the moral order works itself out in community formation is the issue, not primarily what media practitioners by their own standards consider virtuous. The ultimate standard for media professionals is not role-specific ethical principles, but a general morality. This presupposes media workers' knowledge and sharing of the community's general morality.

From this follows a kind of journalism that does not place a high value on objectivity, neutrality, and detachment. In *ubuntu journalism* objectivity is neither necessary nor desirable (see Okigbo, 1996). The journalist is seen to be an involved member of the community and cannot remain a spectator. Through the journalist's work, a voice must be given to the community. Active involvement and dialogue with the community rather than detachment in the name of objectivity and neutrality is required (see Blankenberg, 1999).

As far as the requirement of factuality is concerned, it is argued that the Western conception of truth hinges completely on facts and does little to embed these facts in a network of cultural and social meanings generated within the community itself (see Wasserman and De Beer, 2004, p. 92). In *ubuntuism*, it is then believed that values such as truth, freedom and justice are to be constructed interdependently by and within the community.

In practice, the above may require (see Blankenberg, 1999) reporting that would: stimulate interaction amongst citizens, between citizens and reporters, and between citizens and politicians; enable people to come to terms with their everyday experiences; acknowledge the historical and biographic complexity of a matter or an issue; is not the hurried conclusion of an observer; penetrates the moral dynamics underlying the issue; is interpreted against the background of the community's contexts, beliefs, values and needs.

Most of all, in terms of journalistic practice, whatever goes into print should be assessed in terms of the potential impact of a report on the community. Therefore, subjects, or the community of a story, should have the last say on the media product before it is offered for mass reception (see Blankenberg, 1999). The public interest of the media is thus primarily defined in terms of the *value* of information and knowledge for the/a community, rather than in terms of the need to be informed about a topic in order to be able to make responsible political, social and/or individual choices and decisions.

The question arises if and how the above differs from what is perceived to be the functions and social responsibility of the media in Western normative theory? (See 4.1.) It seems, however, that whereas Western epistemological thought about the media proceeds from a focus on the media primarily in terms of (i) its information, surveillance, entertainment and educational role, (ii) the media's freedom and right to protection in order to be able to fulfil it social responsibility, and (iii) the individual's right to information, surveillance, entertainment and education, the emphasis in *ubuntuism* would first and foremost be on the media's role in bonding and in dialogue towards reaching consensus based on the social values and morals of a community. The emphasis thus moves from the media as informant, gatekeeper, entertainer and educator to the media as mediator; from the media as observer, to the media as participant and negotiator.

4. *Ubuntuism* as an Ethical Framework?

From the above overview of the nature of *ubuntuism* and the kind of journalism it may require as a consequence, a number of questions can be raised with reference to *ubuntuism*'s distinctiveness as an African approach to normative theory: its viability as a model for media performance in the context of a changed African culture and cultural values; the proneness of a moral philosophy such as *ubuntuism* to political misuse; the implications of an *ubuntu* framework for media practice; and the question of the viability of an *ubuntu* framework in the context of normative theory in a globalised world, given that South African society and media demonstrate more characteristics of the post-modern world and media environment than they do of a traditional society.

Apart from the need to probe (any) moral philosophy as a framework for media ethics with questions like these, it is, as raised earlier, also necessary to ask these questions against the background of South Africa's history of apartheid when Christianity was misused as a moral philosophy to breed a kind of patriotic media in support of the white minority.

4.1 Distinctiveness of *Ubuntuism* as African Approach to Normative Theory

How uniquely African is *ubuntuism* as a paradigm for normative theory? In this regard the similarities between *ubuntuism* and Western communitarianism need to be pointed out. Christians (2004), for example, shows how *ubuntuism* can be described as a combination and extension of European and North American communitarian philosophy. It embraces the characteristics of political, feminist and dialogic communitarianism. Like Western political communitarianism, it emphasises the politics of the common good, social fairness and participation guided not by social contracts but by social obligations. *Ubuntuism's* moral 'rules' are grounded in community care, group understanding and group experience. As such *ubuntuism* strongly resembles feminist communitarianism's ethics of care, affection, intimacy, empathy and collaboration. Like Western communitarianism, as understood by for example, Paolo Freire, Martin Buber, and Levinas, *ubuntuism* emphasises that only through *dialogue* about what constitutes the common good we become fully human; that restoring dialogue should be the primary aim of humanity; that interaction between the self and the other should be the guiding principle in public life and of social ethics.

The kind of *ubuntu* journalism described above also closely resembles North American civic journalism founded on the philosophy of communitarianism. Like *ubuntuism,* civic journalism seeks to emphasise a close relationship between the media and the community. It is about establishing connections and contacts between journalists and the communities they cover; about trying to make citizens equal partners. Its purpose is to strengthen civic culture, to rejuvenate public life, to reach consensus rather than conflict, to involve citizens and journalists in an ongoing debate about the aims of journalism, and to treat the public it serves as co-citizens, not as consumers (see Dahlgren, 1998; Schaffer and Miller, 1995).

Similarly, the ideas of *ubuntuism* and the uniqueness of these ideas in terms of existing development and participatory communication theories need to be taken cognisance of. For example: How do the ideas of *ubuntuism*, as far as public communication is concerned, differ from Freire's participatory pedagogy? It can also be asked if and how all of the above differ from the classic Greek idea that the purpose of all public communication should be the promotion of knowledge about identity, belonging, sharing, ability, and the survival of the community in terms of and to the benefit of the community's shared religious, political, and civil values and responsibilities (see, for example, Rosenfield and Mader, 1984).

Consequently, those contemplating *ubuntuism* as a distinctive *African* way of thinking about the role and social responsibility of the media may find entrenched examples of such thinking in both the West and the East.

The point to be emphasised here is not the possible value or usability of *ubuntu* or elements of *ubuntu* as a framework for (global) media ethics, but rather that key elements of *ubuntu* as a moral philosophy cannot be advanced as being *exclusively* African.

4.2 The Changed Nature of Traditional African Culture and Values

Ubuntuism is a general, almost instinctive attitude towards life closely associated with *traditional* African cultures. Being a general attitude, it is not codified in a set of fixed rules or principles. Rather, it can be understood as the lived expression of an instinctive moral attitude and predisposition towards seeing and experiencing the self, others, life, and the world in a communitarian way. Clear rules on which to base professional codes of conduct, are thus difficult to specify. Whereas normative theory is usually based on a framework of ethical values derived from a religious doctrine and/or a political/ideological philosophy that may guide media practice, or with reference to which such practice may be evaluated, it is difficult to see how *ubuntuism* as a *lived moral attitude* could provide such a framework.

This is further complicated by the fact that in contemporary African life, neither the traditional values nor the traditional cultures associated with the idea of *ubuntuism*, or with *ubuntuism* as an attitude, may still exist in their pure form. Over a long period of time, traditional African cultures have been exposed to interaction with Christian and Islamic ethical thought which share numerous similarities with the communitarian values of *ubuntuism*. European colonialism has also, for the better or the worse, but undeniably, brought Africa into contact with new moral and cultural values, the modes of capitalist production, commodity trade and use, urbanisation, et cetera, all of which have eroded traditional African culture. Today, most of the African nations are part of the global economy or exposed to it. Although the residue of precolonial ethical theory may remain, Appiah (1998b) shows how all this makes it extremely difficult to atone *traditional* African ethical ideas about, for example, the community, with contemporary practical life and experiences. Both Appiah and Hamminga (2005, p. 19) argue that traditional communities in the true sense of the word have now almost disappeared and that such traditional values may be far removed from ordinary citizens' experiences.

Nonetheless, as already been referred to, much of what is being written about *ubuntu*, and much of what is being perceived to be the meaning and essence of *ubuntuism* as a possible framework for normative media theory, is motivated by an intellectual quest to rediscover and re-establish the idealised values of *traditional* African culture(s) and *traditional* African communities. Such a search for and idealisation of the past is characteristic of societies during times of turmoil and social and political transformation (see Popper, 1966). Plato, for example, advocated a return to the sublime and perfect state of prehistoric times. He feared that social progress led to moral decay. Other examples include Heraclitus's reaction to the break-up of Greek tribal life; Karl Marx's reaction to the European industrial revolution, Hegel's reaction to the French Revolution, and so on. They all idealised and romanticised a traditional past and traditional values.

After colonial emancipation, African political leaders and thinkers such as Kenneth Kaunda (Zambia), Julius Nyerere (Tanzania), Leopold Senghor (Senegal) and Mobutu Sese Seko (Zaire), likewise emphasised African traditions which, according to them, placed a high value on *ubuntuism*, humanism, negritude and authenticity. Phiri (2006), here paraphrased, summarises these leaders' emphasis on traditional values as follows:

Kaunda preached the necessity of retaining the principles of humaneness or *ubuntu* which, according to him, characterised the African past. He urged that the high value placed in traditional African society(ies) on *humanness* should not be lost in the new emancipated Africa and that this value was "without any sense of false pride" better placed to affect the achievement of a modern ideal society. For Nyerere the African tribal society was the ideal to which modern Tanzania should aspire because all individuals in that society worked for the common good and did not desire to dominate each other. To avoid the emergence of cut-throat capitalism the new Tanzania needed to be built on the African philosophy of *Ujamaa*, or family-hood, which recognises that the whole society is a mere extension of the basic family unit where each member looks after the interests of everyone else. Senghor's ideology of *negritude* was premised upon the rehabilitation of the African past, mystifying it and glorifying some aspects of that worldview through a nostalgic painting of "the imaginary beauty and harmony" that may have existed in the traditional society. Mobutu's emphasis of *authenticity* was meant to encourage Zairians to return to "authentic" African culture through a search for ancestral values and integrating these with suitable foreign ideals.

However, ideal as the above may sound, Phiri (2006) shows how this emphasis on traditional values led these leaders to constrain foreign influences and ideas through various means, including the nationalisation and tight control of the media. They allowed limited equality and democratic participation. Instead of individualism, they promoted communalism and group-thinking.

For Popper (1966, p. 19), this kind of "historicism" runs the risk of seeing social change as social decay and moral degeneration. He shows how it can lead to the establishment of a closed society with rigid institutions, rigid social customs, irrational attitudes towards social life, no room for criticism, and no room for individuals to take personal responsibility for their lives. In such societies, the social group, or the tribe, is everything while the individual is reduced to nothing. In such closed and collectivist societies the institutions are unchallengeable, sacrosanct, magical and based and managed on principles of taboos.

Despite romanticising past traditional values, the African leaders referred to above did not succeed in changing the destiny of many of its citizens. To the contrary, and despite the emphasis on humanness, togetherness and collectivity, famine and genocide continue in many parts of Africa. One of the reasons for this may be that citizens who have been exposed to international influences over a period of decades, no longer share or even know what the *traditional* African values their leaders (and/or intellectuals) may have wanted to cultivate, entail.

4.3 The Political Misuse of Moral Philosophy

Ubuntuism or any moral philosophy can easily be misused or hijacked for ideological and political agendas. The misuse of Christian nationalism by the apartheid government in its claims for a patriotic media in the service of *volk en vaderland* is a case in point (see Fourie, 2002; Hachten & Giffard, 1984). Here, three threats relating to the ideological and political misuse of moral philosophy are highlighted: the danger of intolerance, the danger of indigenising theory not for the purpose of the development of theory, but as a political act, and the danger of masquerading a moral philosophy as part of being politically correct.

4.3.1 The Danger of Intolerance

In writing about communitarianism, and given the close relationship between *ubuntuism* and communitarianism, Buchanan (1998, p. 2) warns that communitarianism as an ethic and as a political philosophy (in its negative use) stands in fundamental opposition to the philosophy of liberalism. He writes: "The success of communitarianism as an ethical theory depends upon whether an account of ethical reasoning can be developed that emphasises the importance of social roles and cultural values in the justification of moral judgements without lapsing into an extreme ethical relativism that makes fundamental ethical criticism of one's own community impossible."

Similarly, authors such as Mbigi and Maree (1995, p. 58) warn that *ubuntuism* can easily lapse into an intolerance of any oppositional opinion or deed, including an intolerance of media criticism and exposure. When "individual conformity and loyalty to the group is indiscriminately demanded and expected, (then) the dark side of *ubuntu* means failure to do so will meet harsh punitive measures such as the 'Dunlop treatment' or 'necklacing' (a burning car tire around the neck of an accused, used in the apartheid era against alleged state collaborators – PJF); the burning of houses and assassination".

As any moral philosophy, *ubuntuism* as an ethical framework is thus prone to political misuse. It can be used to subvert constitutionally entrenched freedom of expression into a form of qualified freedom of expression in the same way a liberal constitution can be circumvented by coopting party loyalists in key judiciary and regulatory positions. Freedom of expression can be circumvented if such freedom is only interpreted from an *ubuntu* perspective and thus as a freedom first and foremost in the service of community values.

4.3.2 The Danger of Indigenising Theory

Urging people to develop indigenous media theory is nothing new. Nain (2000) shows how there have been numerous attempts in Asia, for example, to develop Asian theories of communication and the media and to consider Asian values and Confucianism as viable alternatives to so-called Western values and Western civilisation (see the earlier discussion of comparative theory).

More often than not the results were dubious. Predictably, many of these attempts have been conservative, jingoistic, and 'anti-West', ending up in legitimising repressive regimes, undemocratic practices and tightly controlled media systems whose raison d'être is to uphold and help perpetuate these regimes (Nain, 2000, p. 149).

The same could happen in South Africa with the expectation to develop African media theories. Many examples can be cited of how politicians, union leaders, and members of the public criticise Western news values and journalistic practices (and the teaching thereof), usually with reference to the media's reporting of corruption, nepotism, and malpractices by government officials. It is often in this context that the ideal of an *ubuntu* ethic is encouraged as an ideal ethical framework for the South African media, and to report from 'an African perspective'.

What is meant with an 'African perspective'? If it means that a sound understanding of African culture, the continent's history, its achievements, problems and needs should inform journalists' reporting and academic enquiry, and that African journalists should present a more balanced picture of Africa than non-African journalists and news organisations may do, then an 'African perspective' is commendable. If, however, it means a distortion and an abstention of facts to suit a specific ideology, justified against the background of the principles of a moral philosophy then it is unacceptable, because *ubuntu* is like all moral philosophies often the victim of ideological and political misuse. As Mathatha Tsedu (2005, p. 14), interim chairperson of the The African Editors Forum (TAEF) in 2005, commented at a conference of African editors held in Kempton Park, Johannesburg: "The practice of sunshine journalism is a negation of responsibility. Africa has a history of the misuse of power and no right-thinking journalist can justify a media that subject it to the government of the day".

4.3.3 The Danger of Political Correctness

In South Africa's processes of political and social transformation, often referred to or understood to mean the Africanisation of the South African society, the prescription of *ubuntuism* as a framework for media practice can easily be seen as an act of political correctness. In this regard, Jansen (2004) warns that critical questions need to be asked about the concept of "Africanisation", closely related to the idea of "de-Westernisation" and "indigenising" theory. Isn't Africanisation simply a new mode of conducting inclusion/exclusion politics? Is Africanisation anything other than an essentialist response to ethnic politics and ethnic identity in South Africa? Has the Africanisation agenda taken account of the more powerful counter-force of globalisation? Does the Africanisation agenda recognise and include the multiplicity of ways of being an African, of being a South African?

In other words, is or can a white South African be an African and adopt the philosophy of *ubuntuism*, despite his/her European descent? These questions are politically loaded and dangerous in a young democracy and in a South Africa still struggling to free itself from its racist past. Consequently, care should be taken that *ubuntuism,* being predisposed to political misuse, is not captured and abused in the name of Africanisation and simply as an act of political correctness.

4.4 Practical Implications of an *Ubuntu* Framework for Media Performance

From the discussion of the nature of *ubuntuism* and the kind of journalism it may have as a consequence it is evident that an *ubuntu* interpretation of how the media should behave may have fundamental consequences for the way in which the media may be expected to operate. This may involve a redefinition of what news is and of dealing with news values and concepts such as frequency, threshold, unambiguity, consonance, continuity, et cetera. Would these values need to be reinterpreted and what could the consequences of such reinterpretations be for media practice? To begin with, consulting the community and seeking the community's consent on every issue, even if the journalist is part of and in close contact with a community, is not practical in terms of standardised and almost universally accepted professional practices, even if these practices are not above criticism.

In a study about news in South Africa Du Plessis (2005) found that across the ethnic, linguistic and racial spectrum, political, economic, public, and personal relevance were, like in other parts of the world, the most important constructs in South Africans' perceptions of what constitutes news and newsworthiness. The question thus arises: How would South African journalists and media audiences respond to a form of journalism in which the emphasis is on the value of news for a community as defined by the community in a society characterised by increasing global connectedness, diversity, and heterogeneity?

If the focus should be on the community as an *ubuntu* approach may prescribe, then note should be taken of South Africa's experiences with community media. Despite community-oriented policy[4] emphasising community involvement and participation, shared community values, and shared responsibility, these media (with the exception of a few successful cases) were subjected to the realities of media economics and dynamics shortly after they had been established. The same experience holds for civic journalism (in its different forms and manifestations), which has not been able to disassociate itself from the realities of media economics and the impact and effects of the dominant market paradigm. These (community) media often experience problems with enhancing and keeping alive citizens' involvement, shortly after they have been established.

Finally, if normative theory is about criteria according to which the media should ideally function in order to serve the public's interest in a responsible way, and even though such criteria and the assessment thereof may increasingly be difficult to formulate in the changing social and media environments, thinking about *ubuntuism* as an ethical framework would have to consider how key constructs, principles, and practices related to the media and media performance, such as the following (see McQuail, 1995), will be defined and assessed in an *ubuntu* framework: the freedom of the media, including the impact thereof on censorship, freedom of reception, freedom to obtain information, the independence of the media, and the freedom to formulate editorial policies, diversity in terms of content, variety, choice, access, and in terms of the media being a forum for different interests and point of views, the relevancy of information, objectivity, accuracy, honesty, reliability, and fairness.

4.5 Normative Theory and *Ubuntuism* in a Globalised World

The last question (for the purpose of this chapter) is: How viable is an *ubuntu* framework in the context of the international revision of normative theory and the investigation of the possibility of a global media ethic? From the earlier discussion of both the postmodern and postcolonial perspectives it is clear that normative media theory and media ethics can no longer be based on a single worldview;

that it can no longer be derived from a simple notion of "the press" or "the media" given the context of great diversity (McQuail, 1995, p. 239); that the profound transformation of the media landscape has changed journalism and increased the relevance of entertainment (popular culture) in public life; and, that the nature of the public itself has changed and continues to change (Brants, 1998, pp. 1–6). Given the realities of the new media environment, it may thus be short-sighted to think of a specific indigenous moral philosophy such as *ubuntuism* as an answer for a specific society and even less as an answer to the global questions and problems of media ethics. This, however, does not exclude the possibility of assimilating principles of the *ubuntu* morality in a global media ethic, especially its emphasis on the well-being of the community.

As far as South Africa is concerned, it should be remembered that it is a society marked by diversity and that it has a modern media system which seeks to cater for a vast range of tastes and needs. There are many examples of how not only the public (broadcaster) and community media, who are legally mandated to fulfil social responsibilities such as to contribute to development, moral upliftment and revival and nation-building, but how also the *private* and *commercial* media contribute on an ongoing basis to the development and nation building needs of the country, including fostering a culture of human rights and democracy in a country previously divided along racial and ethnic lines. An abundance of media messages support in one way or another the idea of nation building. The messages are carried by print, broadcast, advertisements, soap operas, talk and phone-in programmes, films, media and government campaigns, et cetera. It is thus possible to identify a clear South African development and nation building discourse and a distinctive dialogue in telling and debating the country and its peoples' histories, fears, hopes and ideals. In short, in telling these stories the media as a whole are contributing to a process of "narrative accrual" (see Attwood, 1996), meaning that through diverse media messages the South African story is told and retold. By so doing, the media's constitution of the South African nation unfolds as being a nation aware of, involved in, and committed to the undoing of its past wrongs and to focus on a better future for all its people.

All this happens in the context of a freer media regulatory environment than has been the case under apartheid (at least for the time being). It happens without any ethical codes based on a moral philosophy or any professional codes forced from above on the media. There are thus ample examples of how a diversity of South African media serves a diversity of communities as well as the broader South African community.

5. Conclusion

In this chapter it was argued that the media and media dynamics of South Africa are highly modernised and, in terms of almost universal trends and developments, on a par with those in the West (and the East – see in this regard, for example, Ma, 2000). In addition, the complexity of the South African society lies in the fact that it is both a developed First World country and a developing (underdeveloped) Third

World country with great diversities and heterogeneity, be it in terms of wealth and poverty, cultures, languages, life styles, et cetera. It has a capitalist economic system, including a media system fully entrenched in Western political economy, and it is governed according to the values and structures of Western democracy.

As far as the nature of *ubuntuism* as a moral philosophy and a framework for media ethics is concerned, it was argued that *ubuntuism* can be understood as a lived expression of an instinctive moral attitude and predisposition towards seeing and experiencing the self, others, life, and the world in a communitarian way. As such, it is difficult to derive specific principles on the basis of which *ubuntuism* can serve as a framework for normative media theory and ethical practice. This is further complicated by the fact that many of the *traditional* values on which the idea of *ubuntuism* is based, may no longer form part of the contemporary African experience. Against the background of a case study of the kind of journalism *ubuntu* may have as a consequence, it was concluded that contemplating *ubuntuism* as an ethical framework would need to consider: the consequences of misusing *ubuntuism* for political and ideological reasons; whether and how *ubuntuism* differs from philosophies such as communitarianism; whether media development and participatory communications theory do not incorporate the ideas of *ubuntuism*; the practical implications *ubuntuism* as an ethical framework may have for what can be seen as universal media practices; constructs and principles related to, for example, freedom of expression, the social responsibility of the media, objectivity, neutrality, et cetera.

Although the idea of postcolonial studies to decolonise Western epistemology, including the dominant way of thinking about the media, may accentuate the need for the media to focus on Africa and to do so from an African perspective, is worthy, the realities of cultural assimilation and globalisation must be acknowledged. This has been proven in other parts of the world where similar expectations to de-westernise media theory have not been able to produce an alternative to what is now, almost universally, accepted as the role of the media in democracy – not that the ways in which the media practise this role are above criticism.

In the light of all this, the chapter concludes that instead of contemplating a moral philosophy as an ethical framework emphasis in South African media policy, normative media theory and in media ethics should be placed on *difference* and *diversity*. By accepting difference (different publics, different public spheres, different audiences, different media), discussion about the South African media would be on par with the realities of the South African society and its media. The challenge would be to search for those common human values that bind all human beings on the basis of which a normative media theory and ethics could begin to be developed in a non-prescriptive and non-pedantic way. Such an approach need not hinder the South African media in fulfilling its social responsibilities related to the development and nation-building needs of the country and its people, nor to interpret South African realities against the background of a sound understanding of Africa from an African perspective. Neither would it prohibit the media and South Africans to honour *ubuntuism's* values of humanness, the public good, dialogue, and consensus. The above 'solution' may also serve as a point of departure in the contemplation of a global media ethic.

Notes

1   Simply defined *ubuntuism* means sharing and belonging. Whereas in contemporary Western philosophy the emphasis is on the individual, *ubuntuism* emphasises the individual's role in and contribution to the/a community. The individual is defined in terms of his/her community.
2   This chapter is a revised version of the following articles published by the author: Moral philosophy as the foundation of normative media theory: The case of African *ubuntuism*, *Communications*, 32 (2007), pp. 1–29; (Publisher: Walter de Gruyter); *Ubuntuism* as a framework for South African media ethics: Can it work? *Communicatio: South African Journal for Communication Theory and Research*, 34(1) 2008, (Publisher: Routledge/ Unisa Press).
3   In ethics and political philosophy the term 'community' refers to a form of connectedness among individuals that is qualitatively stronger and deeper than a mere association. For Buchanan (1998) the concept of a community includes at least two elements: "(1) individuals belonging to a community have ends that are in a robust sense *common* and which is acknowledged by members of the group as common ends, and (2) for the individuals involved, their awareness of themselves as belonging to the group is a significant constituent of their identity, their sense of who they are."
4   To develop the community media sector in South Africa a Media Development and Diversity Agency (MDDA) (Act 14 of 2002) was set up. The Agency encourages ownership and control of, and access to media by historically disadvantaged communities, historically diminished indigenous language and cultural groups. It channels resources to community and small commercial media; encourages human resource development and capacity building in the media industry, especially amongst historically disadvantaged groups; and it encourages research regarding media development and diversity.

References

Ang, I. (1998). The performance of the sponge: Mass communication theory enters the post-modern world. In K. Brants, J. Hermes & L. van Zoonen (eds.), *The media in question: Popular cultures and public interests* (pp. 77–88). London: Sage.

Appiah, K.A. (1998a). African philosophy. In E. Craig (ed.). *Routledge Encyclopaedia of Philosophy*. London: Routledge. Retrieved 2005–09–12 from http://www.rep.routledge.com/article/Z018.

Appiah, K.A. (1998b). Ethical systems, African. In E. Craig (ed.). *Routledge Encyclopaedia of Philosophy*. London: Routledge. Retrieved 2005–09–12 from http://www.rep.routledge.com/article/Z018.

Attwood, B. (1996). (ed.). *In the age of Mabo: History, Aborigines and Australia*. Sydney: Allen and Unwin.

Bardoel, J & Brants, K. (2003). Public broadcasters and social responsibility in the Netherlands. In G.F. Lowe & T. Hujanen (eds.). *Broadcasting & convergence: New articulations of the public service remit* (pp. 167–186). Göteborg, Sweden: Nordicom.

Blankenberg, N. (1999). In search of real freedom: *Ubuntu* and the media. *Critical Arts*, 13(2), 42–65.

Brants, K. (1998). With the benefit of hindsight: Old nightmares and new dreams. In K. Brants, J. Hermes & L. van Zoonen (eds.), *The media in question: Popular cultures and public interests* (pp. 169–179). London: Sage.

Brants, K., Hermes, J. & van Zoonen, L. (eds.). (1998). *The media in question. Popular cultures and public interests*. London: Sage.

Bryant, J.M. (1996). *Moral codes and social structure in ancient Greece: A sociology of Greek ethics from Homer to the Epicureans and Stoics*. Albany, N.Y.: State University of New York Press.

Buchanan, A. (1998). Community and communitarianism. In E. Craig (ed.). *Routledge encyclopaedia of philosophy*. London: Routledge. Accessed 2005–09–22.

Christians, C.G. & Traber, M. (eds.). 1997. *Communication ethics and universal values*. Thousand Oaks, Calif.: Sage.

Christians, C.G. (2004). Ubuntu and communitarianism in media ethics. *Ecquid Novi*, 25(2), 235–256.

Christians, C.G. (2006). Ethical theory in communication research. *Journalism Studies*, 6(1), 3–14.

Crowley, D. and Mitchell, D. (eds.). (1995). *Communication theory today*. Cambridge: Polity Press.

Curran, J. and Park, M-J. (2000). *De-Westernizing media studies*. London: Routledge.

Dahlgren, P. (1998). Enhancing the civic ideal in television journalism. In K. Brants, J. Hermes & L. van Zoonen (eds.), *The media in question: Popular cultures and public interests* (pp. 89–100). London: Sage.

Du Plessis, D.F. (2005). What's news in South Africa? In P.J. Shoemaker & A.A. Cohen (eds.), *News around the world. Content, practitioners, and the public* (pp. 283–307). London: Routledge.

Fourie, P.J. (2002). Rethinking the role of the media in South Africa. *Communicare*, 21(1), 17–41.

Fourie, P.J. (2005). Towards linking normative theory, communication policy and audiences in South African communication research. *Communicatio: South African Journal of Communication Theory and Research*, 31(1), 13–33.

Fourie, P.J. (2007). Moral philosophy as the foundation of normative theory: The case of African Ubuntuism. *Communications*, 32, 1–29.

Fourie, P.J. (2008). Ubuntu as a framework for media ethics: Can it work? *Communicatio: South African Journal of Communication Theory and Research*, 34(1), 210–223.

Gunaratne, S.A. (2005). *The dao of the press: a humanocentric theory*. Cresskill, N.J.: Hampton Press.

Hachten, W.A. & Giffard, C.A. (1984). *Total onslaught. The South African press under attack*. Johannesburg: Macmillan.

Hallin, D.C., Mancini, P. (2004). *Comparing media systems. Three models of media and politics*. Cambridge: Cambridge University Press.

Hamminga, B. (2005). *Epistemology from the African point of view*. Retrieved 2005–04–15 from http://mindphiles.

Hartley, J. (1999). *Uses of television*. London: Routledge.

Jacka, E. (2003). "Democracy as defeat". The impotence of arguments for public service broadcasting. *Television and new media*, 4(2), 177–191.

Jansen, J. (2004). *The Africanisation of the curriculum. Is this a useful articulation of the problem?* Lecture presented at the University of South Africa. Pretoria, March 2004.

Kamwangamalu, N. (1999). *Ubuntu* in South Africa: a sociolinguistic perspective to a Pan-African concept, *Critical Arts*, 13(2), 24–41.

Kasoma, F. (1996). The foundations of African ethics (Afriethics) and the professional practice of journalism: The case for society-centred media morality. *Africa Media Review*, 10(3), 93–116.

Louw, D.J. (2004). *Ubuntu*: An African assessment of the religious other. Retrieved 2005–07–26 from http://www.bu.edu/wcp/Papers/AfriLouw.htm.

Ma, E.K. (2000). Rethinking media studies. The case of China. In J. Curran, & M-J. Park (eds.), *De-Westernizing Media-Studies* (pp. 21–35). London: Routledge.

Mak'Ochieng, M. (2006). Public communication in the national interest: A South African debate. *Communicatio: South African Journal for Communication Theory and Research*, 32(1), 155–169.

Maluleke, T.S. (2005). *Africanization of tuition at Unisa: A perspective from the College of Human Sciences*. Article presented at the Seminar on Africanisation, University of South Africa, 3 March 2005. Pretoria: Unisa.

Mangu, A.M.B. (2005). *Towards the African university in the service of humanity: Challenges and prospects for Africanisation at the University of South Africa*. Article presented at the Seminar on Africanisation, University of South Africa, 3 March 2005. Pretoria: Unisa.

Marshall, T. & Bottomore T. (eds.). (1992). *Citizenship and social class*. London: Pluto Press.

Mbigi, L. & Maree, J. (1995). *Ubuntu: The spirit of African transformation management*. Pretoria: Knowledge Resources.

McQuail, D. (1992). *Media performance. Mass communication and the public interest*. London: Sage.

McQuail, D. (1995). Mass communication and the public interest: Towards social theory for media structure and performance. In D. Crowley & D. Mitchell (eds.), *Communication theory today*. (pp. 235–253) Cambridge: Polity Press.

McQuail, D. (2000). *McQuail's mass communication theory*. 4th edition. London: Sage.

Nain, Z. (2000). Globalized theories and national controls. The state, the market, and the Malaysian media. In D. Crowley & D. Mitchell (eds.), *Communication theory today*. Cambridge: Polity Press.

Nordenstreng, K. (1997). Beyond the four theories of the press. In J. Servaes & R. Lie (eds.) *Media and politics in transition. Cultural identity in the age of globalization*, (pp. 97–109) Leuven: Acco.

Nussbaum, B. (2003). African culture and *ubuntu*. Reflections of a South African in America. World Business Academy, *Perspectives*, 17(1), 1–12.

Okigbo, C. (1996). Contextualising Freire in African sustainable development. *Africa Media Review*, 10(1), 31–54.

Phiri, S. (2006). Media for change? A critical examination of the Open Society Initiative for Southern Africa's (OSISA) support to the media: 1997–2002. Unpublished doctoral thesis. Pretoria: Department of Communication Science, University of South Africa.

Popper, K.R. (1966). *The open society and its enemies*, vol. 1: *The spell of Plato*. London: Routledge & Kegan Paul.

Ramose, M.B. (2002). The philosophy of *ubuntu* and *ubuntu* as a philosophy. In P.H. Coetzee & A.P.J. Roux (eds.), *Philosophy from Africa. A text with readings*, 2nd edition (pp. 230–38). Oxford: Oxford University Press.

Rosenfield, L. & Mader, T. (1984). The functions of human communication. In C. Arnold & J. Bowers (eds.), pp. 475–543 *Handbook of rhetorical and communication theory*. Boston, Mass.: Allyn & Bacon.

Schaffer, J. & Miller, E. (eds.). (1995). *Civic journalism. Six case studies*. Washington, D.C.: Pew Centre for Civic Journalism and the Poynter Institute.

Shome, R. & Hegde, R.S. (2002). Post-colonial approaches to communication: Charting the terrain, engaging the intersections, *Communication Theory*, 12(3), 249–270.

Shutte, A. (1993). *Philosophy for Africa*. Cape Town: UCT Press.

Shutte, A. (2001). *Ubuntu: An ethic for a new South Africa*. Pietermaritzburg: Cluster Publications.

Siebert, F.S. Peterson, T.B. & Schramm, W. (1956). *Four theories of the press*. Urbana, Ill.: University of Illinois Press.

Tsedu, M. (2005, October 15). Beeld van Afrika kom nie tot sy reg. *Beeld*, p.14.

Wasserman, H. & De Beer, A.S. (2004). Covering HIV/AIDS. Towards a heuristic comparison between communitarian and utilitarian ethics. *Communicatio: South African Journal for Communication Theory and Research*, 30(2), 84–98.

Wasserman, H. (2006). Globalized values and postcolonial responses: South African perspectives on normative media ethics. *International Communication Gazette*, 68(1), 71–91.

SECTION 3

Applications and Case Studies

8 Negotiating Journalism Ethics in Zambia: Towards a 'Glocal' Ethics

Fackson Banda

1. Introduction

This chapter argues that the practice of journalism ethics reflects the specificity of the context in question. The point of reference is the practice of journalism in Zambia which has been subjected to differing influences. These influences have manifested themselves in three interrelated historical epochs – colonial, post-colonial and globalisation (Banda, 2007). While the formal aspects of colonialism may end at the historical point of the colony's political independence, the effects of colonisation have much more profound legacies that must necessarily be endured by the postcolony.

Globalisation has resulted in debates about the possibility of a global ethics of journalism. Some debates focus on the comparability of media ethics across various geocultural regions of the world – Europe, the Middle East and the Islamic world (Hafez, 2002). Others hinge on the nature of post-9/11 journalism. The post-9/11 world requires reformulating and rethinking what journalism is and also whether there can be "universal ethical standards for journalism to meet the challenges of globalisation" (Rao & Lee, 2005). The very fact that media have become globalised requires re-examining the global basis of journalism ethics, especially as such media-connectedness has brought together a plurality of different religions, traditions, ethnic groups, values, and organisations with varying political agendas (Ward, 2005, p. 5).

Although journalistic practices in Zambia have been, and are, infused with "Northern standards" of journalism ethics (Kasoma, 1996), such global influences tend to be "refracted through the prism of historical and political contexts" (Banda, 2006, p. 466). My argument is theoretically inspired by the notion of glocalisation

(Robertson, 1992; 1995) and the concept of cultural hybridity (Bhabha, 1994; cf. Kraidy, 2003). Both conceptualisations are fired up by the motive force of postcolonialism (Werbner, 1997).

Firstly, I delineate the theoretical contours of glocalisation, underlining how it represents a formation of identity caught up between the external global influences and the exigencies of the locale. I further make the point that the so-called global influences are themselves not emanating from pure, unadulterated sources. They are, within their own contexts, hybrids of contested epistemic and ontological experiences. Secondly, I sketch the historical and contemporary context of media ethics in Zambia. Here, I highlight three historically interconnected ethical imperatives which seem to describe the media-ethical terrain from the colonial period to the present era of globalisation. Thirdly, I propose a contextual 'glocal' agenda for journalism ethics in Zambia.

2. Glocalisation: Inbetween Globalism and Nationalism

One cannot talk about *glocalisation* without evaluating globalisation, nor can one talk about it without re-evaluating the concept of national identity. Robertson (1992) hints at this tension when he distinguishes between the particular and the universal:

> The relationship between the universal and the particular must be central at this time to our comprehension of the globalization process and its ramifications....Much has been written about universality and universalism in recent years. On the one hand, those ideas have been looked upon with scepticism by communitarians, who are generally resistant to the claim that there can be viable bodies of universalistic ethics and morals. On the other hand, universalism has been rejected by many poststructuralist and postmodernist theories....At the same time, much has been written about particularity and particularism, difference, locality and, of course, community (1992, p. 97).

Given the tension highlighted by Robertson (1992), *globalisation* can be viewed as a contested term, often ending up being a site for hegemonic and counter-hegemonic articulations and re-articulations of reality. In *The myth of media globalization,* Hafez (2007) isolates three forms of cultural change associated with the globalisation debate. These are:
- The adoption of the "other" culture (above all in the form of "Westernised" globalisation);
- The influence of "glocalised" hybrid cultures, which are influenced both by global and local elements; and
- The revitalisation of traditional and other local cultures as a reaction to globalisation (p.14).

According to Hafez, the problem is not so much about the external global influences or the internal traditional character of culture; it is about determining the content and dynamics of the hybrid category 'glocalisation'. Within the context of this problematic, it is possible to comprehend Robertson's definition of *globalisation* as referring "both to the compression of the world and the intensification of consciousness of the world as a whole (1992, p. 8). As a "compression of the world", across time and space, the concept of globalisation can be discussed in terms of the interconnectedness of societies across a range of five dimensions of global cultural flows that can be termed (a) ethnoscapes, (b) mediascapes, (c) technoscapes, (d) financescapes, and (e) ideoscapes (Appadurai, 1996, p. 33).

As an aspect of the intensification of consciousness of the world as a whole, globalisation can be seen as a site of evolutionary action and revolutionary reaction. This idea, seemingly evident in Gidden's (1990) characterisation of globalisation as "a dialectical phenomenon, in which events at one pole of a distanciated relation often produce divergent or contrary occurrences at another", is softened by Robertson's suggestion of a more nuanced analysis that captures the complexities of the global-local theme (Robertson, 1995, p. 27). I have already hinted at the complexities involved in defining, for example, 'national identity'. However, despite this caution by Robertson, the argument can still be advanced in that the process of globalisation, with its associated institutions and symbols, almost always ignites *reaction* from the recipient societies. To acknowledge this fact is to admit that global influences are almost always enmeshed in the counter-hegemonic responses of the 'other'.

For example, the 'export' of liberal democracy that accompanies globalisation is seen by some proponents of the media/cultural imperialism thesis (cf. Herman & McChesney, 1997) as tending towards the universalisation of Western culture. This is often aided by Hollywood, television, pop music, fashion and global news networks such as CNN and the BBC World Service. The symbols associated with liberal democracy – freedom, rights, welfare, sovereignty, elections, representation, environmental protection, cosmopolitanism, and democracy (Appadurai, 1996, p. 36; Sardar & Van Loon, 2004, pp. 162–163) – are thus mediated by global media which act as the new missionaries of corporate capitalism (Herman & McChesney, 1997). The reaction to such mediated symbols is often revolutionary, sometimes consisting of the violent destruction of the symbols of capitalism by anti-globalisation movements. At other times, the resistance is manifested through an affirmation of cultural specificity, as evidenced through the discourse of "Asian values" (Sardar & Van Loon, 2004, p. 166).

Herein lies the motive force behind the idea of glocalisation. Globalisation seems to present a paradox of consequences. While it tends towards homogenisation, often associated with the financial hegemony of the US transnational corporations, it also tends towards what is variously referred to as "heterogenization, hybridization, fuzziness, *mélange*, cut-and-mix, criss-cross and crossover" (Rantanen, 2005, p. 93). Robertson (1992) puts this dialectic aptly when he discounts the notions of "relativism" and "worldism" in favour of preserving "direct attention *both* to particularity and difference *and* to universality and homogeneity". He argues that "we are, in the late twentieth century, witnesses to – and participants in – a massive, two-fold process involving the interpenetration of the universalisation of particularism and the particularisation of universalism" (p. 100). By implication, a focus on 'relativism' would discount any possibility of looking at the world in its diversity. Conversely, a focus on 'worldism' would treat the whole world as one undifferentiated unit of analysis.

What, then, is *glocalisation*? Firstly, as noted above, Robertson (1995) takes it for granted that the debate about global homogenisation versus heterogenisation should be transcended. According to him, "it is not a question of *either* homogenization or heterogenization, but rather of the ways in which both of these two tendencies have become features of life across much of the late-twentieth-century world" (p. 28). Secondly, following from this, Robertson sees glocalisation, originating in Japanese business, as involving the "simultaneity and the interpenetration of what are conventionally called the global and the local, or...the universal and the particular". He sees glocalisation as "an aspect of globalization" (Robertson, 1995, p. 30), "the complex interplay of the global and the local that acknowledges many of the positive aspects that globalization has forced onto local communities" (Creeber, 2004, p. 34).

To demonstrate how the global and the local enmesh, Robertson (1995, pp. 34, 37) gives a series of examples drawn from history:
- Much of the national-state organisation of societies, including the form of their particularities – the construction of their unique identities – is very similar across the entire world, in spite of much variation in levels of development;
- The Global Forum in Brazil in 1992, which surrounded the official United Nations Earth Summit; and
- The attempt by the World Health Organisation (WHO) to promote "world health" by the reactivation and, if need be, the invention of "indigenous" local medicine.

Much of the debate about the paradoxical interface between the global and the local is implicated in the thesis of cultural hybridity. Jan Nederveen Pietersen (1995, p. 45) views globalisation as "a process of hybridization which gives rise to a global mélange", a mixture of often incongruous elements. In the face of globalisation, the notion of nationalism, as a form of bounded cultural identity and identification, is itself subject to a postmodernist rapture. The "fluid, irregular shapes" of Appadurai's cultural "landscapes" (Appadurai, 1996, p. 33) "have intensified cross-cultural contact and spawned a dual process of cultural fusion and fragmentation increasingly captured with the vocabulary of hybridity" (Kraidy & Murphy, 2003, p. 300). For example, Bhabha (1994) rejects the concept of the nation and its implied homogeneity of identification, stressing the position of the migrant who is caught up in two places and maintains a double perspective on social reality. He prefers the concept of cultural hybridity, which places the migrant in a position that transcends the universalising or totalising tendencies of both modernist liberal democracy and Marxist historicism (Sardar & Van Loon, 2004).

As Bhabha (1994, p. 38) suggests, it is possible for people, especially migrants, to be located in the "Third Space", transcending the politics of polarity and emerging as others of ourselves. As such, "hybridity not only displaces the history that creates it, but sets up new structures of authority and generates new political initiatives" (Sardar & Van Loon, 2004, p. 120). In this vein, the modernist notions of stable, bounded national cultures are destabilised in favour of more heterogeneous formations of national identity, allowing for "interpenetrated globalization" (Braman, 1996, p. 27) and Bakhtin's "unconscious, organic hybridity" (in Werbner, 1997, p. 4).

For their part, Kraidy and Murphy (2003) call for an "ethnographic approach to the local-global nexus" because it "is useful to the extent that it contextualizes different hybridities and thus moves away from grand theories such as 'cultural imperialism' and 'cultural globalization' towards a more contextualized and comparative approach to the operation of power in culture" (p. 301, cf. Kraidy, 2003). According to Robertson (1995), the cultural-imperialistic accusation that globalisation carries Western, mostly American, cultural messages can be countered as follows:

* Messages emanating from the West are differentially received and interpreted;
* Major alleged producers of "global" culture increasingly tailor their products to a differentiated market;
* There is evidence of "national" symbolic resources for differentiated global interpretation and consumption; and
* The flow of ideas and practices from the so-called "Third World" to the seemingly dominant societies and regions is underestimated (pp. 38–39).

As Appadurai (1996, p. 17) suggests:

> Globalization does not necessarily or even frequently imply homogenization or Americanization, and to the extent that different societies appropriate the material of modernity differently, there is still ample room for the deep study of specific geographies, histories and languages.

The most vigorous debates on the dynamics of difference in contemporary culture have occurred within the field of postcolonial theory (Papastergiadis, 1997, p. 273; Kraidy & Murphy, 2003). It is not my intention here to dwell at length on postcolonialism. I signal it in order to show that the discussion about evolving global media ethics can be viewed as part of a broader societal debate, grounded in the experience of colonialism and its post-independence legacy. There is an abundance of literature on postcolonial theory (cf. Loomba, 2005; Quayson, 2000; Walder, 1998; Talib, 2000).

Zambia presents a case in which the processes of globalisation, localisation and glocalisation seem implicated in ways that require systematic exposition. Colonialism represented a more geographically defined aspect of imperial globalisation; the postcolonial period between the 1960s and the 1980s marked the intensification of nationalistic responses to the legacy of colonialism; and the postcolonial period from the 1990s onwards became a marker of a more glocalised, diversified response to international pressure for media and other political reforms. By examining these features, it is possible to discern possible trajectories for the search for global media ethics.

3. A Historical Contextualisation of Media Ethics

My description of the media-ethical landscape in Zambia is largely based on participant observations. I was involved in coordinating some of the debates that led to the formation of the Media Council of Zambia (MECOZ). I was appointed secretary to the MECOZ board. I can now assume the critical position of a researcher and the interpretive stance of an insider. My observations can illustrate the tension between the seemingly globalised libertarian values that impinge upon media practice in Zambia and the cultural-relativist responses to those values.

In 2004, the Media Institute of Southern Africa (MISA) Zambia and the Press Association of Zambia (PAZA) set up the Media Council of Zambia (MECOZ). Though still fledgling, MECOZ represents a milestone in negotiating the *institutional* character of journalism ethics in the country. MECOZ has not attracted much positive attention from the public. The few complaints lodged were largely against the privately owned *The Post* newspaper. But *The Post* is not an institutional member of MECOZ and is therefore not subject to the jurisdiction of MECOZ. In addition, the MECOZ members did not seem sufficiently committed. Such a situation does not allow for the flourishing of a media council. As Rønning observes, the effectiveness of a press council in promoting responsible reportage while safeguarding essential press freedoms may be judged, among other things, according to the degree to which newspapers comply with the council's decisions (Rønning & Kasoma, 2002, p. 66).

The following anecdote illustrates the tension I have alluded to above. In 2005, the House of Chiefs complained bitterly against a columnist on the state-owned *Sunday Mail*. The columnist Nigel Mulenga described the chiefs as a bunch of uneducated villagers who could not even sing the national anthem properly, and whose only desire was to squeeze money out of the taxpayers. The background to this article was a news story that alleged that some chiefs were asking the government to give them allowances for their official duties (F. Chembo, personal communication, May 20, 2005).

The MECOZ adjudication committee found the columnist 'guilty' of professional impropriety, in accordance with the MECOZ code of ethics jointly developed and adopted by MISA Zambia and PAZA. The judgement invoked Clause 10.10 which enjoins upon journalists to "respect the moral and cultural values of the Zambian society", concluding that the House of Chiefs needed to be held in high esteem as a symbol of Zambia's cultural and traditional authority.

The judgement also upheld the need for journalists to "defend the principle of freedom of the media in relation to the collection of information and the expression of comment and criticism". To this end, the judgement stated that even the House of Chiefs was not immune from comment and criticism, albeit "fairly, accurately and objectively". The MECOZ board urged the newspaper to publish a full apology to the House of Chiefs (F. Chembo, personal communication, May 20, 2005). The *Sunday Mail* did not accept the ruling, ostensibly because the MECOZ adjudication committee had not given them an opportunity to exculpate themselves. This case, coupled with the *Post*'s reluctance to submit to the jurisdiction of MECOZ, presented special legitimacy problems for the ethics body. This test case was to account for subsequent debates about the desirability of non-statutory media self-regulation. It raised fundamental questions about the *interpretation* of the Western libertarian-journalistic view of media as 'watchdogs' over all forms of authority, on the one hand, and the local demand for respect for 'the moral and cultural values of Zambian society embodied in traditional leadership', on the other hand.

Central to this dilemma is the question of *who* determines the boundaries of application of journalistic ethical standards, and why. This question is partly addressed by examining the historical and political context within which ethical orientations are implicated. I discuss three interlocking historical-ethical imperatives: (i) liberalist-colonial, (ii) nationalist-postcolonial, and (iii) neo-liberal ethical imperatives.

3.1 The Liberalist-Colonial Ethical Imperative

This historico-ethical imperative refers to the normative journalistic framework of intense colonial-imperialist practices of journalism ethics, discernible in the Zambian context from the period of British colonialism in the 1940s up to the point of Northern Rhodesian (Zambian) independence in the 1960s.[1] The ethical imperative here was dictated by the libertarian principles of press freedom, individual liberty, capitalism, et cetera followed by the media in the colonising nation – this seems to be consistent with most literature analysing the nature of colonial media in Africa (cf. Hachten, 1971; Gecau, 1996). As Hachten (1971, p. 147) observes, a major development of the 1940s was the entry of foreign newspaper capital into West African journalism. The London *Daily Mirror* group used its financial and technical resources to establish three West Coast dailies – the *Daily Times* in Nigeria, the *Daily Graphic* in Ghana, and the *Daily Mail* in Sierra Leone.

The policy of these papers was vigorous neutrality between the competing parties: objective reporting of news by African reporters and editors; constructive criticism; volume production; and territory-wide distribution, using air transport for remote areas. According to Hachten (1971, p. 147), such papers were instrumental in establishing a more professional basis for the press and tended to link literate Africans with their new nationalist leaders. In other words, the media was an elite project, reproducing a typically Western-oriented libertarian ethical framework and reinforced by a local elite socialised into the culture of liberal journalism. As Bourgault (1995), citing Ainslie (1966), observes of the *Central African Mail*, it was never really an African paper in the sense of being fully African controlled. It continued to bear the clear stamp of liberal British values which it inherited from the *Observer*.

It was on such papers that 'libertarians' like Zambia's Kelvin Mlenga were to serve, compelling him to remark, some years later as editor of the then *Zambian Mail*: "It is my view that a newspaper owned and run by the State for the purpose of spreading Government propaganda is valueless. A newspaper must have freedom to disagree…with Government policy.…If a Government wants to keep its finger on the pulse of public opinion, it is vital that there should be a free Press in the country…" (in Ainslie, 1966, pp. 19–20). So the central ethical concept to emerge from the colonial era was libertarianism, stressing editorial independence and the Fourth Estate role of the media.

3. 2 The Nationalist-Postcolonial Ethical Imperative

The nationalist-postcolonial ethical imperative was dominant in the period immediately after the end of British colonialism. Its more overt manifestation was the nationalisation of private media and their transformation into mouthpieces of the postcolonial state (Banda, 2003). The ethical imperative, during this period, was influenced by the ideology of national identification and unification sweeping across the newly independent nations of Africa. The media were seen as instruments in forging and sustaining a unified national identity.

This was reflective of similar tendencies across Africa. For example, President Jomo Kenyatta of Kenya urged the press to "always seek to coalesce, rather than to isolate, the different cultures and aspirations and standards of advancement which make up our new nation" (in Wilcox, 1975, p. 26). An important part of this process was the evolution of some politico-philosophical aphorisms to rally the media around the project of national unity and development. The following ideologies each contributed in differing ways to an elucidation of the character of African unity and development: *African Personality* in Ghana; *Negritude* in Senegal; *Harambee* (national unity) in Kenya; *Ujamaa* (togetherness) in Tanzania (Wilcox, 1975, p. 27; Friedland & Rosberg, 1964; Senghor, 2000); *Humanism* (man-centredness) in Zambia; and *Chimurenga* (resistance) in Zimbabwe (cf. Mkandawire, 2005).

Here, it is important to stress that *Negritude* and *African Personality* provided a powerful politico-cultural framework for a strategic essentialisation of African identity and value system (McLeod, 2000; cf. Spivak, 1988). The project of colonial imperialism was, in one sense, a project of what Senghor (2000) decried as "a universal civilisation" (p. 102). As such, he invoked the *essence* of blackness, consisting in "the whole complex of civilised values – cultural, economic, social, and political – which characterise the black peoples" or "the Negro-African world". Senghor was opposed to the French colonialist policy of cultural assimilation precisely because it assumed a universality of application, denying the "black Frenchmen" so assimilated the right to their cultural identity and geopolitical specificity.

This essentialist definition of blackness resonated with Nkrumah's *African Personality* which consisted in Africans developing their "own African personality" and asserting their "own ways of life…customs, traditions and cultures" (in Mutiso & Rohio, 1975, p. 58). This cultural nationalism was aimed at asserting African cultures as the basis of the nationalists' struggles for liberation from colonial rule, mapping out their own unique cultural characteristics as a people (Mutiso & Rohio, 1975, p. xii).

In the newly independent Zambia, this ethical vision for the media, underpinned by a strong anti-colonial and development-journalistic rhetoric (Bourgault, 1995, p. 162), was articulated by then President Kenneth Kaunda. In setting out his ethical vision for the media, President Kaunda castigated the media for failing to reflect Zambian society and for sometimes conducting themselves as if they were an alternative government. He observed that the news media everywhere else in the world reflected the interests and values of the society they served (Kasoma, 1986, pp.104–105).

In Africa as a whole, the ethical debate became implicated in the ideology of "positive neutrality and non-alignment" (in Mutiso & Rohio, 1975, pp. 659–662) whereby the newly independent African countries professed not to take sides in the Cold War but proactively engage the United Nations for world peace. Spurred on by the Non-Aligned Movement (NAM), the Pan-African News Agency (PANA) was created by the Organisation of African Unity (OAU)[2] in 1979. PANA's aims were "to rectify the distorted image of Africa created by the international news agencies and to let the voice of Africa be heard on the international news scene" (in Bourgault, 1995, p. 175). Prior to the formation of PANA, in 1976, the Non-Aligned Movement (NAM) had set up the Non-Aligned Agencies News Pool whose primary news was about international diplomacy, wars, emergencies of various kinds, political and news of other countries (Mytton, 1983, p. 30).

To summarise: the practice of journalism and the determination of ethical questions among many state-owned media organisations are, even today, influenced by the nationalist-postcolonial ethical imperative of national unity and development. This is perpetuated, in part, by the legal and administrative structures inherited from the colonial era (Banda, 1997, pp. 10–11). But this ethical imperative conflicts sharply with the globalised libertarian ethical imperative.

3.3 The Neo-Liberalist Ethical Imperative

From the 1990s onwards, the debate shifted back to a reformulation of what was basically the liberalist-colonial ethical imperative. This recasting was associated with the process of globalisation, interpreted as the interconnectedness of the world through a series of disjunctive global flows of ethnoscapes, mediascapes, technoscapes, financescapes and ideoscapes (Appadurai, 1996, p. 33).

For the purpose of this discussion, globalisation is seen as representing a type of libertarian media culture. Libertarianism, although often varied in detail, typically centres on policies in favour of extensive personal liberties, advocating either limiting or entirely eliminating the power and scope of the state in order to maximise individual liberty (Narveson, 1988). Libertarianism thus lends itself to the economic policies of deregulation, privatisation and commercialisation, which have reconfigured the media landscape in most of sub-Saharan Africa since the 1990s (Banda, 2006).

But the globalising libertarian ethical values, although succeeding in rupturing the nationalist-postcolonial meta-ethical narrative of national unity and development, nevertheless became refracted in the murky waters of the fast changing media politics of the country. What emerged from this conflagration was a hybridisation of normative ethical orientations and practices. This point is particularly important when viewed against the fact that the so-called global influences are themselves not emanating from pure, unadulterated sources. They are, within their own contexts, hybrids of contested epistemic and ontological experiences. In short: glocalisation can be seen as the *unpredictability* of globalisation.

4. Towards a Glocalised Zambian Mediascape

Following from the above discussion of the neo-liberal ethical imperative, and the unpredictability that attended its onslaught on the Zambian media landscape, I now turn to discuss three cases of interpenetration of global-local media phenomena. These are: (i) the internationalisation of libertarian normative ethics; (ii) the libertarian-communitarian dialectic; and (iii) state resistance to libertarian normative media ethics.

4.1 The Internationalisation of Libertarian Normative Ethics

The return to multi-party politics in 1990, with its attendant liberalisation of political space, led to the formation of multiple civil society organisations. These included local non-governmental organisations (NGOs), such as the Zambia Elections Monitoring Coordinating Committee (ZEMCC). US-based organisations, with support from the United States Agency for International Development (USAID), also set up local branches. One such organisation was the National Democratic Institute (NDI).

USAID sub-contracted some of its 'Democratic Governance' cluster of funding to the US-based Southern University. The Chief-of-Party of the project was always an American. The intended or unintended consequence of this situation was that the American brand of libertarian media was imprinted upon any media-and-democracy work carried out within the country. Even the local NGOs were funded by outside agencies, which included the European Union (EU). Given the multiple donor agendas involved, it was going to prove impossible for the country to carry on with the meta-discourse of national unity and development (cf. Kasoma, 1999). Prior to this period, the media ethics debate had largely been carried out around the statist mantra of national unity and development.

The rupturing of the nationalist discourse vis-à-vis media ethics resulted in the impetus to set up media councils for media self-regulation. With greater media pluralism, and a diversified base of sources of news and information, the media became more critical of state and ruling-party functionaries. The instinctive reaction of the state was to legislate media ethics. In this vein, the state introduced, and hastily withdrew, the Media Council of Zambia (MCZ) Bill in April 1997. The law would have required compulsory registration of journalists, apart from giving the council powers to reprimand, suspend, or withdraw their accreditation. Failure to comply could result in prison terms and fines (Amnesty International, 1997).

But American funding, in particular, was linked to the spread of libertarian, individualist values of media and democracy. This reflected the US media system which is predominantly privatised and commercialised (cf. Chomsky & Herman, 1988; Herman & McChesney, 1997). Such a consumerist influence was reflected in the selective issuance of radio broadcasting licences to entertainment-based FM radio stations (Banda, 2003). This amounted to a de-politicisation of broadcasting, and to the marketisation of journalistic practice. Even so, the structure of media ownership changed, with *more and more* private players. In fact, given the near homogeneity of pro-government ZNBC content at the time, this injection of entertainment into the media content menu represented a mark of content differentiation.

This aspect of differentiation subsequently included *political* content, especially through live phone-in programmes. This was probably something the state had not anticipated. It also reflected the general (mis)conception that entertainment-based radio stations could not become politically inclined. Such unexpected outcomes *à la* globalisation are not unusual. As Rantanen (2005) observes, reinforcing Robertson's glocalisation thesis, "one cannot study globalization without acknowledging that the outcome can be either homogenization or heterogenization, or even both, depending on specific circumstances" (p. 74). Often, the outcomes are a very unpredictable *mélange* of actions and reactions. The tendency *away* from libertarian, individualist media forms *towards* other, communitarian media forms is further explored below.

4.2 The Libertarian-Communitarian Dialectic

The emergence of community broadcasting was, to begin with, associated with the infusion of the libertarian agenda into the nationalist media culture. Here, we can perhaps single out the Montreal based World Association of Community Radio Broadcasters (AMARC) as representing the main structural formation that influenced the development of communitarian communication in Zambia (Banda, 2003). Although this debate is hardly empirically developed, it represents a shift in the debate from the almost totalising statist ethic of national unity and development, as well as its libertarian counterpoint of commercialism, individualism and anti-statism, to a heterogeneity of media ethical agendas. It represented, at least in the case of Zambia, an undermining of the encroachment of anti-statism and 'entertainism' as a characteristic feature of the libertarian broadcast media culture inherited from the Global North.

But secondly, while some aspects of such inherited entertainment-based media culture remained, there emerged alongside it a hybrid media culture. This could be attributed to a disenchantment with entertainment *per se* and to a longing for media that could fulfil socio-developmental communitarian goals. For example, discernible were media-cultural orientations towards (i) greater inclusion of women in media representation, and (ii) greater community participation in the production of content. This was evidence that the globalised libertarian value of individual happiness (through media entertainment) was refracted through the cultural prism of greater community happiness (through community broadcasting).

Invoking Bhabha's (1994) liminality, this was neither the particularist postcolonial-nationalist media culture, nor the universalist libertarian media culture. It was a media-cultural hybrid that robbed the postcolonial-nationalist agenda of its state-centrism and the libertarian entertainment media agenda of its individualism. The communitarian ethic, though originating in Western social theory, has been appropriated in terms of its African equivalent – *ubuntuism*. While *ubuntu* as a possible African moral framework for media has been extolled by some scholars (cf. Christians, 2004; Blankenberg, 1999), Pieter Fourie, in chapter seven of this volume, questions how, among other things, *ubuntuism* differs from Western and Eastern feminist communitarians' ethics of care, affection, intimacy, empathy and collaboration.

4.3 State Resistance to Libertarian Normative Media Ethics

The debates cited above signal an underlying philosophical dilemma generated by the apparent split between libertarian utilitarianism as an aspect of the globalisation of journalism *and* cultural relativism as a notion of statist political resistance. The formation of the MECOZ in 2004 was seen as a capitulation to a libertarian 'watchdog' ethic. It was underpinned by a strong resistance to state encroachment on media autonomy, reflected in the media activists' protests to the Media Council of Zambia Bill.

State resistance to the utilitarian basis of MECOZ was not lost on the organisation's founding chairman, Judge Kabazo Chanda. He argued that the operations of MECOZ would be purely to regulate the conduct of media practitioners while at the same time protecting their interests and should not be viewed as an opposition to the state. He noted:

> We are not an opposition to the State but where journalists are oppressed, we will censure the State, just like when a journalist departs from his or her ethics, we will castigate that journalist…

> We are a registered organisation and we have a wide representation on the board. We hope members of the public and the Government will fully utilise this institution (*Times of Zambia*, 2005).

The chairperson's remarks seem to strike a conciliatory tone, as if he needed to reassure the state that MECOZ was not out to be unnecessarily adversarial. Being 'adversarial' is one of the cherished tenets of libertarian journalism, reflecting the so-called 'watchdog' role of the media. This seeming conciliation reflects the tension between the globalising neo-liberal tendency to undermine state authority and the Zambian cultural propensity to 'respect' political authority. The experiential aspect of this tension almost always plays out in the political interface between media activists and state functionaries. For example, this tension was played out in 2005 when the Wila Mung'omba Constitution Review Commission released its draft report to the public for discussion. The Commission was set up in April 2003 to look afresh at the Republican Constitution, as amended in 1996. There were concerns about how restrictive of freedom some of the constitutional provisions were.

The tension between proponents of media autonomy and those of state power manifested in the rejection by Zambia's Attorney General of a proviso guaranteeing freedom of all electronic and print media from interference. The Attorney General also rejected the provision for journalists not to disclose their sources of information except in court. He suggested that a statutory press complaints authority should be set up, arguing that such a statutory body would balance the interests of the media with those of the public and individuals. MISA Zambia countered that a statutory body to hear the complaints against the media was "totally unnecessary because members of the public have recourse to the courts of law or the Media Council of Zambia (MECOZ) to resolve any problems relating to unfair coverage or unethical reporting" (in Adler, 2005).

It can be seen, therefore, that the process of articulating a normative ethical framework for journalism in Zambia is a contested one, usually pitting state actors against non-state actors in a struggle to define the terms of media regulation. As Ward (2005, p. 6) suggests, ethics is the never-completed project of inventing, applying, and critiquing the basic principles that guide human interaction, define social roles, and justify institutional structures.

5. Towards a Negotiated Glocal Journalism Ethics?

The notion of glocalisation explored above suggests that journalism ethics is *always* negotiated. The *practice* of ethics is implicated in the politics of context (cf. Retief, 2002; Sanders, 2003). We cannot treat media ethics as frozen in an essentialist cocoon of media-ethical absolutism. This agrees with Christian's (2000) reasoning that we are "born into a sociocultural universe where values, moral commitments, and existential meanings are negotiated interactively" (p. 187). Negotiating a glocal journalism ethics, then, means engaging with a range of contextual factors.

By 'context', I mean those idiosyncrasies typical of any society – the totality of the social, political, economic, educational, legal, cultural and other factors that have historically influenced the articulation and practice of journalism ethics in that society. I discuss three key contextual variables: (i) process, (ii) ideology, and (iii) concept.

5.1 Processual Negotiation

The call for glocal journalism ethics assumes *process* – a roadmap towards attaining the objective. This process can be democratic, as much as it can be anti-democratic. It can be media-centric, as much as it can be societal. It can be egalitarian, as much as it can be elitist. But, I would argue, it needs to be all-encompassing. It is as much about state intervention as it is about individual agency.

It is in this vein that this idea also seems to agree with what Barger and Barney (2004, p. 191) refer to as "media-citizen reciprocity as a moral mandate". In negotiating glocal media ethics, then, media and citizen alike must accept reciprocal moral obligations related to the distribution and use of information, with journalists facilitating the distribution of information and engaging citizens usefully, fuelling the participatory engine that drives a democracy. As for citizens, they have a reciprocal obligation to expose themselves to information, respond publicly, tolerate (and even encourage) diversity, and protect media autonomy.

This entails that agendas for glocal journalism ethics, no matter what their source of origin, must become implicated within this localised process of negotiation. As I note elsewhere (Banda, 2006), "far from being overriding, globalization is refracted and modified through the prism of historical and political contexts. Globalisation is not a unilinear process, and neither are its results – it is almost always tamed by the historico-cultural specificities of the recipient country" (p. 466).

5.2 Ideological Negotiation

Here, I define *ideology* as meaning in the service of power (cf. Sonderling, 2007). This implies that ideology is always connected to systems of representations such as language and the mass media that communicate dominant meanings and serve the interests of power (Sonderling, 2007, p. 316). As such, it is possible to disentangle from the welter of globalisation those aspects of Western culture which seem to reify and legitimate themselves in the receiving nations. I have already alluded to this by highlighting the role of donor influence on the media in Africa. In this vein, Kasoma (1999), through his "neo-multiparty theory of the press", sought to illuminate the overbearing influence of donors on the media agenda, including the type of ethical normative orientation to be adopted.

What are the key ideological assumptions at play? Is it to export some nationalistic ideology coated with the sugar of universality?[3] These are legitimate questions to pose, particularly in a post/neo-colonial context that defines most of Africa and the developing world. Rao and Lee (2005) treat any efforts at developing a global media ethics code with "postcolonial suspicion". As they claim, "the end of colonialism did not automatically lead to a free press and representational democracy for all ex-colonies, and the postcolonial condition has been characterised by growth of dynastic oligopolies and dictatorial governments" (pp. 106–107). Rao and Lee (2005) conclude that "while highly sympathetic to the development of a global media ethics code, our interviews reveal that Asian and Middle Eastern journalists are concerned that any global media ethics code would be dominated by Western ideas and values" (p. 118).

This historically conditioned postcolonial suspicion does not invalidate the possibility of cultural common ground suggested by Clifford Christians and Michael Traber's protonorms – truth-telling, human dignity and nonviolence, *inter alia* (Christians & Traber, 1997). But, as Christians is quick to point out, human beings enter such "master norms" or "universals" through the immediate reality of geography and ethnicity. In articulating such protonorms, media ethics responds to the simultaneous globalising of communications and the reassertion of local identities (Christians, 2000).

To stretch Christians' reasoning: 'Master norms' always become interpenetrated with the cultural-historical baggage of local contexts, becoming in the process part of the ideological repertoires of those contexts. In Africa, such protonorms, when westernised, become caught up in the ideology of anti-imperialism or 'postcolonial suspicion', a colonial legacy.[4] Detectable within this heated ideological battle is a set of power relations. Bowers, Meyers and Babbili (2004) sketch out the ideological tensions in very poignant terms:

The very fabric of imagination the Western people possess is based on the ability of the media to sketch an imagery that utilizes an established lexicon and vocabularies of Western dominance. This power of journalism in the last two centuries, especially, has resulted in a Western hegemony of ideas and images and in a dominant ideology presented skilfully and disarmingly through its cultural narratives... (p. 241).

5.3 Conceptual Negotiation

The ideological problem extends into the conceptual fabric of journalism ethics. What ideas of knowledge – epistemology – are being championed? What are the underlying conceptions of reality – ontology – that are being promulgated? This ideological-conceptual apprehension seems evident in Zambia. To be sure, one detects in the many conceptual understandings of journalistic ethics strands of both libertarianism and communitarianism, and attempts at paradigmatic harmonisation.

Activists tend to locate themselves in either of these conceptual straitjackets, or find within their own socio-cultural milieu an 'in-between' – a *mélange* – from which to speak about and practise journalism ethics. But Hafez (2002) cautions us that adopting such a dualistic analytical framework is overly simplistic.[5] It masks the complexity of the norms guiding attitudes of *good* journalism. Zambia is a multi-ethnic, multi-religious and multi-racial society – all these factors go to compound the meaning of ethical journalism and constitute an important part of negotiating media ethics. It is possible to negotiate a conceptual middle ground between the universalising tendencies of libertarian utilitarianism and the particularistic traits of Afrocentric communitarianism (Wasserman & De Beer, 2004; 2005; cf. Wasserman, 2006).

Like libertarianism, Afrocentric communitarianism does not brook intervention from a higher (governmental) authority. Libertarianism sees such authority as potentially anti-democratic and anti-freedom, and so presents the media as watchdogs over such state authority. So, too, does Afrocentric communitarianism which abhors control from any authority external to the community. In terms of African philosophy, Kwasi Wiredu (1996), whom Christians refers to in his chapter in this volume, reminds us of the African-communalistic process of consensual-deliberative democracy. According to Wiredu, African communalism is underpinned by:

- Pure morality as a basis for civil interaction – the individual must have impartial regard for the interests of others, motivated by a certain minimum of altruism
- The subordination of individual interests to those of society
- The pervasiveness of consensus as a mode of group decision-making
- Consensual democracy (cooperation, deliberation, compromise, consensus, etc.)
- Non-hierarchy (Wiredu, 2001, pp. 171–178).

A fundamental point raised by Wiredu is one of inter-cultural communication as *prima facie* evidence of moral universals, including *conceptual universals*, which are nevertheless refracted through the particularities of custom (1996, p. 30).

It is for this reason that Christians (2004, p. 242) is convinced that communitarian *ubuntuism* is shared in so many other parts of the world that it has universal appeal. This conception would address some of the concerns of such Zambian media ethicists as Kasoma (Rønning & Kasoma, 2002) who are in favour of a softer form of cultural relativism which is open to truly universal impulses (cf. Wasserman & De Beer, 2004; 2005).

6. Conclusion

This chapter sought to map out how the 'globalisation' of media ethics becomes enmeshed with the specific context in which journalism is practised. I have demonstrated how the trajectories of colonialism, postcolonialism and globalisation have altered the texture of media ethics in Zambia – from colonialism, to post-colonialism to globalisation. The era of globalisation in particular, has reconfigured the media landscape in ways mirroring *both* the influences of globalisation and those of the locale, resulting in the sorts of liminal outcomes anticipated by Bhabha (1994).

In this regard, I have shown the tensions that exist between global, often Euro-American, libertarian ethical values of journalism and the context-based peculiarities of process, ideology and concept. It can be concluded that the question is no longer whether or not globalisation has any impact on the local practices of journalism ethics (Rantanen, 2005; Hafez, 2007). Rather, the question is about the degree of glocalisation or hybridisation of the criss-crossing experience. This somewhat conflicts with the view that suggests that local spaces are populated with pure, unadulterated cultural values that "Northern standards" of journalism somehow render imperfect (cf. Kasoma, 1996).

I have demonstrated how such global influences as liberalisation, privatisation and commercialisation tend to be "refracted through the prism of historical and political contexts" (Banda, 2006, p. 466). In fact, the argument can be stretched to suggest that the so-called global influences are themselves not emanating from pure, unadulterated sources. They are, within their own contexts, hybrids of contested epistemic and ontological experiences. They become more hybridised as they come into contact with the cultures, languages and politics of the other (cf. Robertson, 1992; 1995; Bhabha, 1994; Kraidy, 2003; Loomba, 2005). As such, the adoption of a glocalised media ethics is an exercise in negotiation. As I have noted, such negotiation is implicated in questions of the contextual exigencies of process, ideology and conceptualisation.

Notes

1   The historiography is largely the author's reading of the Zambian press historical data produced by Kasoma (1986) and Mytton (1983). These authors agree that the first media attempts started somewhere in the 1940s, with, according to Kasoma (1983) the setting up of the 'white press'.

2   The Organisation of African Unity (OAU) had its name changed to the African Union (AU) in July 2002. It consists of 54 independent African states and now has an African Parliament headquartered in South Africa.
3   Kasoma (Rønning & Kasoma 2002, p. 134) alleges that some of the so-called 'universal' ethical values, norms and principles in journalism are nothing but national or racial values, norms and principles which certain nations present as universal.
4   As noted already, the debates in the 1970s and 1980s about 'media/cultural imperialism', together with the attendant proposals for a New World Information and Communication Order (NWICO) can be seen partly as a legacy of colonialism.
5   Hafez (2002, p. 245) concludes that the dichotomy of individual Western versus communitarian Eastern journalism ethics is much too simplistic to serve as a general paradigm when comparing European with Middle Eastern, North African, and Muslim Asian ethical codes and discourses.

References

Adler, S. (2005). Zambia: 2005 world press freedom review. Retrieved February 15, 2007 from http://www.freemedia.at/cms/ipi/freedom_detail.html?country=/KW0001/KW0006/KW0182/.
Amnesty International. (1997). Zambia: Donors should seek assurance of human rights improvement. Retrieved February 14, 2007, from http://web.amnesty.org/library/Index/ENGAFR630051997?open&of=ENG-ZMB.
Appadurai, A. (1996). Modernity at large: cultural dimensions of globalization. Minneapolis and London: University of Minnesota Press.
Banda, F. (2007). Media in Africa. In P. Fourie (ed.). Media Studies: media history, media and society (2nd ed., Vol. 1) (pp. 59–86). Cape Town: Juta.
Banda, F. (2006). Negotiating global influences – globalization and broadcasting policy reforms in Zambia and South Africa, Canadian Journal of Communication, 31(2), 459–467.
Banda, F. (2003). Community radio broadcasting in Zambia: a policy perspective. Unpublished PhD thesis. University of South Africa.
Barger, W. & Barney, R.D. (2004). Media-citizen reciprocity as a moral mandate, Journal of Mass Media Ethics, 19(3 & 4), 191–206.
Bhabha, H. (1994). The location of culture. London: Routledge.
Blankenberg, N. (1999). In search of a real freedom: Ubuntu and the media, Critical Arts, 13(2), 42–65.
Bourgault, L.M. (1995). Mass media in sub-Saharan Africa. Bloomington & Indianapolis: Indiana University Press.
Bowers, P.J., Meyers, C. & Babbili, A. (2004). Power, ethics, and journalism: toward an integrative approach. Journal of Mass Media Ethics, 19(3 & 4), 223–246.
Christians, C.G. (2000). Social dialogue and media ethics. Ethical Perspectives, 7(2–3), 182–193.
Creeber, G. (2004). "Hideously white": British television. Glocalization, and national identity, Television & New Media, 5(1), 27–39.
Christians, C.G. (2004). Ubuntu and communitarianism in media ethics, Ecquid Novi, 25(2), 235–256.
Christians, C. & Traber, M. (eds.). (1997). Communication ethics and universal values. Thousand Oaks: Sage.
Friedland, W.H. & Rosberg, C.G. (1964). The anatomy of African socialism. In W.H. Friedland & C.G. Rosberg (eds.). African socialism (pp. 1–11). Stanford: Stanford University Press.
Friedman, J. (1997). Global crises, the struggle for cultural identity and intellectual porkbarrelling: cosmopolitans versus locals, ethnics and nationals in an era of de-hegemonisation. In P. Werbner & T. Modood (eds.). Debating cultural hybridity: multi-cultural identities and the politics of anti-racism (pp. 70–89). London & New Jersey: Zed Books.
Gecau, K. (1996). The press and society in Kenya: a re-appraisal. In B. Andersen (ed.). Media and democracy (pp. 183–212). Oslo: University of Oslo. .
Giddens, A. (1991). Modernity and self-identity. Oxford: Polity.
Hachten, W.A. (1971). Muffled drums: the news media in Africa. Ames, Iowa: The Iowa State University Press.
Hafez, K. (2007). The myth of media globalization. Translated by Alex Skinner. Cambridge: Polity.
Hafez, K. (2002). Journalism ethics revisited: a comparison of ethics codes in Europe, North Africa, the Middle East, and Muslim Asia. Political Communication, 19(2), 225–250.

Herman, E.S. & Chomsky, N. (1988). *Manufacturing consent: the political economy of the mass media.* New York: Pantheon Books.

Herman, E.S. & McChesney, R.W. (1997). *The global media: the new missionaries of corporate capitalism.* London and Washington: Cassell.

Kasoma, F.P. (1999). *The neo-multiparty theory of the press: donor aid and other influences on the media in Africa (Professorial inaugural lectures).* Lusaka: University of Zambia Press.

Kasoma, F.P. (1986). *The press in Zambia.* Lusaka: Multimedia.

Kraidy, M.M. (2003). Globalization *avant la letter?* Cultural hybridity and media power in Lebanon. In P.D. Murphy & M.M. Kraidy (eds.). *Global media studies: ethnographic perspectives* (pp. 276–296). New York and London: Routledge.

Kraidy, M.M. & Murphy, P.D. (2003). Media ethnography: local, global, or translocal? In P.D. Murphy & M.M. Kraidy (eds.). *Global media studies: ethnographic perspectives* (pp. 299–307). New York and London: Routledge.

Loomba, A. (2005). *Colonialism/postcolonialism* (2nd ed.). London and New York: Routledge.

McLeod, J. (2000). *Beginning postcolonialism.* Manchester and New York: Manchester University Press.

Mkandawire, T. (ed.). (2005). *African intellectuals: rethinking politics, language, gender and development.* London and New York: Zed Books.

Mutiso, G.C.M. & Rohio, S.W. (eds.). (1975). *Readings in African political thought.* Nairobi, Ibadan and Lusaka: Heinemann.

Mytton, G. (1983). *Mass communication in Africa.* London: Edward Arnold.

Narveson, J. (1988). *The libertarian idea.* Philadelphia, Pa.: Temple University Press.

Nyamnjoh, F. (2005). *Africa's media: democracy & the politics of belonging.* London, New York & Pretoria: Zed Books & UNISA Press.

Papastergiadis, N. (1997). Tracing hybridity in theory. In P. Werbner & T. Modood (eds.). *Debating cultural hybridity: multi-cultural identities and the politics of anti-racism* (pp. 257–281). London & New Jersey: Zed.

Quayson, A. (2000). *Postcolonialism: theory, practice or practice?* Cambridge: Polity Press.

Rantanen, T. (2005). *The media and globalization.* London, Thousand Oaks and New Delhi: Sage.

Rao, S. & Lee, S.T. (2005). Globalizing media ethics? An assessment of universal ethics among international political journalists. *Journal of Mass Media Ethics,* 20(2 & 3), 99–120.

Retief, J. (2002). *Media ethics: an introduction to responsible journalism.* Cape Town: Oxford University Press Southern Africa.

Robertson, R. (1995). Glocalization: time-space and homogeneity-heterogeneity. In M. Featherstone, S. Lash & R. Roland. (eds.). *Global modernities* (pp. 25–44). London, Thousand Oaks and New Delhi: Sage.

Robertson, R. (1992). *Globalization: social theory and global culture.* London: Sage.

Rønning, H. & Kasoma, F.P. (2002). *Media ethics: an introduction.* Pretoria: Juta & Nordic/SADC Journalism Centre.

Sanders, K. (2003). *Ethics & journalism.* London, Thousand Oaks and New Delhi: Sage.

Senghor, L.S. (2000). Negritude and African socialism. In D. Brydon (ed.). *Postcolonialism: critical concepts in literary and cultural studies* (Vol. 3). (pp. 998–1010). London and New York: Routledge.

Sonderling, S. (2007). The ideological power of the media. In P. Fourie (ed.). *Media Studies: media history, media and society* (2nd ed., Vol. 1) (pp. 306–323). Cape Town: Juta.

Spivak, G.C. (1988). *In other worlds: essays in cultural politics.* London: Routledge.

Talib, I.S. (2002). *The language of postcolonial literature: an introduction.* London and New York: Routledge.

Times of Zambia. (2005). *Media Council of Zambia launched.* Retrieved February 15, 2007, from http://www.times.co.zm/news/viewnews.cgi?category=4&id=1089594399.

Walder, D. (1998). *Post-colonial literatures in English: history, language, theory.* Oxford: Blackwell.

Werbner, P. (1997). Introduction: the dialectics of cultural hybridity. In P. Werbner & T. Modood (eds.). *Debating cultural hybridity: multi-cultural identities and the politics of anti-racism* (pp. 1–26). London & New Jersey: Zed Books.

Ward, S.J.A. (2005). Philosophical foundations for global journalism ethics, *Journal of Mass Media Ethics,* 20(1), 3–21.

Wasserman, H. (2006). Globalized values and postcolonial responses: South African perspectives on normative media ethics, *International Communication Gazette,* 68(1), 71–91.

Wilcox, D.L. (1975). *Mass media in black Africa: philosophy and control.* New York: Praeger.

Wiredu, K. (2001). Society and democracy in Africa. In T Kiros (ed.). *Explorations in African political thought: identity, community, ethics* (pp. 171–184). New York and London: Routledge.

Wiredu, K. (1996). *Cultural universals and particulars: an African perspective.* Bloomington and Indianapolis: Indiana University Press.

Young, R.J.C. (2001). *Postcolonialism: a historical introduction.* Oxford: Blackwell Publishers Ltd.

9 Journalistic Ethics and Responsibility in Relation to Freedom of Expression: An Islamic Perspective

Ali Mohamed

1. Introduction

In an age of global and transnational media – characterised by a worldwide system of production and consumption, and a proliferating new electronic media that cross political and cultural boundaries – an urgent need has developed to consider new parameters of global ethics for media practice as a way to begin to meet the challenges of globalisation (Ward, 2005; Rao and Lee, 2005; Callahan, 2003). For example, has it become necessary to craft a transnational media ethics capable of addressing such issues as the Danish cartoon controversy? Transnational codes of ethics, unlike those established within the frame of the nation-state or in the context of parochial professionalism, must take into account the values and traditions of diverse cultures and seek common and universal principles that can be endorsed cross-culturally (Christians & Nordenstreng, 2004).

The traditional ethical mission of journalism is to serve the common good and to tell the truth. Moreover, journalists have been given freedom, protection, and privilege to help fulfill their commitments and moral obligations (Callahan, 2003). A failure to fulfill these commitments and moral obligations (due to the concerns of self-interest) cancels the rationale for this journalistic freedom (Christians & Nordenstreng, 2004, p. 14). A truly free press is always accompanied by responsibility – a pledge to do no unjustified or unnecessary harm to others. Perhaps the most recent example of this difficult responsibility placed on a free press occurred when European newspapers published the Danish cartoons of the Prophet Muhammad, an event closely accompanied by violence and acts of protest in some countries of the Muslim world. In particular, the case of the

Danish cartoons raises the issues of press freedom and freedom of expression in the context of globalisation, cultural pluralism, and new media that enable the rapid reproduction and circulation of controversial images and texts across borders. This ethical responsibility applies to the decisions made with respect to the original publication and republications of the cartoons and to the subsequent press coverage of the reaction to the cartoons in the Muslim world.

Many of the debates about press freedom and the ethics of publishing these cartoons were carried out on the assumption – either implicit or explicit – that Western notions of press freedom are nearly absolute and universal. This assumption was the basis of both the defence of the initial publication of the cartoons and the subsequent stereotypical mischaracterisation of the Islamic perspective on freedom of expression. In this sense, the debates that followed the publication and republication of the cartoons were as great a symptom of misunderstanding and insensitivity to difference and pluralism as the cartoons themselves.

The Danish cartoon controversy has raised anew the question of the value of freedom of expression, both as a core principle of journalism ethics and as a principle for assessing the publication of the cartoons and the Muslim reactions to them. Discussing freedom of expression from an Islamic perspective is important when considering journalism and communication ethics because of the particularity of the position of Islam among Muslims. The specific purpose of my essay is to explain the standpoint of Islam, as a religion, on the issue of freedom of expression through a reading of the primary Islamic scriptural sources (the Qur'an and the Prophetic tradition [*Sunnah*]) that reflect Islam's support for the common ethical value of freedom of expression and the responsibility it entails. In addition, this essay uses Islamic principles to evaluate the cartoon case, and describes how the application of these principles may differ from other ethical approaches. The centrality of Islam among Muslims helps to justify the growing importance of discussing how an ethics based on Islamic principles may be impacting globalised journalism. This realisation also provides a starting point for understanding the reactions of Muslim countries to the Danish cartoon controversy, especially considering the special meaning of religious symbols to those who hold them sacred.

2. The Position of Islam among Muslims

The role and status of religion in any professional ethics differ from one culture to another. In the Arab-Islamic culture, where politics and religiosity simply cannot be separated, religion occupies a unique status and "makes a uniquely powerful demand on its adherents" (Taylor, 1989, p. 118), and for that reason, this religious necessity may help to explain the Muslim reaction against blasphemous representations (Taylor, 1989, p. 121). Religious virtues, consciously or unconsciously, are often at the core of many contemporary ethical systems. Even in the erstwhile secular societies of the West, one finds Christian religious principles and commitments – for example, the Bible's "Golden Rule" – at the root of a wide range of ethical practices. In the context of comparative ethics and diverse religions, the most recognised and agreed upon values cross-culturally are free expression, responsibility, truth-telling, justice, respect for human dignity, and the sanctity of the innocent (Christians & Traber, 1997, p. xv). These morals and principles, which are based on the sacredness of human life, reverence for life on earth, and the right to live in human dignity, constitute the ground, in a broad sense, for universal human and social responsibility that is the solid foundation for a universal global communication and media ethics (Christians, 1997, pp. 6–7).

Since Islam is an important constituent in the everyday lives of Muslims, Islamic ethics and morality must be reflected in all walks of life of Muslims. Islam is not merely a faith; it is an entire way of life, as the prophet Muhammad said, "Iman (faith) is what you embrace in your heart and apply to your actions". The connection between words and deeds is indivisible, and this consistency between them represents a central constituent of Islamic ethics. In the Islamic faith, one has to associate his/her actions with good intentions so to give moral legitimacy to them. Particularly, this solid association between action and speech is described by the Prophet when he said: "God would not accept any speech unless substantiated by action and would not accept any act unless it is based on intention" (Ayish & Sadig, 1997, p. 108).

The ultimate goal of the individual Muslim – men and women – is to worship God and seek His satisfaction and pleasure. Consequently, this goal "leads them to a high level of God-consciousness and a sense of accountability to God, whose pleasure they seek, and which lies in serving humanity with humility and justice" (Siddiqui, 2000, p. 12). In other words, the ultimate goal of the individual Muslim is guided by the same principle that governs the ethics of freedom of expression – the principle of piety (*taqwa*). From an Islamic perspective, freedom of expression should be a means for a Muslim to reach *taqwa* and should not go beyond the boundaries and limits set by God, especially since the goal of a Muslim is to please God. No sovereignty should exist over the individual except for the sovereignty of God as exemplified by Islamic principles (Mowlana, 1993, p. 18). In the Islamic context, piety is the prior value that makes freedom thinkable and meaningful. To act impiously is not to demonstrate, but rather to negate one's freedom. The believers devote all their deeds and actions to reach this goal, meaning that they liberate their soul from all things that prevent it from reaching *taqwa* (Mowlana, 1989, p. 145).

Islamic teachings confirm the existence of moral and ethical consciousness in human beings, and encourage people to resort to their conscience for judging conduct or behaviour. Moreover, it can be argued that, as a whole, Islamic religious ethics have more of an influence on Muslim journalists around the world than the codes of ethics formulated by professional organisations. This phenomenon has been attributed to the important role that Islam plays in the lives of individuals in Islamic nations, hence, it provides them with the cultural framework through which they perceive the world. In this context, a distinction should be made between Western liberal societies, which give priority to the separation of church and state, and the Islamic cultural view that politics and religion simply cannot be separated. Islam is not only a religion; it is a total life system and a public affair, and Islamic principles are the supreme guide of conduct for all the human activities of Muslims (Mowlana, 1993, p. 18). This integrated relationship between religion and politics may contribute to the interpretation of the discourse surrounding the publication of the Danish cartoons.

Nevertheless, a question may be raised as to the applicability of the Islamic perspective for the practice of journalism ethics in Western liberal democracies. It is interesting to note that this question is ethnocentric from the outset. Perhaps a more appropriate question is: To what degree is Islam compatible with global human rights and global journalism ethics in general? It could be argued that the ethical virtues in all cultures and religions are universal and that the degree of agreement among different religions and cultures is much broader and deeper than the narrow space of disagreement. A global journalism ethics grounded in equal recognition and respect may require Western liberals to reconsider claims regarding liberalism's alleged cultural neutrality (Taylor, 1994, p. 62).

3. The Place of Freedom of Expression in Islam

The fact that freedom of expression, whether in the everyday practice of media and journalism or at the level of personal communication, may not be adequately protected in Arab and Islamic countries does not decrease the importance of this value in Islam. Therefore, to avoid confusing the protection of freedom of expression in Islamic countries with the stance of Islam towards this value, this essay investigates how Islam itself encourages freedom of expression and protects it from abuse by identifying certain limits, as are reflected in Islamic Scripture. As Kamali (1994) argues: "Islam not only validates freedom of expression but it also urges Muslims not to remain silent nor indifferent when expressing an opinion which is likely to serve the cause of truth, justice, or be of benefit to society" (p. 16). Necessarily, one should distinguish between Islamic principles that ground a set of fundamental human rights and the prevailing lack of support for these rights in Muslim countries where censorship and oppression prevail.

In the Islamic context, a fundamental freedom is the freedom of religion and belief. Everyone has the right to choose and embrace their own religion with conviction and without any coercion, as the Qur'an states: "Let there be no compulsion in religion" (Chapter 2, Verse 256). Also, this support for freedom of religion and belief is found in the Qur'anic verses which were addressed to the Prophet, for example: "Say: 'The truth is from your lord.' Let him who will, believe, and let him who will, reject (it)" (Chapter 18, Verse 29). Moreover, freedom of religion requires an environment characterised by a permissive tolerance which disdains the ridicule of other religious beliefs, lest the opposing party blaspheme against one's own religion: "Do not revile those whom they call upon besides Allah, lest they out of spite revile Allah in their ignorance" (Chapter 6, Verse 108). On the basis of this direction, Islam gives special attention to the sanctity of religion, particularly within the context of the practice of freedom of expression.

Islam provides all the guarantees that encourage people to get involved and declare their opinions publicly, to criticise the views and opinions of others without any fear or hesitation, provided that the expression of these opinions accords with truth and upright behaviour. When a believer trusts that their life and sustenance are in the hands of God (Chapter 51, Verses 22, 58), and that only God determines life and death (Chapter 50, Verse 43), they can be free from control and domination, and freely express their diverse opinions and criticism with the assurance that their most significant life needs are guaranteed. In Islam, the Qur'an and the Prophetic traditions not only emphasise and support freedom of expression, but also encourage followers to declare their opinions and to be active participants in society. This participation, according to the prophetic tradition, is a condition of membership in the Muslim community.

The Prophet Muhammad encouraged members of the community not to remain silent or be indifferent when he said: "He who remains silent about truth is a dumb devil" and "the best form of *jihad* is to utter a word of truth to a tyrannical ruler" (Kamali, 1994, p. 51). This directive is consistent with the Scriptural principle of "commanding to the right and prohibiting from the wrong", which is considered to be the foundation for social responsibility in Islam in that it implies the responsibility of all Muslims, including all forms of media, to establish Islamic principles and to encourage others to adopt these principles in their lives (Mowlana, 1989, p. 142). Moreover, this principle is a collective obligation and duty for those who have the ability to influence the entire community.

To guarantee an interaction between different opinions in the interest of making good choices, Islam invites people to hold their own opinions and not to follow others without belief or conviction in what is being done. The Qur'an denounces those who follow others who stray, imitating them blindly without using their minds (Chapter 31, Verse 21). Islam discourages this kind of indifference, and the Prophet Muhammad instructs Muslims: "Let none of you be turned into a tail (*imm'ah*): that is a person who does good work or embarks upon evil only when he sees others doing the same. But make up your minds. Let everyone join others in good deeds and avoid participation in evil conduct" (Kamali, 1994, p. 53).

Freedom of expression necessitates that people have the right to obtain the information and knowledge they need for deliberation and discussion to formulate their opinions – the necessity of the right to know. This position is supported by the prophetic traditions. When the Prophet Muhammad acquainted his companions with his plans and policies before their implementation, he was careful to disseminate all information pertinent to the general populace. An implication of this action is that leaders must consult the public about matters affecting the community. Information must be truthful, and the one who gathers it must verify its veracity before broadcasting or announcing it to the public. Not only are the senders of information and news obliged to tell the truth, but also the receivers of it must seek the truth by obtaining information from more than one source to be sure of its veracity. Veracity is the cornerstone of the Islamic model of communication, emphasising personal responsibility and accountability in news production and dissemination. Islam supports people in the expression of their opinions publicly, while, at the same time, mandating that respect must be shown to the opinions of others.

4. Responsibility as the Complement of Freedom

The Islamic teachings emphasise the limits of freedom of expression and the responsibility that should restrain its use. In particular, attention is directed towards the moral guidelines that extend beyond what is articulated in laws and codes, with an emphasis on human dignity and the common good. Followers are encouraged to avoid every public action or speech that could potentially harm society or hurt its individuals or groups. Spoken or written words are of great consequence and represent the most potent weapon in opposing oppression and, at the same time, affect the prosperity of the community, changing it for better or worse. In Islam, freedom of expression is framed by a set of principles, which emphasise and guarantee the responsibility of that freedom. These principles encourage people not to abuse this freedom and not to transgress the rights of others.

Freedom of expression necessitates that the individual uses the best of his cultural and scientific ability to engage in discussion, dialogue, and argument. Some issues and topics, especially specialised ones, necessitate technical knowledge. Accordingly, only specialists in this field are consulted for solutions. Naturally, when opinion comes from experts and specialists or from those who have the knowledge and competency in discussing the issue, authority and legitimacy are given to that opinion. The Qur'an says: "If you realise this not, ask of those who possess the Message" (Chapter 21, Verse 7). Thus, Islam encourages people to learn and obtain knowledge, as the Prophet said: "seeking knowledge is mandatory for every Muslim".

Also, people are discouraged from expressing themselves when their opinion is bereft of purpose, when the discussion centres on matters of no concern to them, or when no occasion exists for them to speak. In these cases, silence is recommended, as the Prophet says: "It is indicative of piety for a Muslim to remain silent in regards to matters which do not concern him" (Kamali, 1994, p. 122). When expressing one's opinion, one must think about the rest of the community. Public interest moderates individual behaviour, ensuring that individual freedom does not harm others or subject the community to threat. Freedom of expression must be harnessed for some type of benefit. Speaking about an evil in public is permitted if this public proclamation rights some wrong or establishes justice. Individuals should feel that they are responsible to others, and recognise that they also are part of the larger community.

The measure and limits of freedom of expression can be perceived collectively rather than individually. If conflict should arise between an individual and community interests, priority is given to those of the community. This suggests a different picture than the one drawn, for example, by John Stuart Mill's emphasis on the importance of the individual's freedom of expression. The concept of *ummah* or "community" in Islam is not illuminated by Mill's cautionary account of "the tyranny of the majority" exercised by public authorities, or the force of collective opinion and public feeling, with its implications of threat to the individual's freedom (Mill, 1978, p. 4). The Islamic teachings that emphasise the limits and responsibilities of freedom of expression, which have been discussed throughout this essay, can contribute to a determination of "the legitimate interference of collective opinion with individual independence" (Mill, 1859/1978, p. 5). The community, the *ummah*, as Mowlana (1989) puts it, "must be exemplary, setting the highest standards of performance, and be the reference point of others" (p. 144). The concept of community implies that all people are equal, and preferential status does not arise based on race, gender, or social status (Chapter 49, Verse 13). With respect to sacred or moral authority, the individual renounces "the imperatives of self-maintenance, for personal interests, he [or she] enters into communion with all other believers; he [or she] merges with the impersonal power of the sacred which reaches beyond all that is merely individual" (Habermas, 1984, p. 49). Such a moral stance is simply inconceivable within the framework of Mill's liberalism, a fact that may indicate the limits of liberal ethics in a multicultural, global context.

5. Freedom, Privacy, and Human Relations

In Islam, freedom of expression is perceived within the larger framework of respect for human dignity. Everyone has the right to live his life as he desires, so long as his choices do not threaten the rights of others. This limit or principle is a common thread in different ideologies. For example, it is highlighted in Mill's position on an individual's freedom when he states: "The liberty of the individual must be thus far limited; he [or she] must not make himself a nuisance to other people" (Mill, 1859/1978, p. 53). To protect society and an individual's right to honor and a good reputation, Islam elucidates moral restraints against defamation, backbiting, and derision. The abuse of freedom of speech through the violation of the human dignity of others is also emphasised in the clearest manner in the Qur'an and the prophetic traditions. For example, the Qur'an instructs believers to protect and respect others, and forbids any act that may hurt others or expose any aspect of their private affairs, regardless of their social situation (Chapter 49, Verse 11). Moreover, God asks people to speak well of others and not to engage in suspicion and espionage (Chapter 49, Verse 12).

Another set of ethical imperatives regarding human relationships direct the devotees of Islam when they exercise freedom of speech. A person's property, life, and private matters are sacrosanct in Islam. In addition, Islam warns people against unleashing their tongues in backbiting or hurting the reputations and honour of others, especially when those harmed are innocent (Chapter 24, Verse 23). The Qur'an condemns rumor-mongering or the circulation of rumors, especially those that affect public safety or stir fear and chaos among people, and encourages veracity in news and information gathering by consulting those who are knowledgeable (Chapter 4, Verse 83). The Scripture also warns people against defaming others and disseminating evil: "Those who love (to see) scandal published and broadcast among the believers will have a grievous Penalty in this life and in the hereafter" (Chapter 24, Verse 19). However, it is important not to misinterpret these Islamic instructions and thus use them as an excuse to obscure the truth or to pass over the corruptions and wrongdoings of others.

The revelation and exposure of the truth, and the investigation of all kinds of mischievous acts, are obligatory duties in Islam as long as they are justified and for the sake of the public interest. The difference between the violation of others' privacy and the defamation of their reputation is clear, though it does demand discretion and judgment. The fundamental principles of Islam regarding the freedom of expression are clear in the Islamic Scripture. How these statements are interpreted and applied in reality is quite another matter.

6. The Danish Cartoons: Freedom of Expression and Irresponsibility

On September 30, 2005, the Danish newspaper *Jyllands-Posten* published twelve offensive cartoons depicting the Prophet Muhammad. The newspaper announced that the publication of these cartoons was justified to overcome self-censorship, especially, regarding criticism of Islam. According to Carsten Juste, the editor-in-chief of *Jyllands-Posten*, "the newspaper asked a number of Danish illustrators to submit their own personal interpretations of how the prophet might appear" to assess "exactly how widespread self-censorship is" in Denmark over Islamic issues ("The Story Behind The Drawings", 8 February 2006, cited in Ghazi, 2006, p. 18). Subsequently, these cartoons were republished in other European newspapers to show their solidarity with *Jyllands-Posten* in defense of freedom of expression. The cartoons ridicule the Prophet Muhammad and portray him with a bomb in his turban, and ultimately equate Islam with extremism and terrorism. Many Muslims feel that they were deliberately and maliciously humiliated and insulted through the degradation of a sacred religious personality, especially considering the Prophet Muhammad's central role in Islam and the lives of Muslims.

Was the publication and republication of the Danish cartoons an example of, or a misuse of, freedom of expression? From a Western perspective, freedom of expression is a basic right not easily denied; it also is a basic element of identity in Western liberal societies in which the publication of these cartoons is a legitimate right with respect to the right to free speech. Surely, free expression as materialised through a free press has been central to the development of liberal democracies in the West, and part of this freedom has entailed the protection of speech that is highly controversial or considered even 'offensive' in one respect or another by particular interests. In addition, no one can underestimate the value of freedom of speech and freedom of the press for any democracy to function. Hence, free speech is protected as a basic human right and guaranteed by the Universal Declaration of Human Rights of the United Nations, as well as being protected by many constitutions and legal systems around the world. However, the debate over the limits of freedom of speech never ends. Even in liberal democracies with their ethos erring on the side of permissiveness, free speech has considered limits at which it is unacceptable to cross some lines. As Siebert (1971) explains, all libertarian philosophers agree that freedom of expression is not absolute but has some limits. However, the problem is, as he points out, in defining the proper limits of freedom of expression, which always has been an area of debate in democratic societies (Siebert, 1971, pp. 49–56). I recognise that the question of where to draw the line of permissiveness in relation to 'offensive' speech has been a persistent topic of debate in the liberal tradition. The Danish cartoon controversy has brought these tensions to the surface once again.

Islam prohibits the publication or representation of any of the prophets, whether it is Muhammad, Adam, Joshua, or Jesus. Moreover, respect for religious symbols is part and parcel of ethical behaviour. Therefore, as Ramadan (2006) argues, the publication of these cartoons, from a Muslim perspective, was a gratuitous provocation and, at the same time, difficult to defend under the concept of freedom of expression. According to a statement issued by the International Union for Muslim Scholars, the Danish cartoons "were presented in a way that could never be acceptable to any person of good faith, nor ever approved of by any person having sound morals. This depiction is unbefitting of a prophet who delivered the divine message" (Islamonline, 2006).

From an Islamic viewpoint, freedom is not devoid of limits. For example, the violation of sacred symbols, slander, and blasphemy are prohibited by the Qur'an: "God loves not the public utterance of evil speech except by one who has been wronged" (Chapter 4, Verse 148). Freedom of expression must be harnessed for some type of benefit. Speaking about an evil in public is permitted in the case that this public proclamation rights some wrong or leads to the establishment of justice. Justice, a basic principle in Islam, is essential to the discussion of the value of freedom of expression. Islam places great emphasis on the provision and administration of justice and on the right of the individual to have just and fair treatment. In reference to the principle of justice, all contradictions and paradoxes associated with the value of freedom of expression can be weighed and resolved.

From an Islamic point of view, the concept of justice is crucial for understanding the scope of freedom of expression in relation to the responsibilities it entails. Islam gives priority to justice as the supreme value that underpins other values such as freedom and equality. The concept of justice in Islam epitomises how to approach the issue of rights and obligations to others, and so provides a compass of good conduct, while at the same time, indicating how to arrange personal priorities to accord with the common and public good. In the case of the Danish cartoons, Islam was prejudicially depicted without justification.

With growing changes in the structure and complexion of traditional societies where cultural, and especially religious frames of reference, have multiplied, informal traditions play an increasingly important role in constituting freedom of expression (Rosenberg, 2006, p. 20). These informal traditions, which are not codified by legislation, derive from the ethics established and rooted in religion and in the general human heritage throughout history. Allen and Voss (1997) argue that "when laws don't suffice, we must be guided by ethics". Since laws cannot keep pace with the growing transformations and changing circumstances in society that have accompanied the revolution of new communication technologies, the ethical perspective must serve as the criterion for proper behaviour (pp. 99–101).

My argument is that a global/transnational/pluralist journalism ethics cannot simply assume that political decision-making about where to draw the line of offensiveness for freedom of expression can adequately, or solely, occur within a secularist arena. Taking a religious perspective into account, rather than discounting it prejudicially, produces a different ethical response for cases such as the Danish cartoon controversy. Religious sensitivities are a matter of fact, and freedom of expression should be limited when it causes offence to a religion or members of it through the defamation and ridicule of their sacred personalities. Any media ethics that does not take this perspective into account, and that makes a universalist assumption about secularism, undermines the very pluralism that liberal ethics purports to serve. In his response to the Danish cartoon controversy, Kurtis Cooper (spokesperson for the US State Department) illustrates the principle discussed above: "We all fully recognize and respect freedom of the press and expression, but it must be coupled with press responsibility. Inciting religious or ethnic hatreds in this manner is not acceptable" (cited in Raboy, 2006).

By ignoring the importance of informal rules – those rules not stated in legislation – that moderate freedom of expression in the context of public discourse, Danish and European newspapers have misconstrued the limits within which freedom of expression can be justified, productive of the public good, and meaningful. The ethical virtue of prudence – the commonsense ability to weigh universals (such as freedom of expression) against particulars (such as the religious sensitivities of Muslims) – was apparently absent in the decision by the Danish newspaper to publish these cartoons, and by other media outlets to republish them. They did not consider that the universal principle of freedom of expression should be moderated according to the time and place, or the "communication situation", in which it is being practised. J. S. Mill touches on this point when he states: "Opinions lose their immunity when the circumstances in which they are expressed are such as to constitute their expression a positive instigation to some mischievous act." He goes on: "Acts, of whatever kind, which without justifiable cause do harm to others may be, and in the more important cases absolutely require to be controlled by the unfavorable sentiments, and, when needed, by the active interference of mankind" (Mill, 1859/1978, p. 53). Hence, the responsibility taken on by journalists is more than just telling the truth or conveying information. As Callahan (2003) argues, truthfulness is not just telling the truth to make a story and present facts; it also means that journalists should not misrepresent these facts and "try to interpret the meaning of the day's news" (p. 4); or, according to the Hutchins Commission 1947, journalists should be urged to provide a "truthful, comprehensive, and intelligent account for the day's events in a context which gives them meaning" (Peterson, 1971, p. 87). Rao and Lee (2005) conclude from the statements of the journalists whom they interviewed that "the idea is that journalists should always be cognizant of the ethical values of their readers and viewers... and that their own values should not overshadow the values of the people and regions they are reporting about" (p. 115).

From the Islamic perspective, a consideration of the characteristics of the target audience is important to avoid creating misunderstanding, a position that is supported by the statement of one of the Prophet Mohammad's companions: "You should preach to the people according to their mental caliber so that they may not convey wrong things" (Bukhari, 1979, p. 95). This suggests that prudence may be the core virtue of a truly transnational media ethics. Freedom of expression is always wrapped in responsibility; boundaries and limits always exist. Respect for sacred and religious symbols has nothing to do with limiting freedom of expression or censorship. Therefore, publishing the Muhammad cartoons was an unjustified, morally unacceptable act.

The debate over the Danish cartoons was also about the Muslim response, which appeared irresponsible and inconsistent and had nothing to do with the essence of Islam. Islam does not encourage hateful speech or action; no one has the right to defame or ridicule any human being. Moreover, Muslims are strictly forbidden from burning any living being (humans or animals) or cities, properties, farmlands, etc., even during a war. The burning of a fellow human being, or even their effigy or flag, is abhorrent and not desirable (Ghazi, 2006, p. 36). Although no one can deny that Muslims have the right to seek the legal and peaceful use of the media to express their grievances, and while peaceful demonstrations and legal action were a legitimate response against *Jyllandus-Posten* and the newspapers that republished the cartoons, the violence which accompanied the publication of the controversial cartoons was unjustified and definitely *not* in line with the righteous values and ethics of Islam. In this context, the reality of Islam contained in its original scriptural sources can also be brought to bear to critique the choices of some Muslims who responded to the violation represented by the Danish cartoons.

The Islamic teachings show how the Prophet Muhammad treated those who hurt him and his fellows. One of the prominent examples of the Prophet's tolerance, mercy, and forgiveness is that after the conquest of Mecca, he pardoned those who previously had oppressed, tortured, and starved him and his fellows. Instead of taking retaliatory measures against them, he pardoned them instead saying: "Go, for you all are free" (Maccido, 2004, p. 15). The other directive comes from the Qur'an when God orders faithful believers to be patient at a time of anger and to excuse those who treat them badly: "Nor can goodness and Evil be equal. Repel (Evil) with what is better. Then will he between whom and you there was hatred become as it were your friend and intimate" (Chapter 41, Verse 34). The Prophet is recorded to have said: "The strong is not the one who overcomes the people by his strength, but the strong is the one who controls himself while in anger" (Bukhari, 1979, p. 87). This tolerance is based on sound scriptural precedent that unambiguously demonstrates that the violent reactions committed in respect to the Danish cartoon controversy are not consistent with the morals and ethics of Islam and are against what is called for by the Prophet Muhammad. However, at the same time, this does not mean that social injustice should be tolerated or that one should abandon or weaken one's convictions, or accept the imposition of the views of others (Maccido, 2004, p. 13).

Stephen Ward's (2005) contractualist perspective towards journalistic ethics assumes that the relationship between journalists and the public takes the form of a contract in which "duties and responsibilities arise out of fair contracts whereby agents claim rights and impose duties on themselves and others" (p. 7). He also argues that "in all contracts the public grants (or guarantees) certain freedoms and privileges to the press on the expectation that journalists will act responsibly, fulfill a range of functions, and provide benefits" (Ward, 2005, p. 8). When this view is applied to the case of the Danish cartoon controversy, it could be argued that the Danish *Jyllandus-Posten* newspaper and the other newspapers that republished the cartoons broke the rules of the social contract between them and the public, since they did not consider the three principles of the social contract that Ward identifies – credibility, justifiable consequences, and humanity. These principles are justifiable restraints on the liberty of journalists and combine an emphasis of freedom of the press with social responsibility (Ward, 2005, p. 14).

According to this social contract approach, the Danish *Jyllandus-Posten* newspaper intentionally or unintentionally failed to fact-check information about the character of the Prophet of Islam and instead perpetuated stereotypes about Islam based on terrorist personalities who claim Islam as their religion. This conduct undermines the principle of credibility that journalism always claims. Also, from the perspective of the second factor of the social contract – justifiable consequences – the initial publishing and then the republishing of the Danish cartoons caused unjustifiable and gratuitous harm to Muslims by ridiculing the most sacred symbol of Islam. In addition, the Danish cartoons are unjustifiable from the perspective of freedom of expression, since that very expression tramples on the religious and ethnic rights of Muslims. Lacking moral responsibility, the free expression supposedly represented by the Danish cartoons has violated ethical norms of "good" journalism (Callahan, 2003). Even if one legally defends the right of the *Jyllandus-Posten* to publish offensive materials, including those that offend religion – under the assumption of raising the discussion about the limits of freedom of expression and to overcome self-censorship concerning Islamic issues – the question becomes, for example, as Charles Taylor (1989, p. 121) inquires in his paper about the Rushdie controversy: "Is any other way available by which to investigate this issue without insulting and denigrating depictions of religious symbols, including depictions of Muhammad?"

From the Islamic perspective, a jurisprudential rule states that it is impermissible to inflict harm upon others if it returns a benefit to the doer, and also if it does not result in any benefit to the doer. Harm is prohibited by common sense and by legal reasoning except for that which can be tolerated because it results in a benefit which surpasses its negative effects. An example of this is the just penalties that are imposed by law to protect the common good. In the liberal tradition, a similar concept is preventing harm to others (Mill's harm principle), which is the justifiable reason to rightfully restrict an individual's freedom (Mill, 1859/1978, p. 8). The ultimate point is that doing harm should be a last resort, and justifiable, only when its use benefits the public interest and the common good. Also, according to Islamic teachings, people must tell the truth even against themselves or their own people, whoever and whatever they may be; hence, journalism must tell the truth even if this truth is offensive, and regardless of whom it hurts (Pasha, 1993, p. 75). Furthermore, news must have a utility value and provide people with a benefit. As reported in the Qur'an: "...God makes truth and falsehood clash. As a result the froth evaporates and vanishes, while that which benefits the people remains on earth" (Pasha, 1993, p. 75). Mill's strong defense of the freedom of expression and his consideration of all the possibilities of the liberty of thought and discussion seeks to find and develop the truth (Mill, 1859/1978, pp. 15–44).

The publication of the Danish cartoons incited action harmful to others without any benefit and without truth. From the contractualist perspective, newspapers do not owe their primary allegiance to humanity, since they do not consider the public interest of all their potential readers, especially minorities within their own country, and thus, they do not consider the offensive impact, for example, of the controversial Danish cartoons.

In this case and those similar to it, arguments have been made that the contemporary media does not encourage a voluntary commitment to the good of society, does not have any meaningful relationship with an audience, and is less ready to enter into dialogue with the public. In other words, both assigned and self-imposed responsibilities are lagging behind while contracted obligations or denied responsibilities are rising (McQuail, 1997, pp. 516, 518). From the perspective of the practical reality of the media, it can be concluded that the Western idea of freedom of expression suffers from an ethical shortcoming and lack of balance. From an Islamic perspective, freedom is always associated with responsibility: absolute freedom does not exist. The ethical standards of freedom of expression are provided by the guidelines of the Qur'an, and the prophetic traditions stress the justice of freedom that is based on self-imposed responsibilities. These guidelines offer a form of accountability that can meet the three general aims put forward by McQuail (1997): the promotion of media freedom, the prevention of harm which the media can cause, and the promotion of the positive benefits of media for society.

Conclusion

Under the present circumstances in which struggles and wars are increasing all over the world and in which the media participates in terms of its lack of ethical reliability and decreasing credibility, the study of journalism in relation to ethics at a global level constitutes an important turning point in mass media studies. The practice of provocation is crucial to the craft of journalism, and it is supported by freedom of expression. However, freedom without responsibility is harmful and can lead to horrible consequences. Given the growing violations associated with freedom of the press and expression in regards to current events, and the misrepresentation of freedom of expression (from an Islamic perspective) stimulated recently by the offensive Danish cartoons, this paper has examined the ethical value and characteristics of freedom of expression from an Islamic perspective based on references in the Qur'an and the prophetic traditions, with an attention to the compatibility of Islam with global human rights.

From the Islamic viewpoint, freedom of speech is not an absolute right without limitations; rather, it is modified by certain limits realised within the framework of the concept of justice. Moral and social restraints against defamation, backbiting, derision, acrimonious speech, and the exposure of the weaknesses of others – as well as an affirmation of the right to privacy and the right of honour and a good reputation – help to emphasise and guarantee the responsibilities associated with freedom of expression and the press.

These moral and social restraints have nothing to do with the value of freedom of speech as a basic human right useful for discovering the truth and for building a healthy democratic community; moreover, these restraints are not censorship or the repression of free speech. Islamic morality and the moral limits of freedom of expression are self-imposed obligations, since the ultimate goal of human beings is to seek and acquire the satisfaction of God. To accomplish this goal, individuals must devote their deeds and actions to liberating their soul from all things that prevent it from reaching true piety – the framework in which freedom gains its legitimacy and meaningfulness.

In an age of transnational and cross-cultural communication, civic responsibility and moral ethics could be the parameters by which journalists make important decisions to exercise their right of freedom of expression, especially when: "there isn't a universal definition of freedom of expression, because there isn't a single world culture" (Taylor, 1989, p. 121). In this context, the ethical virtue of prudence might become the core virtue of a truly transnational media ethics. Moreover, the issue is not primarily contained by the legal limits of freedom of expression or in the professional codes of journalism practice. The issue *is* the ethical culture that underpins these laws and codes.

The recent example of the offensive Danish cartoons represents a similar violation of freedom of expression. However, at the same time, freedom of expression requires an environment characterised by a tolerance that permits open argument and accepts the free expression of oppositional opinion. Ethical standards for freedom of expression provided by the Qur'an and Sunnah not only avoid hurtful speech but also promote peace and mutual understanding in society. In sum, if media ethics are to be truly transnational, they must adequately take into account the enduring religiosity of many non-Western populations, and this means that society must contemplate limits on offensive speech, limits that might enforce greater restraint than is typically allowed by liberal media ethics based on the assumption of secularism. Failing this, liberal media ethics simply enforce secularism upon religious peoples, thus violating the very principles of openness and tolerance upon which liberal ethics are purportedly built.

Notes

1   I relied on Abdullah Yusuf Ali's translation for references to the Qur'anic material: *The Meaning of the Glorious Qur'an*, Trans. Abdullah Yusuf Ali (Istanbul: Asir Media, 2002). References to the canonical traditional collection of al-Bukhari were from al-Bukhari, *The Translation of the Meanings of Sahih al-Bukhari*, Trans. Muhammad Muhsin Khan (Chicago: Kazi Publication, 1979).

Acknowledgement

I would like to thank Professor Darin Barney, the Canada Research Chair in Technology and Citizenship, for his helpful editorial comments as this paper evolved through several revisions. His generous provision of resources through the Canada Research Chair were of inestimable value to the completion of this project. I also am grateful for the thoughtful editorial comments and careful reading by co-editor Professor Stephen Ward. Finally, I would like to acknowledge the funding assistance provided by the Beaverbrook Graduate Travel Grants from Media@McGill.

References

Abdul-Fattah, S. A-D. (2006, May 17). Freedom and the cartoon crisis from the incident to the approach. Retrieved December 20, 2006, from http://www.islamonline.net/English/contemporary/2006/03/article03.shtml.

Allen, L., & Voss, D. (1997). *Ethics in technical communication: Shades of gray.* New York: John Wiley & Sons, Inc.

Ayish, M. I., & Sadig, H. B. (1997). The Arab-Islamic heritage in communication ethics. In C. Christians & M. Traber, (eds.), *Communication ethics and universal values* (pp. 105–127). Thousand Oaks, London: Sage Publications.

Callahan, S. (2003). New challenges of globalization for journalism. *Journal of Mass Media Ethics* 18(1), 3–15.

Christians, C. G. (1997). The ethics of being in a communications context. In C. Christians & M. Traber, (eds.), *Communication ethics and universal values* (pp. 2–23). Thousand Oaks, London: Sage Publications.

Christians, C., & Nordenstreng, K. (2004). Globalizing media ethics? An assessment of universal ethics among international political journalists. *Journal of Mass Media Ethics* 19(1), 3–28.

Ghazi, M.T. (2006). *The cartoons cry.* Bloomington, Ind: AuthorHouse.

Habermas, J. (1984). The theory of communicative action, Volume Two: *Lifeworld and system: A critique of functionalist reason.* Trans. Thomas McCarthy. Boston: Beacon Press.

Kamali, M. H. (1994). *Freedom of expression in Islam.* Kuala Lumpur: Berita Publishing Sdn. Bhd.

Khan, M. M. (1979). *The translation of the meanings of Sahih Al-Bukhari. Arabic-English.* Chicago, Ill.: Kazi Publications.

Maccido, M. (2004). The Qur'anic handling of tolerance and peaceful co-existence (empirical examples in Madina, Najran and Mekkah). *Tolerance in the Islamic civilization. The sixteenth general conference of the Supreme Council for Islamic Affairs.* Cairo, Egypt: Ministry of Al-Awqaf, The Supreme Council for Islamic Affairs.

McQuail, D. (1997). Accountability of media to society: Principles and means, *European Journal of Communication,* 12(4), 511–529.

Mill, J. S. (1978). *On liberty.* Ed. Elizabeth Rapaport. Indianapolis, Ind.: Hackett Publishing Company. Original work published 1859.

Mowlana, H. (1993). The new global order and cultural ecology., *Media, Culture and Society,* 15, 9–27.

Mowlana, H. (1989). Communication, ethics, and the Islamic tradition. In T. W. Cooper, C. G. Christians, F. F. Plude, & R. A. White (eds.), *Communication ethics and global change* (pp. 137–146). London: Longman Inc.

Pasha, S. H. (1993). Towards a cultural theory of political ideology and mass media in the Muslim world, *Media, Culture and Society,* 15, 61–79.

Peterson, T. (1971). The social responsibility theory of the press. In F. S. Siebert, T. Peterson & W. Schramm, (eds.), *Four theories of the press* (pp. 73–103). Urbana, Ill.: University of Illinois Press.

Raboy, M. (2006). *What can we learn from the cartoon controversy.* Unpublished manuscript. McGill University, Montreal, Quebec, Canada.

Ramadan, T. (2006). The Danish cartoons, free speech and civic responsibility, *New Perspectives Quarterly,* 23(2), 17–18. Retrieved October, 2006, from http://www.Blackwell- synergy.com/doi/abs/10.1111/j.1540-5842.2006.00799x.

Rao, S. & Lee, S. T. (2005). Globalizing media ethics? An assessment of universal ethics among international political journalists, *Journal of Mass Media Ethics,* 20(2 & 3), 99–120.

Rosenberg, G. (2006). The freedom of what's not said, *New Perspectives Quarterly* 23(2), 19–22.

Siddiqui, D.A. (2000). A comparative analysis of the Islamic and the Western models of news production and ethics of dissemination. Retrieved October 21, 2006, from http://www.islamist.org/images/News.pdf.

Siebert, F. S. (1971). The libertarian theory of the press. In F. S. Siebert, T. Peterson & W. Schramm, (eds.), *Four theories of the press* (pp. 39–71). Urbana, Ill.: University of Illinois Press.

Taylor, C. (1994). The politics of recognition. In A. Gutmann, (ed.), *Multiculturalism: examining the politics of recognition* (pp. 25–73). Princeton, N.J.: Princeton University Press.

Taylor, C. (1989). The Rushdie controversy, *Public Culture,* 2(1), 118–122.

Ward, S.J. A. (2005). Philosophical foundations for global journalism ethics, *Journal of Mass Media Ethics,* 20 (1), 3–21.

Ziadah, M. (2004). Al-tasamuh al-islami bayn al-haqiqa wa al-iftiraa (Islamic tolerance between reality and libel), *Tolerance in the Islamic civilization. The sixteenth general conference of the Supreme Council for Islamic Affairs.* Cairo, Egypt: Ministry of Al-Awqaf, The Supreme Council for Islamic Affairs.

10 Media Ethics in Ethiopia

Gebremedhin Simon

1. Introduction

Ethiopia is perhaps predominantly known to the world by the striking reports of prominent BBC journalists such as Jonathan Dimbelby and Mohammed Amin. These journalists and others visited the country during its times of crises. Pictures of emaciated cattle and children dying of famine due to persistent drought and conflicts caused uproar all over the world and provoked a number of nongovernmental organisations such as Band Aid, Save-the-Children, Oxfam, and World Food Programme to start providing relief and rehabilitation. A number of journalists and nongovernmental organisations have saved many lives during the times of recurrent drought and famine since the 1970s. Unfortunately, the negative image of Ethiopia drawn by the international media seems to persist, although many Ethiopians are now in a better position to cope with similar catastrophes, and the local picture is not as gloomy as originally portrayed. Recent unofficial reports by the Disaster Preparedness and Prevention Commission indicate that the number of people dependent on food aid has dramatically decreased. Nonetheless, the older framing of the country by the international media seems to persist as evidenced in their reports on the May 2005 elections in Ethiopia, and Ethiopia's recent dealings with Eritrea and Somalia. Some sceptics may resist credulity and may want to know whether the picture of poverty is all there is to be known about Ethiopia. Others may take the label 'poverty' as a baseline when they select news and commentaries about Ethiopia. International media seem not to take heed of this diversity of perspectives on the country.

It is evident that there is a general reluctance on the side of international media, especially Western media, to revise their framing of Ethiopia. It is apparent that the international media tend to refer to a particular framing of a country such as Ethiopia, or a region such as Africa, as a basis for the interpretation of their reports. African framings such as a continent of conflict, poverty and underdevelopment, and corruption would seem to be at the centre of the interpretation of news, features and other related media output. The various reports about Somalia, and even about Iraq, reinforce the idea that the international media operate based on some semi-permanent framing of countries or regions. Ostensibly, framing provides the perspectives for making meaning of the news. However, framing should be understood in relation to time and space. It is likely that these framings outlive their time-space settings. Apparently, this disparity may give rise to unbalanced reporting and may go against the conventional codes of ethics in journalism such as balance, objectivity, and accuracy. It is indeed a challenge for all media to investigate this dimension and to be able to operate as per the stipulations of media ethics if claims of global media ethics are to make sense.

In fact, one wonders why such depictions persist. Is it because they are true and continue to be true, or are there other factors that govern the operations of media houses and the journalists working for them that possibly challenge the conventional codes of ethics in journalism? Is the Western media output acceptable because of their own Western public, and are the media acting on the basis of their own 'local' codes of ethics consistent with their Western publics? This polemic would lead one to assert that since the Western codes are fundamentally local, they would not be appropriate to address global issues. Another may say that since Western media are dominating during the age of globalisation, they should form the global media codes, and journalism schools should teach these as journalistic codes of ethics. Others suggest a form of global-local combination would be the most appropriate content for global media ethics (see Banda in this edition).

One may also follow a linear prescriptive paradigm in which regions and countries are assumed to follow 'similar' patterns of development and manifest similar perspectives and 'worldviews' and thus display universally predetermined codes of ethics in similar social ecologies. This trend may corroborate the first point of argument mentioned above.

Researchers now face the challenges of not only local versus global in media ethics, but also the philosophical interpretations of the concept 'ethics' and the codes. Studies indicate that there are some philosophical contentions regarding the conventional elements that constitute media ethics (Kieran, 1998). According to Kieran

> Accusations of bias, press cynicism, media manipulation, condemnations of journalistic intrusions into privacy, worries about the damaging or distortive effect of the televisual medium and hotly contested pronouncements about the appropriate forms of media regulation or censorship have all hit the headlines with ever greater frequency. The aim ... is to focus upon some of the key questions about the media's ethical responsibilities and rights. For only by critical reflection upon what, rationally, we may legitimately demand of the media, in terms of their duties and responsibilities, can we hope to arrive at any substantial basis for claiming that a particular press intrusion or media programme is immoral (p. x).

In other words, Kieran (1998) indicates that there may not be consensus regarding the conventional codes of ethics. He adds:

It may be that many people assume political spin-doctoring, cheque-book journalism or the broadcasting of pornography on satellite channels are immoral and thus should be prohibited. But even if there were a social consensus about such matters, it does not follow that these things are indeed wrong. For, as we are all aware, people's preferences and moral judgements can be mistaken. Hence, in order to understand what the ethical issues involved are, what responsibilities, rights or duties exist and how they might conflict, we need to pursue a philosophical analysis of things like the nature of objectivity, privacy, the influence of sexual and violent programming and censorship (pp. x–xi).

There is also abundant literature on the effect of cultural and technological developments, in short, the dramatic effects of globalisation on media and media ethics. As shown below, some indicate that the journalist is tied between two contending commitments – the national interest and the professional commitment.

It is essential to see a link between the occupational ideology of journalism and the self-perception of journalists. How journalists perceive themselves to be and what they think their roles are will influence what they consider to be appropriate and professional. This surely would reflect on what they consider to be ethical or unethical. Although this carries with it the issue of universality – the dialectic relationship between how one perceives himself or herself and his or her professional identity – it is evident that the conclusions arrived at will be rooted in the journalist's specific social and cultural orientations.

Likewise, Ramaprasad (2001) relates the perspectives of the Tanzanian journalists about their profession as follows:

> (They) rate western journalistic functions – accuracy, analysis, investigation and entertainment – highly, and they place considerable importance on the public affairs benefits of their jobs. At the same time, their Tanzanian conceptions of the role of the press – portraying the country positively, using traditional media, ensuring rural coverage and thinking of news as a social good, all for national development – are also important to them (p. 539).

Such a duality in fidelity or commitment towards journalistic professionalism (usually of the Western type) and the devotion to the interests of one's country or nation as that of the Tanzanian journalists is said to be uncommon among Western journalists who may set their priorities based on the concrete Western reality. However, it is apparent that the perspectives used to describe media in other, non-Western, parts of the world are highly Western-oriented. According to Fourie (2005), the Western worldview with its focus on individualism, cause and effect, and measurable and observable evidence is not appropriate for the innate spirituality of Africa's various cultures and ethics (quoted in Botha & de Beer, 2006). Koltosva (2001) strongly argues against such a perspective by making a reference to descriptions about post-communist media in Russia:

Strangely enough, when it comes to post-Communist media, the scope of academic enquiry has been predominantly narrowed to normative theories of democracy, often merged with the theory of modernization. Though the latter may not be used explicitly, it enters the analysis of non-western media in a more latent way. Modernization theory implies that all societies move (or should move) along the same trajectory: from inferior (premodern, precapitalist, authoritarian) to superior (modern, capitalist, democratic). So, with or without reference to the notion of modernization, the role of post-Communist media is usually evaluated according to their ability to promote this unitary course of development....Sometimes media are even expected to *want* to become independent from normatively undesirable forms of control (political, economic) and to subject themselves to normatively approved forms (legal, control by public opinion). The main problem with this approach is that it tends to substitute descriptive or explanatory concepts by prescriptive categories, which weakens analysis of *any* society – either 'eastern' or 'western'. In the beginning of the 1990s it led to 'developmentalist' and 'transitional' hopes for rapid post-Communist westernization that never came true (p 316).

These are, indeed, challenges to the efforts of working out or discovering the ingredients for global media ethics. On the other hand, this may be evidence for the existence of glocalisation – a mix of global and local traits (see Banda in this volume). Although he admits the prevalence of local equivalents, Krüger (2004), for instance, criticises Francis Kasoma who has argued that the standards generally accepted by media in Africa remain based in European morality and advocated that African journalists should rather look to their own moral heritage for establishing a code of ethics for media. Krüger (2004) recommends:

Perhaps the contrast being drawn is less between two sets of values than between African ethics and the *practice* in Western journalism. There are many voices who would agree with these criticisms of Western practice, without necessarily making reference to African values. Rather than seeking sharp differences between Western and African ethics, we should recognise the common ground (p.11).

He mentions the works of Clifford Christians and Michael Traber (1997) who set out to find values applicable to communication shared by different cultures – what they call protonorms (see also Christians in this volume) – as the basis for global media ethics.

The above implies that, whatever arguments may be raised, defining global media ethics remains complex and contentious. This case study represents an instance of specificity rather than generality, not necessarily a repeat of Kasoma's rationalisation or a return to African traditional values as the basis for media ethics, or glocalisation – a mix of both global and local, but the issue of the specific socio-cultural ecology – which provides both the substance and the perspective – as the basis for moral values and ethics.

This case study investigates media ethics as understood and practised by journalists in Ethiopia by way of addressing the general versus the particular paradigm as an aspect of global media ethics. The study is based on the general framework that ethics is culturally sensitive, that it is defined, interpreted and practised according to the beliefs and value systems of a given society. In other words, ethics is set, defined, practised, and interpreted by a particular social ecology. Although there is abundant literature in philosophy pertaining to the evolution of morality and ethics, it seems that, while the notions of 'good' and 'bad' are universal, the specifications of what is considered to be 'good' and 'bad' may not necessarily be universal. Value systems thus thrive in their own respective social ecologies, and although there seems to be some universality, there are aspects of specificity that deserve consideration. In trying to work out the global ethics for a profession such as journalism, these specificities deserve some attention. This study tries to question Krüger's (2006) claim:

> I was considering this question of whether ethics are universal or we need a new set of ethics for Africa. My view is that it can't be just about cultural sensitivity. I don't think the argument that we need to be culturally sensitive is not enough to say we need the whole new set of ethics. Cultural sensitivity can easily be accommodated within the existing framework (taken from the oral presentation).

It is also possible to argue that taking Africa as a single cultural entity is quite misleading. Africa is a huge continent with people displaying significant contrasting socio-cultural assets. The majority of people in North Africa may not share similar cultural values to those found in East Africa or Southern Africa. One may argue that a perspective that pits 'African ethics' against 'Western ethics' clouds the specific features of cultural entities. Krüger provides instances to justify his arguments by referring to some common codes evident both in African and Western notions, such as building consensus and working for the common good, and the need to call for less authoritarianism and more collective decision-making.

As indicated above, the argument is not as such between African and Western value systems (which may as well be sustained due to the presence of significant cultural and historical peculiarities). By making a reference to the historical evolutions and deviations of values, morals and ethics, it is argued that there could be different perspectives and interpretations of reality. Some attribute this to the notion of linguistic determinism or relativity which is commonly labelled as the Sapir-Whorf hypothesis which stipulates that our perception of reality and the world around us is determined by thought processes we have developed which are shaped by the languages we have learned. A corollary of this notion is that our symbol systems make it easy for us to see reality in one way rather than in another way. It is this that would help us develop our unique value systems. Although it is admitted that we have similar properties as *homo sapiens* such as the human brain that is 'programmed' for learning language and the schema for evolving and storing knowledge, the social ecology we find ourselves in may have a significant role in the way we develop and use language.

According to Korajian (2006), ethics is more of an individual behaviour in a narrow sense. He says it is a

...standard by which individuals evaluate their own conduct and the conduct of others. However, most ethical decisions do not hold one's life in balance. They are day-to-day decisions people make and often take for granted in the world of work: treating others with respect, keeping promises, making personal decisions, looking out for friends, giving and accepting gifts, padding expense vouchers, or reporting wrongdoing (p. 3).

Conceptually, it is normal to assume that some notions in journalism are quite homely for most of us familiar with Western culture. It is to be understood that journalism education is based on Western notions of the profession, and so those who have had the training would be familiar with the notions, albeit their philosophical contentions. For those who are not familiar with Western culture, these notions are either attached to similar local equivalents, or they are just ignored. The general trend is to 'import' the codes of conduct and the codes of ethics and teach them in schools of journalism in isolation, with the expectation that prospective journalists practise them irrespective of the environments they are supposed to operate in. There are several cases where journalists have acted as per the specifications of their training and, although their behaviour may not have produced any major social uproar in the West, it has caused social catastrophes in some parts of Africa where ethnic relationships are delicately handled in a traditional way. Some argue that, for instance, media acted 'irresponsibly' to worsen the recent ethnic strife or genocide in Rwanda. Common media excesses were also evident in some conflict-ridden parts of Africa.

Although accepting in principle that there are universal prototypes that may be identified to become the basis for global media ethics, this study intends to raise a strong argument in support of the prevalence of specific socio-cultural assets that dictate the perspectives for creating meaning and for the interpretations of such 'universal' values. The presence of specific socio-cultural elements challenge such universality and demands an interpretation within localities. In the Ethiopian context, it seems that the codes of ethics are simply imported without paying attention to their local interpretations and contexts.

2. Exploring the Social Ecology

Ethiopia is situated in north-east Africa surrounded by Sudan, Kenya, Somalia, Djibouti and Eritrea. It is estimated that the country has an area of about one million square kilometres with a population estimated at 77 million in 2005.[1]

Various ecological features, such as the high rugged mountains, flat-topped plateaux, deep gorges, incised river valleys and vast rolling plains, have conditioned the unique settlement patterns and the evolution of contrasting cultural entities; on the one side we see isolated entities of sedentary farming cultures with concomitant traditions, beliefs and value systems, on the other side there is a roving pastoralist culture with all its attendant norms and values. Such a difference is accentuated further by the fact that the people living in the highlands are mostly Orthodox Christians, while the ones in the lowlands are predominantly Muslims. Besides this, the people in the highlands are mostly Amharas, Tigrians and Oromos, while the lowlanders are mostly Afars, Somalis, and others. In short, the country is home to several ethnic and religious groups. The topography of the country coupled with the ethnic, linguistic[2], religious and cultural diversities, makes even the above description of the country and its peoples an oversimplification. In other words, Ethiopia is home to people with several religions, languages, and histories.

The complexity of the Ethiopian population is further accentuated by historical factors. There is now evidence that Ethiopia is a possible origin of humankind. The recent discoveries in the Afar region attest to this assertion. The obelisk in Axum, the Lalibela rock-hewn churches, the city of Harar, and the Fasiledes castle in Gondar are but a few relics of ancient, medieval and early modern history in Ethiopia. The history of the country can be categorised into ancient, medieval and modern periods – the history of ancient civilisations stretching from the BC era to the 13th century (the introduction of various religions: Judaism, Christianity, and Islam, the founding of schools of thought in monasteries, the development of local literature and philosophy in an ancient language, *Ge'ez*, the development of church literature, music and arts, the development of Qur'anic schools in Arabic in Harrar, etc.), a period of feudalism (from the 16th century to the late 19th century), a period of modern times (from the late 19th century to present times), and the emergence of modern Ethiopia. In general, most of the history of Ethiopia is a history of a protracted feudalism characterised by rivalries among various groups that involved over 80 national groups speaking about 80 languages with over 200 dialects.[3]

> Ethiopia's history is characterised by internal rivalries among regional warlords. The country for a long period of time (for about 1,650 years or so) had been under the iron grip of feudal dynastic rules (http://www. moinfo. gov.et/; Desalegn and Meheret, 2004).

However, in the words of the prominent South African journalist, Alistair Sparks (2006),[4] the country has a different image:

> And I remember in the date of independence column, there you had Ghana 1957, Nigeria 1960 and so on, until one came to Ethiopia where, there in that column, was no date but the mathematical symbol for infinity. What a wonderful boast to be able to make. Forever free!

> Of course there was a brief interruption in that infinite span of independence, when Benito Mussolini's Italy colonised you for five years from 1936. But that is barely a nano-second in the long sweep of your 2000-year history.[5]

It is apparent that the people who have lived in such a situation will create their own unique identity based on their experience. This provides the basis for their values, morals and ethics. In other words, it is not the long history that brings about uniqueness but the psychological make-up people develop about themselves and their relationships with others throughout their history. The values and ethics that reflect their perspectives of interpretations of themselves and their relationships with others normally guide their actions. If a new profession such as journalism is imported with its codes of ethics that may have some relationship with domestic value systems, the local or indigenous perspective would guide the new profession. In this sense, one can see that the applicability of postcolonial media ethics for African media is going to be remote (Rao, Wasserman in this volume).

Coming back to the history of the country that may colour the local value systems (unlike those mentioned by Rao, Wasserman in this volume), the past four decades have been spectacular in the history of the country. During this period there have been major shifts in political, economic and other aspects against the backdrop of the established traditional and cultural factors.

> In this period the country has had three radically different political regimes involving in each case economic, legal and administrative reorganisation.... The imperial regime, which was one of absolute monarchy, ruled the country during much of the first half of the 20th century; it was overthrown in 1974 by the *Derg*, a ... military ... regime. The Derg in turn was ousted from power in 1991 by rebel forces combined in the Ethiopian Peoples Revolutionary Democratic Forces (EPRDF) .... Following the setting up of the transitional government in 1991, there were a number of important political developments (Desalegn and Meheret, 2004, p. xix).

During the periods of the imperial and the military regimes, there was no private press and no legal framework for press freedom. All media work had to pass the requirements of the censorship office, which censored government media output as well. The present government abolished any form of censorship in the 1994 constitution. Freedom of expression and press freedom have been taken as legal and fundamentally essential for the democratisation process. Such an environment has favoured the creation of legally operating opposition political parties. It is now common to observe the airing of a diversity of views and perspectives and the mushrooming of private press. As might be expected, the diversities have taken a strong political stance and journalistic work has been coloured by such a stance.

Desalegn and Meheret (2004) summarise the events as follows:

> Following the setting up of the Transitional Government, there were a number of important political developments. The country's administrative map was redrawn along ethnic lines and a 'regional state' for each of the major nationalities was created. These regional states were given wide administrative and legislative power: the goal was devolution of power within a federal framework. Ethnic federalism was further formalised by the drafting of a constitution in 1994, following elections were held to the constituent assembly whose job was to ratify the Constitution. The Constitution established a federal state the component elements of which were "nations, nationalities and peoples". It endorsed respect for human rights, the rule of law and a multi-party electoral regime (p. xix).

These developments have encouraged for the first time in the history of the country the establishment of various human rights groups[6] and others interested in expressing the rights of citizens in general and the groups they represent in particular. For instance, the above study categorises such groups into four, based on convenience. These include a) those that monitor human rights violations and make public reports; b) those that promote gender equality and defend the rights of women; c) those that generally enhance public awareness about civil liberties and promote respect for the rule of law by providing training on human rights; and d) those that undertake civic education, in particular voter education, to enable citizens to make well-informed decisions during elections. Since the proclamation, a significant change in the media environment is the attempt to introduce changes to the state media, the proliferation of private newspapers and the pronounced division among journalists, thus making way for the formation of different journalist associations. The recent establishment of the Broadcast Agency has also encouraged private investment in the area.

A significant attempt made in the state media is to transform them to be accountable to management bodies selected by the parliament. Each media institution has been encouraged to draw up its own editorial policy, including its accepted code of ethics. A case in point is the Ethiopian News Agency. The Ethiopian News Agency has outlined in detail its editorial policy, including its code of ethics which includes seeking and recording truth, serving the public's right to know the truth, promoting public interest, and the like.

Similarly, various journalist associations have attempted to draw up their own code of conduct and code of ethics. However, these associations came with different brands and challenged the veteran Ethiopian Journalists' Association and organised themselves in line with 'who supports the government' and 'who does not support the government'. Instead of working towards evolving a common set of codes and ethics – either based on the Ethiopian experience and resources for values and ethics, the journalists were engaged in accusing each other. While all seem to adopt the codes of conduct and ethics stipulated elsewhere, the division among them became a strong barrier for working together to ensure press freedom and to improve the situation of journalists (see Banda in this volume for a similar case). At the moment, it seems that there are only a few operating journalist associations in Ethiopia.

A point that is made above is the tendency by these journalist associations to accept and adopt codes of ethics and codes of conduct used elsewhere. The Ethiopian Free Journalists' Association, for instance, urged its members to follow the professional code of ethics, such as informing the public of the malpractices of officials, revealing the truth, not disseminating information that endangers the national unity, security and sovereignty, abide by the 'code of ethics', and so on.

Currently, there are attempts by some sectors to bring together all Ethiopian journalists and to work out a common code of conduct and code of ethics by establishing an editors' forum, a press council and similar organisations that can be used to promote the profession. A meeting of over 55 journalists – state and private journalists – was organised, and in the meeting the journalists established an ad hoc committee to formulate a press club and outline a code of conduct.

The journalists who attended the meeting agreed that the role of journalism is to promote the process of democratisation in the country, which has both a universal and a local tone. The problems facing journalists were identified as lack of awareness of regulations and ethical responsibilities, misinterpretation and self-censorship. On the part of the government, the journalists felt that there was lack of transparency, denial of access to information, and the discrimination between state and private media journalists. It was recommended that press freedom orientations be given to police officials, lawmakers, and public relation officers. A brainstorm of the code of ethics included the sought-for truth, upholding the integrity and freedom of the press, and remaining faithful to serving the public by providing clear, accurate, properly tested, balanced and unbiased information. It is apparent that these are universal issues in journalism despite the fact that one may assume that these are ideals taken from international codes of conduct and ethics. It seems there is no reference made to their recognition of the nascent democracy that is evolving in the country. There seems to be no bridge linking the two spheres[7].

Journalists' self-perceptions and professional ideologies are at the centre of the journalistic operations. It has been mentioned above how Ethiopian journalists perceive their conditions and the conditions the country finds itself in. An earlier study made by Wall (2000) clearly indicates how journalists conceive of their role as journalists. Her interest was not directly related to media ethics *per se*, but that the notions the journalists have about their profession imply what they consider as ethical. Her work revolved around models of journalism suggested by the journalists' discourses about a) the relationship between journalism and the government, b) between journalism and the public, and c) the identities of the journalist. Through interviews and ongoing conversations, and text analysis of materials produced by the journalists themselves, she categorises three different discourses based on the above research question. The first category is what she calls the 'Westernizer'. This group follows the Western capitalist, liberalist philosophy which, apparently, purports that the media should be a watchdog. The second category is the 'Developer' – who follows the established pattern in many African countries of using the media to contribute to nation-building and to support the government in this effort. The last group is the 'Azmari'.[8] This group reflects previously identified cultural tendencies toward a political, populist press. She comments that unlike the first two, the last group takes audience as active and participative.

Besides some work done by Krüger (2005) on media in Ethiopia, there are related studies made on media ethics in Ethiopia by postgraduate students in the Faculty of Journalism and Communication as part of their MA study at the Addis Ababa University.

One study is made by Haile-Gabriel Endeshaw (2005). Haile-Gabriel intends to identify ethical problems in news writing. He takes the state-owned *The Ethiopian Herald* as a point of reference. He employs a content analysis accompanied by questionnaires and interviews. He states that the majority of the election 2005 news stories do not fulfil some of the code of ethics – fairness and independence.

The other study is conducted by Solomon Alemu (2005). His study deals with the practice of censorship and its ethical effects on broadcasting in Ethiopian Television. He claims government interference as a factor in affecting the established code of journalistic ethics. Based on his findings he argues that, despite the fact that censorship has been abolished by law, there is direct censorship in Ethiopian Television.

A recent study made by Hallelujia Lulie (2008) deals with the political history of the private press. He confirms that the private press was predominantly unethical and acted irresponsibly, although the journalists knew the codes of conduct and codes of ethics of journalism.

3. The Results of the Case Study

As indicated above, baseline research was conducted to find out a) the journalist's awareness of the code of ethics, and b) the journalist's awareness of the practice of the code of ethics in Ethiopia. The idea was to find clues for arguing the specificity versus generality of identified codes of ethics – whether these codes are understood to mean what they conventionally mean, or are given local meanings by employing one's own interpretation[9], or they are not clearly understood. In most instances, the former is likely to happen.

The questionnaire consisted of two main parts. The first part requires the respondent to scan his/her environment in order to list as many codes of ethics as possible. In the second part, the journalist is required to identify the levels of frequency of use of identified codes of ethics practised by the journalist in Ethiopia – those that are adopted as codes, those that are never practised, those that are sometimes practised, and those that are often practised. Here the list included those codes of ethics that are usually mentioned as codes of ethics in journalism.

The questionnaire was distributed to 74 journalists who were currently senior students of the undergraduate division of the Faculty of Journalism and Communications, Addis Ababa University. Out of the expected total of 70, only 51 responses were valid enough to deserve consideration. The age range was found to be between 22 and 44. 15 of the journalists reported that they were below the age of 30. Six journalists reported that they were above the age of 40. Very few were inexperienced journalists. Only ten of them reported that either they did not have any experience in journalism or that they had only worked for a maximum of a year. About 21 of them reported that they had worked as journalists for ten years and more. Only six were female. Ten of the respondents reported that they were working for private papers. The remaining journalists claimed to be working in state media. 14 of the respondents were broadcast journalists while the remaining were print journalists. Some reported as working as both.

Asked why they would like to continue to work as journalists, their most frequent response was that they liked the profession. The reasons they may not like to continue working as journalists included low payment, lack of independence, and an unmotivating environment. Some of the local values that they thought may be used to develop a local code of ethics for journalism included respect for elders, collective work, coping with challenges, and keeping secrets. The list below indicates the values and beliefs that the respondents mentioned as being the basis for media ethics:

Values and Beliefs as Basis for Media Ethics

- cooperative system of the society, working together
- coping with danger, threats
- respect for others
- Christian beliefs (Orthodox belief ...)
- theft forbidden
- secrecy
- telling the truth with editing
- sociability
- respect for elders
- loving one's country with zealousness
- helping the needy
- responsibility, accountability for social aspects
- credibility and hardworking
- social interaction with neighbours
- support
- honesty, openness, integrity, respect
- fear of God, tolerance
- accept things after careful weighing (due to exposure to conflict/strife)
- work cooperation, traditional ways of dispute settlement, being passionate about the needy
- hard work (endurance under difficult circumstances), consistency and rigidity, sense of boldness
- peaceful coexistence
- the 'gada' system and all beliefs surrounding this system

Apparently, some of the items mentioned overlap. Some are socio-cultural specific, such as the 'gada' system.[10] The elements considered negative were forwarding what you know without editing, jealousy, cheating, stealing, not respecting elders, lying, etc. Finally, the respondents pointed out that the basis for the development of the code of ethics for media in Ethiopia should include responsibility, honesty, fairness, being credible, cooperation in work, and helping each other. Moreover, some included transparency, empathy, neutrality, respect, endurance, and the love for work. Some also added not cheating, humanness, and respecting others.

The second part of the questionnaire indicated a possible list of code of ethics which required the subjects to identify which ones were adopted as codes and which ones were practised. The responses are more or less non-conclusive and one may assume that the journalists may not clearly know some of the items or their practices.

Another complementary study revolved around the editorial policies of the media houses, which in most instances included the code of conduct and the code of ethics. A general observation of the data compiled from in-depth interviews shows that the media houses, or even the journalists, do not follow the principles, possibly because of lack of professional skills, motivation or self-censorship, or a disparity between professional ideology and self-perception. State media refer to the Ethiopian Constitution, the press law and related other documents as the basis for standards of media ethics.

The responses show that there are a number of 'universal' values that are moral values that can be applied to media ethics in a global context. However, there are some tensions that seem to be clearly localised issues, or, at least, would predominantly seem applicable in non-Western societies, where the traditional values of local communities such as the high status of the elders, the well-being of the community, traditional ways of dispute settlement, etc., have been passed on from generation to generation and are still valid and practised today. These may also provide the 'appropriate' and 'local' meanings of the code of ethics which are based on Western value systems.

Conclusion

The study was initiated as part of the global effort to seek universal code of ethics for global media. Despite the fact that there is generally a point of reference for the code of ethics for global media, there is the possibility that this may not necessarily address local issues and concerns. Or at least, this is not what is in practice in local contexts. It is considered that codes of ethics are culturally sensitive, that ethics is an amalgam of various socio-political and cultural aspects, including the way people see and interpret their reality, which includes the relationships among themselves and other people in different areas. Without denying the fact that there are universal issues that are true across several cultures, the research for a code of ethics for global media will have to address such a reality.

With this in mind, a draft survey of the Ethiopian ecology was undertaken by making a reference to the geocultural and historical features. Besides, a questionnaire was distributed among journalists to find out their level of awareness about the Ethiopian media code of ethics. The study attempted to draw an organic relationship between the ecology and the perceived codes of ethics. It was not possible to unequivocally state that codes of ethics are highly culture sensitive. However, there were some indications that this could be true. At least, in reality, what is usually binding is the local circumstances and realities. This study implies that there is a need for further investigation in the areas of culture-specific codes which are at work in determining the perceptions of the journalists and their professional ideology. While it is possible to say that, in the development of universal codes of ethics, traces of specific local tendencies will remain, these should be explored further. This exploratory study makes it evident that arriving at global media ethics is challenging.

Notes

1 The Central Statistical Agency has made all the preparations to collect all essential data on the country. It is hoped that the necessary figures will be available towards the end of 2008 – possibly just in time for the beginning of the new Ethiopian millennium.

2 There are about 80 mother-tongue languages in Ethiopia.

3 Ethiopia is home to four important language families in Africa: Afro-Asiatic or Semitic (12), Cushitic (22), Omotic (18), and Nilo-Saharan (18) languages.

4 When he came to Ethiopia the first time, he came to report on the opening of the Organisation of African Unity. He was given some information about member countries; and, that is what he is referring to.

5 A speech made by Alistair Sparks, the prominent South African journalist, during the opening ceremony of the School of Journalism and Communication, Addis Ababa University.

6 It is apt to note here that these human rights groups were established on Western models and their codes of conduct are based on Western value systems, although one may argue that there are some overlaps between the local and the global – mainly Western value systems.

7 The journalists admit the following: Ethiopia is a nation in transition from an autocratic past to a democratic future. A vibrant, free, and responsible press is of vital importance for a democratic society. Ethiopian journalism as a whole is in a developing stage. We believe in abiding by a dynamic press law that is transparent, enabling, judicial, and democratic in intent and scope. We believe in the vital importance of a well organised and self-regulating news industry. We believe that our raison d'être is to serve the public by providing clear, accurate, properly tested, balanced, and unbiased information. We believe it to be our professional duty to closely monitor the workings of public institutions, the government, industries, and commercial enterprises on behalf of the public. We believe in striving to achieve excellence in international standards of professionalism in our practice. We believe in the importance of diligent and consistent practice of critical thinking. We believe in being constructive, proactive, and circumspect in our engagement with all stakeholders. We commit ourselves to the principles enshrined in Article No. 29 of the Ethiopian Constitution.

8 Amharic – The word literally means 'singer'.

9 The terms such as 'independence' are thought to be clear and a 'local' meaning may be attributed.

10 A traditional 'democratic' system of rule among the Oromos in Ethiopia. The mention of this system goes in line with the argument raised by this study – the social ecology should be the reference point for developing a code of ethics for the profession.

References

Alemu, S. (2005). *Censorship and Ethics: Practice and Problems in Ethiopian Television.* Faculty of Journalism and Communications, Addis Ababa University. Unpublished MA thesis.

Christians, C. and Traber, M. (eds.) (1997). *Communication Ethics and Universal Values.* Thousand Oaks: Sage.

Endeshaw, H-G. (2005). *Ethical Issues of News Reporting with Particular Reference to the Ethiopian Herald Newspaper.* Faculty of Journalism and Communications, Addis Ababa University. Unpublished MA thesis.

Fourie, P.J. 2005. Journalism studies: The need to think about journalists' thinking. Ecquid Novi, 26(2): 356–359; quoted in N. Botha & A.S. de Beer. 2006 (Spring). *Revisiting South African Journalism Education in the Post-apartheid Era.* Global Media Journal – Polish Edition. No. 1.

Lulie, H. (2008). *A Political History of the Private Press in Democratic Ethiopia 1991–2007*. Faculty of Journalism and Communications, Addis Ababa University. Unpublished MA thesis.

Kasoma, F. (ed.). (1994). *Journalism Ethics in Africa*. Nairobi: ACCE.

Kieran, M (1997). *Media Ethics: A Philosophical Approach*. Westport, CT: Praeger.

Kieran, Matthew. 1998. *Media Ethics*. London: Routledge.

Koltosva, O. (2001) News Production in Contemporary Russia: Practices of Power. *European Journal of Communication*. Vol 16(3): 315–335. London: Sage Publications.

Korajian, G. (2006, May) *Ethics and Journalism: Skills in Developing an Organisational Code of Ethics*. Paper presented at the Faculty of Journalism and Communications, Addis Ababa University.

Krüger, F. (2004). *Black, White and Grey: Ethics in South African Journalism*. Cape Town: Double Storey Books.

Krüger, F. (2006). Media Ethics. Faculty of Journalism and Communication, Addis Ababa University Symposium on *Media Response to Democratic Imperatives*. (unpublished paper).

Rahmeto, D. and Ayenew, M. (2004, July). *Democracy Assistance to Post Conflict Ethiopia – Building Local Institutions*. Working Paper 27. Democratic Transition in Post Conflict Societies Project. Unpublished.

Ramaprasad, J. (2001) A Profile of Journalists in Post-Independence Tanzania. *Gazette* Vol 63(6): 539–555. London: Sage Publications.

Wall, M (2000, June). The Westernizer, the Developer and the Azmari: Journalism Discourses in Ethiopia. A paper presented to the International Communication Association, Acapulco.

Index